THE HISTORY OF THE LEFT
FROM MARX TO THE PRESENT

THE HISTORY OF THE LEFT FROM MARX TO THE PRESENT

THEORETICAL PERSPECTIVES

Darrow Schecter

continuum

NEW YORK • LONDON

2007

The Continuum International Publishing Group Inc
80 Maiden Lane, New York, NY 10038

The Continuum International Publishing Group Ltd
The Tower Building, 11 York Road, London SE1 7NX

www.continuumbooks.com

Library of Congress Cataloging-in-Publication Data

Schecter, Darrow.
  The History of the left from Marx to the present : theoretical perspectives / Darrow Schecter.
      p. cm.
  Includes bibliographical references and index.
  ISBN-13: 978-0-8264-2849-3 (hardcover : alk. paper)
  ISBN-10: 0-8264-2849-5 (hardcover : alk. paper)
  ISBN-13: 978-0-8264-8758-2 (pbk. : alk. paper)
  ISBN-10: 0-8264-8758-0 (pbk. : alk. paper)
  1. Socialism--History. 2. Radicalism--History. 3. Right and left (Political science)--History. I. Schecter, Darrow. II. Title.

  HX39.S25 2007
  320.53--dc22

                                                                2007012466

To Costantino and Manuela, and the future

CONTENTS

ACKNOWLEDGEMENTS

Over the past few years many people have facilitated the difficult task of providing a systematic account of theoretical perspectives on the left from Marx to the present. Many are or have been undergraduate, MA and DPhil students at the University of Sussex, including Penny Adamson, Leo Allen, Ned Birkin, Tim Black, Arianna Bove, Steve Brown, Nick Butler, Jennifer Cooke, Joanna Dawson, Claire Edwards, Erik Empson, James Furner, Ulrich Gelb, Catherine Hollis, Mark Hopkinson, Timo Juwellen, Peter Kolarz, Burak Köse, Wil Kuo, Charles Masquelier, Teodor Mladenov, Richard Mullin, Dave Murphy, Simon Mussell, Chris Okane, Jorge Ollero Peran, Leena Petersen, Patricia Priestly, Luke Stevens and Sam Thomas. I'd also very much like to thank all of the students who took my Methodological Approaches to the History of Ideas seminar in the autumn of 2006. Finally, very special thanks go to David Mieres.

Others include faculty at Sussex, such as Paul Betts, Peter Boxhall, Andrew Chitty, Rafe Hallet, Kathryn Macvarish, William Outhwaite, Roberta Piazza, Stephen Robinson, Neil Stammers, Daniel Steuer, Céline Surprenant, Chris Warne, Richard Whatmore and Chris Wyatt. Academics at other universities have also helped me a great deal. I'd like to thank Eric Jacobson, Jeremy Lester, David McLellan, Drew Milne, Alan Norrie, and especially Alex Thomson and Fabio Vighi. In writing this book, as others, Chris Thornhill has made me challenge my assumptions, reread history and rethink the relation between theory and practice.

The constant input of friends has been equally important. Many thanks to Fernand Avila, Gary Barber, Valerio Chiessi, Costantino Ciervo, Fine Ciervo, Jean Demerliac, Diana Göbel, Thorsten Göbel, Katharyn Lanaro, Luca Lavatori, Manuela Linti, Volker Lorek, Mand Ryaïra, Jarret Schecter and Imke Schmincke.

It has been a pleasure to work with David Barker and Christina Garbutt at Continuum, and I very much look forward to joint projects with them in the future.

If thesis 11 remains the categorical imperative, the point is now *how* the world is to be changed for the better. This study hopes to make a small contribution to looking at the question anew. Although all the people cited above have aided me a great deal, I bear full responsibility for the exposition and conclusions drawn in the book. I'd be happy to be wrong about everything if in the process it clarifies the way forward.

INTRODUCTION

The only real critique was and remains *the critique of the left.*
Why? Because it alone is based upon *knowledge.*[1]

In his wide-ranging and scholarly study *Demanding the Impossible: A History of Anarchism,* Peter Marshall accomplishes the impressive feat of providing an account of anarchist thought and action that dates back to ancient Greece, moving through the Middle Ages and including valuable information on the English Civil War and the role played in it by groups such as the Levellers and Ranters. His study then proceeds right up to the new left and ecological currents within the new left anarchism of the 1960s and 1970s.[2]

This book sets out to do something quite different. In addition to looking at anarchism, it examines a range of other ideas and movements on the left. The book begins much later than Marshall's study and concludes with a look at contemporary movements against neoliberal globalised capitalism. Although it is a history, as the title suggests, it is for the most part a history of theoretical perspectives. Major events such as the Paris Commune, the Russian Revolution, the Spanish Civil War, May 1968, Seattle 1999, and the founding of the first World Social Forum in Porto Alegre in January 2001 are all discussed in varying degrees of detail. But they are usually analysed against the background of a series of theoretical arguments that run from Karl Marx to Michel Foucault, Gilles Deleuze and Antonio Negri. The quotation above from Henri Lefebvre offers a good indication of the central theme addressed throughout the book, which is the relation between knowledge, left politics and human emancipation.

In order to provide theoretical and analytical coherence to the study of this theme, it has been necessary to bypass a number of important episodes in the history of the left that other authors may well have considered essential. There is not a great deal about new social movements

(NSMs) such as peace, feminist, ecology, gay and related networks that have been politically active on the left. The book does not provide a history of the former Soviet Union or the regimes associated with Mao, Castro and other state socialist leaders, nor does it look in any detail at the evolution of social democracy.

Some readers will consider the account here excessively Euro-centric, and may be inclined to argue that there is not nearly enough on anti-colonial struggles or movements such as the Sandinistas, Zapatistas, the Sendero Luminoso, etc. In short, it may be objected that the history of the left in this book unnecessarily privileges marginal offshoots of the European labour movement without (until the last chapter) adequately engaging with international developments. These criticisms are in some measure justified. Yet the chapters here on Marx, Western Marxism, critical theory, libertarian socialism and anarchism, the critique of everyday life, and the critique of power cover a very wide array of thinkers and ideas. It has proved impossible to do justice to the complexity of the material in question while at the same time examining NSMs, social democracy and anticolonial struggles. To have attempted to do so in the space allowed would have resulted in the trivialisation of those struggles. The relative neglect of these topics in this book is indicative of the wealth and diversity of left political struggle, and is in no way symptomatic of any intention to minimise their importance.

Although there are many ways of presenting the history of the left, the one offered in this book begins with Marx and the diverse struggles for human emancipation that have characterised European and world history since the French Revolution. The reasons for this choice of approach will become clear in due course. Rather than being a series of casual reflections on marginal offshoots of the European labour movement, each chapter builds on the previous one in an attempt to analyse the emergence and development of a specifically left-wing understanding of the relation between knowledge, left politics and emancipation. For the thinkers and movements in question, this methodology poses a series of even more fundamental questions about humanity and nature. The crucial question is how to institutionalise the relation between humanity and nature in a free society of fully humanised individuals. By the end of Chapter 6 it becomes clear how and why fundamental left concepts such as humanism and human emancipation are now problematic. The conclusion takes up the issue of what this impasse might mean for the future of the left.[3]

If the crisis of humanism is a relatively recent problem for left thinkers and movements, it is compounded by the older problem that the capitalist and liberal democratic systems first analysed in a systematic and critical fashion by Marx continue to be hegemonic. At first glance it appears that liberal democracy remains hegemonic because it succeeds in imposing the view that it is liberalism, as opposed to all other political doctrines, that protects individual liberty within a democratic framework that in practice makes individual freedom compatible with collective political accountability. Moreover, this view seems to be confirmed by the history of state socialism in the former USSR, China, Cuba, North Korea, etc. On the one hand, there is broad agreement among the various thinkers and movements considered in this book that liberal democratic liberty is for the most part negative individual liberty: i.e. it is freedom not to be interfered with rather than a positive or creative affirmation. There is also broad agreement that institutionalised negative liberty legislates an oppressive obsession with one's own career, property, children and future. On this reading the obsession leads to the degeneration of liberty into narrow-minded consumerism and private retreat from political life. The conclusion is that negative liberty undermines the democratic bases of collective political accountability by destroying the channels of communication between citizens that genuine political accountability requires.[4] On the other hand, the history of the left has also been a history of the (at times violent) disagreements about how to counter these tendencies, and about what might serve as a libertarian alternative to liberal democracy. If this alternative exists, it offers the key to answering the question about how to institutionalise the relationship between humanity and nature in a free society. It will be seen in Chapter 1 that the modern search systematically to understand the conditions under which such an alternative could exist begin with Marx.

Notes

1 Henri Lefebvre, *Critique of Everyday Life* (*Critique de la vie quotidienne*), p. 130 (his emphases). (In most cases in this text I shall work with the original text and provide a translation of the title in the notes for readers who may be interested in consulting an English translation of the work in question.)

2 Peter Marshall, *Demanding the Impossible*.

3 Prior to the French Revolution there was no meaningful distinction between left and right. Indeed, these terms arose on the rather arbitrary basis of the seating arrangements in the French National Assembly in the wake of the events of 1789 and the issue of the royal veto. One group espoused the view that the will of the people, as expressed through its elected representatives, must have priority on all issues concerning property reform, religious education, etc. A second group, comprising the representatives of the nobility and upper clergy, defended the right of the monarchy to intervene in these matters. The first sat to the left of the speaker's platform, the second to his right. Moderate voices with no definite opinion sat in the middle, thus inspiring the anger and sarcasm of the ostensibly more principled positions at the extremes. In a somewhat polemical vein one might argue that the current crisis of the left has distant origins, since there has always been something slightly problematic about the left–right spectrum. If it is true that the extremes meet in terms of

intransigence and intolerance (in which case there is not a great deal to separate them), while the centre is the meeting point of the relatively indistin-
guishable moderates, it looks as if the extremes meet at the ends and the rest
converge in the middle. The end result is that there is little meaningful difference anywhere! Chapters 5 and 6 of this book explore some of the problems of
thinking about politics in terms of a spectrum or continuum from right to left,
or 'less' humanist to 'more' humanist. For a very good historical introduction
to these issues, see David Smith, *Left and Right in Twentieth-Century Europe*. For a
defence of the continued relevance of the left–right distinction, see Norberto
Bobbio, *Left and Right*.

4 Matters are complicated further if one considers that this analysis of the degeneration of liberty is also shared in large measure by liberals such as Alexis de
Tocqueville (1805–59) as well as by some right-wing thinkers, such as Vilfredo
Pareto (1848–1923) and Gaetano Mosca (1858–1941). That is, it is a problem
addressed by thinkers at the centre and right of the political spectrum, not
only by those on the left. This issue will be raised at various points in the chapters to come.

1
Marx

Marx's writings can be roughly divided into three periods. The first is characterised by his grappling with the philosophies of Kant (1724–1804) and Hegel (1770–1831). The second is marked by a turn away from his concentration on philosophy, and a transition to the detailed study of politics and economics. The third is the period of maturity in which Marx wove together all the various strands of his thinking, writing the *Grundrisse* in 1857–58, as well as the three volumes of *Capital*, which, along with the *Communist Manifesto* (1848), is perhaps his most famous work.

In terms of Marx's prodigious output as a whole, it is often remarked that the system he develops is derived from three principal sources. These sources are German idealist philosophy (Kant, Hegel), French utopian socialism (Fourier, St Simon), and English and Scottish British political economy (Adam Smith, Adam Ferguson, Dugald Stewart and David Ricardo). It will be seen below that another key figure from the first period, Ludwig Feuerbach (1804–72), provides him with the tools he needs to criticise Hegel in a specifically materialist direction, and that the shift in emphasis from idealism and anthropology to historical materialism has a tremendous impact on Marx's project as a whole. This shift should not be misunderstood as a radical break, however, for there is a fundamental continuity between the young Marx on philosophy and politics, and the mature Marx on sociology and political economy. What emerges across the three periods is a many-sided but ultimately very coherently synthesised critique of religion, philosophy, law, political economy and the state. In terms of the themes in this chapter, the first period is the most important for two principal reasons, which elucidate the trajectory of the left in Europe from Marx to the present.

Firstly, and most importantly, in grappling with the ideas of Kant, Hegel and Feuerbach, Marx takes up a line of inquiry that is pursued in different ways by the theorists of Western Marxism (Chapter 2) and critical theory (Chapter 3) in the inter-war period and again in the 1960s. In the subsequent decades of the twentieth century, this line of Hegelian–Marxist inquiry is substantially revised by some of the poststructuralists as a result of the incorporation of selected ideas from the work of Friedrich Nietzsche (1844–1900) into their social theory (Chapter 6). Following Marx, the leading representatives of Western Marxism, critical theory and poststructuralism explore the idea that the critique of epistemology (i.e. of the ways in which we know), is implicitly and at times explicitly also a critique of the society in which we live, and of the way we conceive of the relation between theory and practice.

Secondly, while Marx's oeuvre can be seen to culminate in his mature writings on political economy, the critique of political economy is ultimately a development of the theory of historical materialism, and the latter is itself a development in the critique of idealism and Hegel's theories of subjective and objective spirit. Hence this chapter begins with a brief excursus on Kant, Hegel and Feuerbach, and then moves on to examine Marx's attempt to project epistemology beyond traditional philosophy in theory, while projecting economics and politics beyond capitalism and the democratic parliamentary state in practice.

The Precursors: Kant, Hegel and Feuerbach

At the core of Kant's critical philosophy is an attempt to rescue epistemological inquiry from a cul-de-sac. He starts from the intuition that the attempt to explain the knowledge process by relying on the primacy of mind or human consciousness variously defended by rationalists such as Descartes, Leibniz and Spinoza is as questionable as the empiricist primacy of nature espoused in different ways by Berkeley, Locke and Hume. The impasse reached by the diametrically opposed positions taken up by these two schools leads Kant to say that the question as to whether knowledge is to be sought in humanity (mind) or in nature (the world external to the mind) is falsely posed, just as the fundamental question of whether we have knowledge or merely whims and opinions is falsely posed. He maintains that framing the key questions of epistemology in this way results in a stand-off between rationalist knowledge, which is monolithic and dogmatic (because all minds must be the same), and empiricist knowledge, which is arbitrary and relativist (because there is a potentially unlimited number of versions of individual experience with no way to adjudicate between their different claims). Kant asserts that the choice between dogmatism and relativism is highly unsatisfactory, and in any case inadequate to the challenges of Enlightenment and modernity. Hence he attempts to rescue epistemological investigation from the rationalist versus empiricist dilemma by arguing that the real question is not whether or not we have knowledge, or if knowledge is to be sought in consciousness or in nature. The more pertinent question is: *Under what conditions is knowledge possible?*

In the *Critique of Pure Reason*, Kant identifies the condition of possible knowledge as the existence of a transcendental subject that can reflexively unify itself with reason, and thereby have formal knowledge of the phenomena that present themselves to the twelve categories of the understanding (causality, unity, plurality, possibility, necessity, substance, etc.) in time and space.[1] In furnishing a critique of 'pure' reason, Kant is arguing that though we can have *formal* knowledge of the phenomena of perception that is objective, we cannot have *essential* knowledge of the noumena—the things in themselves, unmediated by conceptual form— that is absolute. Against a rationalist understanding of the relationship between humanity and nature which is *dualistic*, and an empiricist understanding of that relation that can be described as the *identity* of humanity and nature, Kant reintroduces the Greek emphasis on *dialectics* into philosophy. In other words, rationalists posit a dualism between humanity and nature due to the existence of the human mind, while empiricists posit an identity between mind and nature based on the idea that the mind is a natural organ. According to a more dialectical understanding, dualism and identity are both inadequate, since humanity is itself part of nature because of the simple reality of hunger, thirst, birth and mortality, etc., though not reducible to nature because of consciousness and our ability to reflexively unify ourselves with reason.

The dialectical approach, which was adopted in different ways by Hegel and Marx and subsequently taken up in a more critical vein by later figures on the European left such as Marcuse, Adorno and Sartre, attempts to think in harmony with the paradox that humanity is located both inside and outside nature. Hence, whilst dualistic and identity approaches tend to be analytical and static, the dialectical approach recognises that thinking is moved by contradiction and tension because the world itself is comprised of a dynamic *totality* of contradictory and at times opposing forces. Hence for dialectical thinkers trying to ascertain the bases of knowledge, it is the forms of *mediation* between humanity and nature that count, and they reject attempts to establish an essential primacy of the human mind or of nature. Whether the thinkers in question acknowledge it or not, however, this way of looking at reality is initiated by Kant.

One of the central questions for all thinkers after Kant is how to conceive of the mediation between humanity and nature without making what they take to be the Kantian error of assigning permanent validity to the two forms of sensible intuition (space and time), and the twelve categories of the understanding. Kant posits an insurmountable limit to reason and what we can know by insisting that we cannot know the things in themselves. Many of the thinkers on the left who will be considered in this book pursue the question: Might not a different society be capable of producing more perfect forms of mediation, and, as a result, more perfect forms of reason and freedom?

Modern dialectical thinking becomes historical when Hegel discovers that the forms of reason mediating between humanity and nature are in a process of constant unfolding, and are never at rest for long. Indeed, it is Hegel's implicit claim that, while moving philosophy beyond the dualist and identity approaches, Kant's philosophy is not dialectical enough precisely because it is not sufficiently historical. For Hegel, it is not enough to realise that the relationship between humanity and nature is mediated. If one stops there, one runs the risk of settling for the idea that humanity and nature are forever separated by the mediating processes in a manner analogous to the separation of form and content or essences and appearances. It is Hegel's contention that Kant does just this by categorically separating the phenomena and the forms of our knowledge from the noumena and the objects of our knowledge themselves. From Hegel's standpoint, Kant forgets that, in addition to being mediated, the relation between humanity and nature is dialectical. Kant also forgets that it is inherent in the notion of historicised dialectics that the mediation processes reach successively higher and more complete resolutions as history progresses. Hegel sees this happening in a movement from unmediated unity (thesis), to mediated disunity (antithesis), to mediated unity (synthesis). This is a movement that he believes culminates in absolute knowledge at the level of the individual subject. In a parallel development, the same movement results in the achievement of absolute freedom at the level of world history. The theory of individual knowledge is outlined as a theory of what Hegel calls 'subjective spirit' in the *Phenomenology of Spirit* of 1807. In the *Philosophy of Right* (1821) and in the *Lectures on the Philosophy of World History* (1830), Hegel develops his theory of history as the unfolding of what he refers to as objective spirit. As will be seen presently, Hegel's theories of subjective spirit and objective spirit mark a decisive break with Kant, and at the same time clearly foreshadow Marx's particular approach to dialectics and his explanation of historical change and political revolution. For the time being one might say that Hegel regards history as the story of spirit's journey from unmediated unity to mediated unity, traveled along a difficult and winding succession of progressively more perfect stages of mediated disunity. This idea is briefly explained below.

In terms of subjective spirit, Hegel imagines that humanity once enjoyed a relationship of unmediated unity with nature, which was broken (or, to anticipate Feuerbach and Marx, *alienated*) in the realisation that consciousness is always consciousness of something foreign to one's own consciousness. At some point in history, people become acutely aware that this 'something' is no longer identical with consciousness, but rather an entity external and hostile to it. From that stage in the development of consciousness onwards, subjective consciousness perceives the relationship with the objects of consciousness as mediated disunity.

Although they are no longer united in identity, consciousness and the objects of consciousness are nonetheless united in the dynamic non-identity of subject and object, and the corresponding perception that there can be no subject without an object and vice versa. As such, subject and object, like humanity and nature, constitute a totality, so that even if the terms of the totality are not identical (dogmatism), they are nonetheless not dualistically separated (relativism/positivism). That is, that in spite of their nonidentity, a form of mediated unity is operative in the relation between subject and object, and between consciousness and nature. This is part of what it means to think dialectically about human-ity's paradoxical location in the world: mediation processes *unite* know-ing subjects (1) and known objects (2) at the same time that they *separate*; the paradoxical dimension that unites as well as separates—i.e. medi-ates—is what Hegel refers to as spirit.

A temporary form of mediated unity is achieved when consciousness adjusts the concepts and categories it adopts in order better to grasp the objective quality of the object of perception. But before long, mediated unity gives way to mediated disunity again, as consciousness perceives that the concepts and categories invoked to understand objective reality are deficient and in need of further adjustment. In Hegel's estimation, Kant implies that there is an inevitable stalemate between subjective con-sciousness and objective reality that precludes the possibility of pure rea-son and knowledge of objects without the mediation of conceptual form. Hegel is thus determined to move philosophy beyond Kant's static con-ception of mediation, and beyond what he considers to be Kant's inade-quate conception of epistemological form.

For Hegel, Kant's great achievement is that he shows that all objective knowledge is mediated by the twelve subjective categories of the under-standing: i.e., he shows that *all objectivity is mediated by subjectivity.* Hegel takes the argument further by showing that *all subjectivity is mediated by objectivity.* In this context, what Hegel means by 'objectivity' is the histor-ical evolution of social and political institutions. It is the ongoing contra-diction between subjective consciousness and the concepts developed to explain objective historical reality (thesis), on the one hand, and the actual historical reality as it is really operative at any particular time in real institutions (antithesis), on the other, that always indicates that the concepts invoked to explain reality are in need of further revision in order to become even more real (synthesis). Another way of expressing this idea is that subjectivity is historically created, superseded and recre-ated as a result of the changing conditions of objectivity and the unfold-ing of objective spirit in ever-new sociopolitical institutions that produce qualitatively new, more perfectly knowing subjects at every stage of the historical process. Thus Hegel attempts to show that all subjectivity in the guise of consciousness is mediated by objectivity in the guises of history and society. From that moment on, Hegel submits, one cannot convincingly rely on the notion of twelve fixed categories of the understanding, nor can one rely on some static conception of 'human nature' or 'the human condition'. Humans are products of nature as well as products of history, and the latter, in particular, has a dynamic structure that tends towards overcoming the limits on knowledge at the same time as tending towards overcoming the limits on freedom. This theory of objective spirit is systematically developed in the *Philosophy of Right*.

In the Prologue Hegel says that the actually existing world is rational, and that the rational is what actually exists. There are two closely related consequences that follow. First, there can be no credible Kantian juxtaposition between what is, in terms of ethics and morality, and what ought to be, in terms of politics and the state. What is and what ought to be might seem like discrepant realities, but for Hegel they are in fact in a process of slow but inexorable convergence. This analysis points to the second consequence, which is that all of reality can be understood as a mediated totality of humanity and nature in which the structure of the mediations is knowable. It is a rational configuration of mediating concepts that is gradually uniting mind (subjective spirit) with institutions (objective spirit) over the course of the historical process. The theory of objective spirit in the *Philosophy of Right* thus brings philosophical idealism to a culminating point of no return which, as will be shown in the rest of this chapter, Marx seeks to transcend with his ideas on historical materialism and revolution. To anticipate the argument, Marx sees the motor of historical change in a series of contradictions between our human capacity to transform the natural world through creative labour power, on the one hand, and the legal, political, ideological and cultural impediments to the full development of that productive capacity, on the other. Hence for Marx it is not the contradictions within the movements of spirit that mediate between humanity and nature, but rather human labour power. This means that Hegel is absolutely right in his objections to Kant, and is also right to insist on the dialectical nature of reality. But for Marx, Hegel is wrong to suppose that the mainspring of dialectics is consciousness. (This raises several questions, which will be revisited later in this book.) While he resolutely criticises Hegel, it is also clear that to a significant extent Marx adopts key aspects of the structure of Hegel's epistemology to his own epistemological and political programme. Does Marxism in particular and the left in general need to be even more resolute in challenging Hegelian thought? Or does Hegelian thought on the contrary offer political and epistemological possibilities that are not fully recognised as a result of Marx's haste to dispense with Hegel and idealism? Does Marx exaggerate the centrality of technology and labour in the mediation of humanity and nature? It will be seen in Chapter 2 that Western Marxism arises as a response to technologically deterministic and economically mechanical interpretations of Marx and their manifest incapacity to explain historical phenomena such as working-class nationalism during World War I and fascism. Dissatisfaction with this explanatory inadequacy on the part of mechanical and evolutionary models of Marxism leads the theorists of Western Marxism to reconsider relations between the economic base and the legal, cultural, political and aesthetic superstructure. Before moving on to these discussions it is therefore imperative to clarify Marx's relation to Hegel.[2]

In his exposition of the theory of ethical life in the third section of the *Philosophy of Right*, Hegel argues that the movement from unmediated unity to mediated disunity to mediated unity at the level of subjective spirit finds its parallel in the movement from the family to civil society and from there to the state at the level of objective spirit. Prior to Hegel, modern legal and political philosophy from Hobbes to Kant attempted to formulate the conditions of political obligation in secular terms by explaining, albeit in substantially different ways, why and how the free individuals existing in the state of nature unanimously agree to abandon their natural advantages in order to form a civil society. Thus, before Hegel, the state of nature is juxtaposed to civil society, and the latter term is synonymous with the state. Hegel abandons the state of nature versus civil society dichotomy for his tripartite system of mediations because, among other reasons, he is determined to give the state a firmer foundation than his predecessors, who generally rely on different versions of the idea of a social contract. Social contract theorists posit that individuals leave the state of nature by making a contract with the state that guarantees their rights in a more stable form than would be possible without the state. The state of nature is sometimes depicted as violent, as in Hobbes. It is also described in more consensual and peaceful terms, as in Locke and Rousseau. In all cases, however, contract is regarded as the medium through which the modern state can be seen to be founded: on a fundamental form of unanimous agreement rather than force, the divine right of kings, tradition, or some other specious argument.

It is clear to the social contract theorists that agreement must underpin secular forms of modern authority. Arguments in favour of the divine right of kings are no longer tenable given the trajectory of political thought and action since the appearance of Renaissance republicanism and humanism in the fifteenth and sixteenth centuries. While Hegel agrees that modern authority must be based on rational agreement rather than divine right, aristocratic privilege, tradition, force, etc., he is nonetheless certain that this agreement cannot be based on the model of individual interest and contract. He explains that it is futile to attempt to derive the terms of political obligation from a contractual model, since a valid contract presupposes a valid state which makes a contract binding in the first place. In other words, the difference between ownership and mere possession is law and the state. In a manner analogous to the movement from unmediated unity to mediated unity by way of mediated disunity, and corresponding to the idea that all subjectivity is mediated by institutional objectivity, Hegel argues that it is actually the substantive and noncontractual forms of agreement that make the contractual dimension based on interest and contract possible. Universality and legitimate authority make particularity and the pursuit of interest possible and in fact dictate the terms under which the latter may be pursued—not the other way round.[3]

Hegel is confident that the fabric of the modern state is particularly strong and elastic, since it can assimilate and harmonise a great many particularist and individualist threads. To this extent he concurs with social contract theorists who argue that individual rights and interests are a key component of modern consciousness. He also has a certain amount of sympathy with the ideas voiced by a number of his contemporaries who would like to see the Greek *polis* resurrected, in order to recreate a form of unmediated unity between the individual citizen and the political community. But such 'creations', however desirable they might seem, are in fact arbitrary interventions in the course of spirit's long journey toward self-discovery and mediated unity. An attempt to recreate unmediated unity between the citizen and the state is bound to fail, for it fails to acknowledge the moment of truth in particularity, conflict and divergence, i.e., in institutionalised forms of mediated disunity that are characteristic of modern civil societies and the struggles for mutual recognition within them. In the section of the *Philosophy of Right* dedicated to the role of the corporation within civil society, Hegel implicitly warns that attempts to eradicate contractual ties, pluralism and associational life embodied by churches, universities, guilds, competition, commerce, etc., is bound to fail. After the experiences of Christianity, the Reformation, the Renaissance, the Enlightenment, the scientific revolution, and the nascent industrial revolution of his own day, it was clear to Hegel that it is not possible for us to return to ancient Greece and the forms of politics that flourished there. Moreover, the episode of the Terror in the French Revolution indicates that political projects designed to create unmediated unity between citizen and state will result in tyranny.

In terms of the complicated relation between consciousness (theory) and institutions (practice), therefore, it might be that Hegel is in a position to enter into a critical dialogue with those who preceded him, such as Robespierre and the Jacobins, as well as those who came after him, such as Lenin and the Bolsheviks. He implies that despite all the many problems in the civil sphere, any attempt to incorporate civil society into the state in the name of the General Will and a resolution of the tension between equality of citizenship and inequality between classes is destined to fail. Marx, by contrast, is sure that history does not stop with the French Revolution and the modern state. He thinks that far from resting on a fundamental form of agreement, the modern state represents the political compromise resulting from the conflicts arising between, on the one hand, waning feudal-aristocratic power based on land ownership and, on the other, ascendant bourgeois-industrial power based on the ownership of capital. Rather than being an expression of mediated unity, the state is largely an expression of mediated disunity institutionalised as bourgeois-industrial power, which can in its turn be criticised and overthrown. Like Hegel, Marx is sure that mediated unity is inscribed within the unfolding of history. This means that for both thinkers a harmonious community between humanity and nature and between humanity and other humanity is an historical inevitability. Unlike Hegel, Marx refuses to regard the arrival of the modern state as the last stage of that process.[4]

To begin with, Marx does not share Hegel's confidence in the capacity of the modern state to bear the strains of associational pluralism and forms of commercial exchange predicated on contractually mediated individual and class interest. However, the path of inquiry that leads Marx to this conclusion and beyond to his theory of historical materialism and the critique of political economy begins with a critique of religion. This is a critique in which Feuerbach's concepts of species-being, alienation and fetishism play a key role.

Feuerbach develops his ideas on these subjects in detail in *The Essence of Christianity* (1841). Here he anticipates Nietzsche's critique of religion by arguing that in attributing humanity's best characteristics to God in heaven, humanity itself becomes incapable of unifying theory and practice on earth. For Feuerbach, there is an answer to why humanity is largely neither happy nor free, and it is decidedly not original sin or some other curse of nature or God. To the extent that God is said to be omniscient, omnipotent, creative, loving and forgiving, humanity becomes ignorant, weak, unimaginative, petty and vengeful. In this process, people take what rightfully belongs to the human species, and they alienate it to some kind of deity. That is, the creation of God consists in a series of steps in which humans defer the earthly realisation of their own freedom, happiness and creativity by projecting that realisation on to an already perfect being who exists in another world. Projection results in passivity and conformity instead of active, world-transforming practice. What makes this process difficult to criticise and change is that what begins as an array of human qualities comes back to humanity in a form they no longer recognise as human. This can be explained with a look at Feuerbach's twin critique of religious thinking and Hegelian philosophy.[5]

One must bear in mind that Hegel regards history in terms analogous to a journey in which the spirit mediating humanity and nature experiences first unity, then loss, and then unity again on a higher, more richly articulated plane. Feuerbach interprets Hegelian philosophy as a rather inconclusive break from religious thinking. He observes that by reasoning in terms of spirit's journey towards self-discovery, Hegel endows thought itself with a life independent of humanity and individual thinking humans. The journey of spirit attains a kind of otherworldly quality that is at odds with sensuous, practical and earthly realities. As a consequence of Hegel's garbled terminology, philosophical thinking about this journey becomes opaque and wrapped up in its own closed system of abstract concepts and categories. By the time one has read it, one forgets that it is the result of active, creative thinking, because it seems to come from another world. It is not important whether one accepts it as dogmatic truth or dismisses it as wholly foreign and unintelligible. More crucially, one forgets that it is the product of the mind of an intelligent man with physical needs, material hopes, sentiments of love and so forth.

Feuerbach suggests that there is nothing fundamentally alienating about philosophy or religion unless we forget that they have their common origins in the struggle of humanity to understand its relation with nature. Taking the case of religion, one sees that in theory, religious thought teaches us about love, kindness, forgiveness and hope. But when we are confronted with the rules, codes, organised hierarchies and punitive sanctions of existing religious institutions, God and religion appear to humans as something strange, terrifying and otherworldly. In the end humans no longer recognise a product of their own earthly existence and imagination in religion. Religion becomes a phenomenon created by an alien being or deity to which humans must submit.[6] Feuerbach credits Hegel with the insight that history develops in stages, and that the institutional results (Hegel's objective spirit) at every stage are increasingly complex and rich in possibilities for knowledge and freedom. However, he thinks that Hegel gives us a theological account of history in philosophical language that obscures the anthropological fact that both philosophy and religion are the result of human interpretations of history and society. Hegel perpetuates rather than solves the problem that when we grapple with theological and philosophical systems, we all too often lose sight of our own mental activity and imagination in them. Philosophies and religions can then assume the objective form of doctrines and institutions that command deference and obedience.

Marx interprets Feuerbach's critique of Hegel to mean that the critique of religion and the critique of philosophy are related enterprises. Not only are humanity and nature, and subject and object dialectically mediated in history—so are theory and practice. Hence Marx acknowledges the importance of Feuerbach's critique of Hegel, but hastens to add that by placing sensuous and thinking humanity at the centre of reality instead of philosophers and priests, Feuerbach offers an ultimately anodyne form of anthropological humanism in place of organised religion and academic philosophy. He does not show or explain what kinds of institutions and relations between people must obtain if there is to be a truly humanised world. From Marx's perspective, revolutionary practice must supersede religion, philosophy and Feuerbach's brand of generic humanism.[7]

What Marx proposes in his early writings of 1843, and particularly in the *Critique of Hegel* and *On the Jewish Question*, is to think through the questions raised by Feuerbach in relation to Hegel by retaining Hegel's dialectical method and infusing it with the revolutionary materialism implicitly suggested by Feuerbach's anthropological humanism. Marx seeks to do this by transferring Feuerbach's critique of Hegel to the domains of the state, law, politics, and from there to political economy and the labour process. While retaining the dialectic in Hegel, Marx retains Feuerbach's genealogical notion that ideas and practices start out in one institutional form, and subtly evolve towards a different form. Ideas and practices then return to actual citizens in a new institutional form in a series of stages that over time tend to become opaque to most of the participants in the historical process. This makes the power relations governing the historical process appear unfathomable and unchangeable. On the basis of his reading of Feuerbach, the young Marx argues that humans create religious systems and forms of authority that enslave their minds and find their real, terrestrial expression in the power of the church hierarchy over concrete individuals. But he takes a decisive step further by explaining that something analogous happens in our political and socioeconomic institutions. In the writings of 1843–45, Marx traces the social mechanisms in which human relations (which are always capable of being reformed or even revolutionised) acquire the objective institutional form of relations that are unchangeable either because they are natural or because they are things that are not of our own creation, to which we must submit.

While Kant proves that consciousness is neither identical with nature nor wholly separate from it, and Hegel proves that consciousness is modified by history and determinate forms of society, the young Marx sets out to prove that it is within humanity's power to liberate itself from all forms of consciousness and social relations that reduce its individual members to passive roles in the hierarchies operative in the church, state and civil society. As will be seen, in the course of his analysis Marx locates the economy as the key to understanding civil society and the state.

Marx on Fetishism, Reification and the Difference between Political Emancipation and Human Emancipation

The tendency to attribute natural and otherworldly properties to human creations and relations is a phenomenon Marx calls fetishism. He diagnoses a related problem in the tendency to attribute thinglike qualities to human creations and relations, which he calls reification. The question of reification and reified consciousness is taken up in detail by a number of influential Western Marxists and critical theorists, as will be seen in Chapters 2 and 3. For now it is important to note that systematic reflections on these topics appear for the first time in the *Critique of Hegel* and *On the Jewish Question*. They are then developed further in the *Economic and Philosophical Manuscripts of 1844*. In the introduction to the *Critique of Hegel*, one reads the now-famous lines about religion being the opiate of the masses. Marx goes on to explain that the critique of reified social, political and economic relations must begin in his native Germany as a critique of religion and philosophy, since, historically speaking, Germany is less advanced in the field of industrial production than other countries, most notably England. He is already thinking along lines that will recur in the works of the next few years, such as the *German Ideology* (1845) and the *Communist Manifesto* (1848): that the economically most developed countries indicate to the lesser developed ones their future course of development. This process can take unusual turns, making the key issue appear to be religion in one place, philosophy in another, and politics in a third. Marx suggests that what must be grasped in dialectical fashion is the notion of the totality of mediations, even if at any particular historical juncture in a given country its religion, philosophy or politics may appear the most visible point of social conflict and political rupture.[8]

The best way to understand the totality of mediations is still somewhat unclear to Marx in 1843, though he says that what it means to be radical is to take a problem by the root. This implies that behind the religious, philosophical, artistic and political disputes of a time and place, there is a primary key of interpretation. At this stage, however, Marx is still defining his own position in relation to the ideas of Hegel and Feuerbach. Two points emerge in the introduction to the *Critique of Hegel*. The first appears with Marx's demand that 'The criticism of religion ends with the doctrine that for man the supreme being is man, and thus with the categorical imperative to overthrow all conditions in which man is a debased, neglected and contemptible being.' Marx follows these remarks at the end of the introduction, where he talks about a class that is the dissolution of all classes, a sphere that has a universal character because of its universal suffering, which lays claim to no particular right, because the wrong it suffers is not a particular wrong but wrong in general. He then announces the appearance of a social class that—precisely because it represents the total loss of humanity—bears within itself the possibility of the total redemption of humanity.[9]

It is striking that Marx remains under Hegel's influence to the extent that the process preparing the emancipation of humanity is seen to be preceded by a stage of total loss and alienation. But in contrast to Hegel and many of the thinkers who will be examined in this book, he is firmly committed to revolution. For Marx, the only way to answer philosophical questions about reality, knowledge and freedom is to put theory into practice; he likens this transformation to making philosophy redundant by realising philosophy in practice. Just as the critique of religion must give way to the critique of the social relations that give rise to religious institutions, for Marx the critique of philosophy must give way to a radical reorganisation of the institutions that encourage people to understand the real, material problems in their lives in abstractly philosophical terms. This line of argument is pursued further in *On the Jewish Question*, in which Marx turns his attention to that particular aspect of Hegel's philosophy that fascinates him most in 1843–45. This is Hegel's marked departure from the social contract theorists and his corresponding theories of the state and civil society. Following Feuerbach, Marx reasons that just as humans create God, religion, and the material conditions that give rise to religious penitence instead of active transformation, so too do humans create law and the state. As in the case of church hierarchy, law and the state confront the citizens as alien institutions that dominate the very people who brought them into existence.

To the extent that the state is imagined to be communitarian, democratic, transcendent of particular interests, and the embodiment of freedom, the citizens in civil society are compelled to understand themselves as engaged in egotistic, nondemocratic and competitive pursuits. The capacity of self-government, which at least in theory starts with the autonomous citizen, is unconsciously bestowed upon the state by the citizens. The state then seems like an objective phenomenon with its own objective imperatives and rights against the citizens. Like God, the state becomes a reified entity that inspires incomprehension and fear. Citizens forget that the capacity for democracy and freedom is their capacity, because in the state they are confronted with alienated institutions that they no longer recognise as the result of their own activity. For Marx this is a disastrous situation, which Hegel consciously seeks to defend (in the *Philosophy of Right*) by declaring state institutions to be the bearers of mediated unity. In *On the Jewish Question*, Marx recognises the profundity of Hegel's critique of the social contract theorists as well as his diagnosis of the separation of the state and civil society as a key feature of the structure of modern industrial countries. He goes on to explain that the real issue involved in the 'Jewish Question', and his polemic with the Young Hegelian Bruno Bauer in that text, is not the political enfranchisement of the Jewish population of European nation states. The real issue is political enfranchisement or emancipation versus more universal human emancipation for everyone, not just the Jewish members of the state. What is meant by this distinction between political and human emancipation?[10]

Marx does not belittle the struggle for Jewish enfranchisement. He uses the example of the struggle in order to make the point that the key to the emancipation of the Jewish people is not their political emancipation but the emancipation of the state from Judaism. That is, the more the state can portray itself as a neutral state that makes no distinctions between Christians and non-Christians, the more it can be seen to be impartial and neutral. It is then the entire people's state, a democratic state, not the Christian state, Jewish state, or any other state championing particular interests—it attains true universality and appears to embody Hegelian mediated unity. Marx is always aware of the pitfalls of fetishism and reification. Accordingly, he implies that the term 'state', like the term 'capital' in his later analyses, denotes a *relation* rather than a thing to be seized, smashed or occupied. When Marx speaks of the emancipation of the state from Judaism (or from any other religion for that matter), what he means is that the relations of power in society are in a constant process of reorganisation and redeployment. At a particular historical moment, it may well be that the advancement of determinate power interests requires a legitimating discourse, and it is characteristic of modern societies that the exercise of power becomes increasingly detached from visibly identifiable figures such as kings, queens and the nobility.

In emancipating itself from religion, the network of power relations and interests denoted by the word 'state' becomes even more of an abstraction to the citizen than it is when the state is directly identified with one religion or a definite set of rulers. The process that runs parallel to the state declaring itself the embodiment and guarantor of reason and universality is that the citizens become passive recipients of universal human rights. In theory, all people—regardless of race, religion, class and other distinctions—are henceforth proclaimed equal, and political emancipation becomes synonymous with human emancipation. Marx suggests that what is really happening is that the arrival of this particular form of political emancipation is tantamount to the realisation of a new kind of religiosity in the fetishising of law, property and human rights. It is true that the restructuring of the state in order to make religion a personal matter allows citizens across different denominations to practise their religions. But it simultaneously becomes difficult to see that along with religion, the real obstacles to a credible form of universality are becoming private and increasingly unaccountable to public authority.

What Marx means by the 'real obstacles' is of course property and capitalist forms of exchange based on production for profit rather than need or intrinsic creativity. One is in fact tempted to say that the first analyses of what is today referred to as globalisation, in terms of the power of private economic interests to elude public and political accountability, are actually implicitly contained in the 1843 writings. Chapter 6 and the Conclusion will take up this point.[11]

By granting religious emancipation, Marx explains, humans are not freed from religion—they are granted religious freedom. The more important result is that they are not freed from the social relation denoted by the term 'property'. They are granted freedom to acquire as much property as they like—if they can. Marx uses the issue of religious emancipation in order to analyse a more fundamental development in the evolution of different forms of state. He traces the processes by which the modern state, far from being universal or neutral, and far from reconciling clashing particular interests, as Hegel claims it does, actually secures the bases of newly emerging interests of a very specific kind which are in the process of emancipating themselves from feudal political control. Hence Marx is convinced that the French Revolution is much more than a French affair. It marks the transition from the feudal-aristocratic epoch to the bourgeois-democratic epoch in Europe, North America, and eventually on a global scale. He has no doubt that the defeats of Napoleon Bonaparte in 1812–13 and the partial restoration of hereditary power in places such as Italy thereafter would be only small parentheses in the otherwise inexorable movement of history towards more perfect forms of freedom and knowledge. However epochal in scope, the movement for political emancipation inaugurated by the French Revolution is nonetheless crucially limited. This is the gist of Marx's critique of Hegel and the argument developed in *On the Jewish Question*. The Revolution proclaims the sovereignty of the citizenry as well as the Right of Man and Citizen. However, Marx objects, if the citizens were really sovereign, there would be no separation between them and the machinery of government. Political emancipation guarantees each citizen's right not to be infringed upon in the private sphere in which they gain their livelihood. In framing freedom in this way, each individual has the negative freedom not to be infringed upon in the buying and selling of property. In effect this means they have the freedom necessary to secure the conditions under which the interests of private property become synonymous with general interests.

Prior to the French Revolution, guilds, estates, and various kinds of corporation in civil society perform the mediating function between individual and state assigned to them at the theoretical level by Hegel. The events in France signify the culminating point of a process in which the authority of these mediating institutions is gradually undermined. According to

Marx, civil society increasingly becomes a de-politicised battlefield of struggling individuals and classes, whilst the state becomes an increasingly centralised and distant form of largely symbolic political authority. It is largely symbolic authority, he argues, because real authority is dispersed in power networks in civil society. This diagnosis prompts Marx to say in *On the Jewish Question* that 'political emancipation was at the same time the emancipation of civil society from politics, from its even having a semblance of a universal content.'[12] While Hegel is confident that the associational life of the corporations provides a kind of pre-state-level form of organisation that involves citizens in semipolitical pursuits beyond the struggle for survival, Marx regards this as a quickly diminishing institutional reality in the individualist age of the Rights of Man and Citizen. Marx does not yearn for a return to the age of guilds and corporations, for this was what he calls in the *Critique of Hegel* the 'democracy of unfreedom'.[13] Moreover, as will be seen in the next section, he is also persuaded that the demise of associational corporatism and the rise of bourgeois individualism will result in an increase in humanity's productive capacity on an entirely unprecedented scale. This productive capacity prepares the ground for the 'democracy of freedom' by emancipating people from the various forms of physical necessity and material scarcity that have shackled the imagination to the daily grind of winning the battle of survival. The immediate task in the early writings, then, is fully to grasp the processes leading to the restructuring of power relations that brings about the formation of the modern state. An analysis of these processes will offer the key to understanding what more legitimate forms of political community might in their turn replace the newly established institutions of bourgeois power.

Marx interprets the advent of political emancipation in terms of two important developments. First, modern economic institutions are given an individualist basis on the foundation provided by formal legal equality in general and by civil law in particular. The first consequence is that various forms of serfdom are abolished (not until 1861 in Russia) in favour of the contractual right to buy and sell labour as a good or *commodity*; the second consequence is that the state emerges as a powerful and largely politically unaccountable force, reigning in the name of a spurious general interest on behalf of particular interests linked with contract, exchange, and the sale and accumulation of capital and property. In view of these tendencies, Marx is at first sceptical of, and soon after categorically opposed to the idea of a parliamentary solution to the divorce between the state and civil society. He begins to see that economic interests related to property and exchange cannot have a basis separate from political and community interests in a truly legitimate democratic polity. Hence the question arises: what does Marx envisage as an alternative to political emancipation and the negative forms of liberty guaranteed by parliamentary democracy? Towards the end of *On the Jewish Question* he affirms that '. . . only when man has recognised and organised his "forces propres" (own powers) as social forces, and consequently no longer separates social power from himself in the shape of political power, only then will human emancipation have been accomplished.'[14] While he does not specify exactly what he has in mind by this in institutional terms, one can reconstruct his argument to mean broadly that in a humanly emancipated society commonly owned property replaces private property, and that alienated political power no longer exists.

The *Communist Manifesto* and the Revolutions of 1848

In his early writings and up to the period culminating in the revolutions of 1848, Marx intuits that the solution to the problem of class relations is intimately bound up with the solution to the problem of the relations between citizens and the state. He intuits further that the next revolution, the revolution to follow the French Revolution and complete the transition from political emancipation to human emancipation, would have to abolish class distinctions simultaneously with political hierarchies and bureaucracies. He reasons that while class distinctions prevail in civil society, and particularly in the economy, where the bourgeoisie buys labour power and the proletariat sells labour power, political alienation is perpetuated in the gulf between citizens and their government. Marx suggests that formal legal equality obtaining between citizens is undermined by the real inequality between those who buy and those who sell labour power in civil society. Hence the step from political emancipation to human emancipation will be a unification of civil society and the state in a more legitimate form of political community than the parliamentary democratic republic. That more legitimate political form he has in mind is communism.

Marx is sure that communism is the answer to the riddle of history and the key to squaring the manifest inequality between social classes with the formal equality of citizens. During the 1840s, however, he is not quite sure about the precise path of the process culminating in communism as the first truly nonantagonistic form of sociopolitical and epistemological mediation between humanity and nature. The question is: does Marx see the arrival of communism primarily as a transition from political to human emancipation occurring in stages, or does he see it as a revolution that abolishes every form of alienated power in one stroke with the reappropriation of all of humanity's 'forces propres'? This leads to the related question concerning the kind of new institutions that are to be operative in a new, humanly emancipated society.

The background to the *Communist Manifesto*, written with Marx's friend and political comrade Friedrich Engels (1820–95), is the democratic revolutions across Europe of 1848 and the attempt to carry on with renewed vigour the project initiated in France in 1789. The *Manifesto* is a political pamphlet taking up organisational and strategic questions rather than a theoretical work like *On the Jewish Question*. In addition to the now famous opening lines about the spectre haunting Europe, Marx and Engels write:

> The history of all hitherto existing society is the history of class struggles . . . The bourgeoisie finds itself involved in a constant battle. At first, with the aristocracy; later on, with those portions of the bourgeoisie itself whose interests have become antagonistic to the progress of industry; and at all times with the bourgeoisie of foreign countries. In all these battles it sees itself compelled to appeal to the proletariat, to ask for its help, and to drag it into the political arena . . . The bourgeoisie itself, therefore, supplies the proletariat with its own elements of political and general education, in other words, the bourgeoisie furnishes the proletariat with the weapons for fighting the bourgeoisie.[15]

Two key passages follow, in which the authors explain their position on the state and democracy in 1848. First, they define the state as nothing more than an executive committee for managing the affairs of the entire bourgeoisie. Second, they affirm that the proletariat must 'win the battle of democracy'. This leaves unanswered the question of peaceful reform or violent revolution, since winning the battle of democracy could be interpreted to mean replacing the representatives of other political parties with communists in the legislature. This is one plausible interpretation, given the at times positive remarks Marx makes about the potentially revolutionary dimension of universal suffrage and the possibility of applying the principle of 'one person one vote' to all areas of socioeconomic life which had once been the bastions of power, privilege and inequality. It is also the case that in their written correspondence with friends and contemporaries, both Marx and Engels make reference to the possibility of arriving at communism through the ballot, especially in countries with no cumbersome aristocratic-feudal heritage, such as Holland and the United States.

Hence the notion of winning the battle of democracy in the *Communist Manifesto* could be interpreted to imply a parliamentary-democratic solution to the problem of the separation between state and civil society first systematically analysed by Hegel. The implication of this solution is that there is nothing inherently capitalist about parliamentary democracy, and indeed this is the political position adopted later by the German Social Democratic politician Karl Kautsky (1854–1938) and other leading figures in the international communist movement during Marx's day and after. At the end of the second section of the pamphlet, the authors assert, 'In the place of the old bourgeois society, with its class antagonisms, we shall have an association, in which the free development of each is the condition for the free development of all.' This can be seen as an attempt to formulate a positive response and a programme of action after the earlier critiques of Hegel and of political emancipation. In effect, they propose to revolutionise the locus of freedom. They want to shift the basis of freedom from liberal democratic noninfringement, in which each individual citizen is regarded as at best a possible trading partner and at worst a potential threat to the freedom of every other citizen, to positive community, in which each citizen recognises in their fellow citizen the possibility of their own freedom and full development. The form of mediation between humanity and nature needed to make this emancipated form of community possible is one in which individuals recognise their creative powers in the actual products of their labour, and not, as in capitalism, by passively receiving a generic wage in return for labour performed. It remained for Marx and Engels to continue outlining in more detail the most appropriate political form for the emancipation of human labour power from the capitalist wage system.[16]

Although they seem to accept that there is nothing essentially capitalist about the functioning of the modern state, they nonetheless also suggest that the new institution, which they refer to as an 'association', will at some point be a fully legitimate vehicle making collective decisions and adjudicating what little remains of conflict after private property has been replaced by commonly held property. It was theoretically and strategically important to concretise the issues in 1848. Following England's very early transition to parliamentary government and modern forms of capitalist production, the modern state was now entering a decisive phase of restructuring in key European countries such as France, Italy and Germany. In France the regional political cultural differences between Brittany, Languedoc, Alsace, etc. were gradually being eradicated with the incorporation of the regions within a unified state claiming sovereignty over all of French territory and centrally administered from Paris under a republican ideology and the ideals of 1789. The republican struggle against the restoration forces attempting to retard this work of consolidation resulted in street barricades and parliamentary clashes, which inspired Italian and German patriots to press forward with their aims to unite Italy and Germany as independent nation states. The articulation of republican discourses about liberty in conjunction with democratic discourses concerning popular sovereignty at this time results in a constellation of concepts centred around nation, state, the people, sovereignty and democracy. For partisans of national unification and republican government, the democratic self-government of a sovereign people is thought to be achieved in a state, where one state presupposes the existence of potentially hostile other states.[17]

Put in these terms, democracy, within the borders of the emerging modern state, is framed as a national question, that is, as a question of common legal concern for all people within the nation, regardless of their location in the class structure. Although Marx and Engels reject this idea of a common national identity beyond the class divide, they have to engage with it in 1848 as part of the contradictory reality of class struggles in the bourgeois époque of political emancipation. They favour working-class solidarity and internationalism, but this leaves a crucial question unanswered: what should the organised working class within the boundaries of the nation state do in the immediate term? (For it is here that elections and other concrete issues of practical importance are fought out.) Should the working class in different countries struggle for control of the state, as if democracy, state control and communism are to be considered complementary political gains, or is international working-class solidarity the more appropriate goal? In the *Communist Manifesto*, Marx and Engels suggest that both a national and an international perspective is necessary. Yet until the establishment of the First International in London in September 1864, the question of the co-ordination of the struggles remained provisional and tentative. It would in fact remain so, as long as it was unclear exactly what winning the battle of democracy meant in theory as well as in practice. This entailed, among other things, explaining how, within the contradictions and limitations of a class-ridden society, the state could be replaced with a much more communal form of association. After some initial uncertainty and hesitation about how theoretically to grasp the relation between class, nation, state, and democracy in a way that best indicated the path to revolutionary practice, the experience of Bonapartism helped Marx and Engels define their position.

From Bonapartism to the Paris Commune

In his writings on Bonapartism as an historical phenomenon connected with Louis Bonaparte, the younger cousin of the great leader Napoleon Bonaparte, Marx analyses the changing structure of the relations between state and civil society first culminating in the French Revolution of 1789 and then in the revolutions of 1848. These are transformational processes, which confirm Marx's belief that, contrary to what Hegel argues, the efficacy of the mediating institutions in civil society has been definitively undermined. Not only does this depletion of the explicitly political character of civil society result in the sanction of the more exploitative aspects of civil life in a supposedly private and neutral sphere of legal equality; it also results in the emergence of the modern state as an independent entity that is alienated from popular control, and entitled to reign over civil society as an autonomous force. The development of the state in this potentially authoritarian direction reaches a particularly acute phase with the tyrannical rule of Louis Bonaparte, which is the subject of Marx's brilliant analysis in the *Eighteenth Brumaire of Louis Bonaparte*, which covers the events of 1848–51 and the dictator's ascension to power.

The study registers a decisive shift in Marx's thinking about politics and the state that anticipates some of the concerns of the theorists of Western Marxism. While in the *Communist Manifesto* the state is dismissed as being nothing other than an executive committee for managing the affairs of the entire bourgeoisie, by the time of the *Eighteenth Brumaire* Marx develops a much more subtle analysis of the state and power relations among contending social classes. This more nuanced version of state theory implicitly recognises what is problematic about the idea of 'winning the battle of democracy', if what is meant by this is putting the working class at the head of government, regardless of whether one considered the new government a state or an association. Marx's analysis of Bonapartism shows that at a particular junction of the class struggle, a stalemate in the relative power of each of the struggling classes in civil society can lead to a political situation in which the state can no longer be considered an executive committee or tool of the bourgeoisie. Instead, the state emerges as a political force in its own right, enjoying a certain degree of relative autonomy from class-based socio-economic power. This increased room for manoeuvre of state institutions, and especially the executive, is likely to occur under modern conditions when divisions within the bourgeoisie between its agricultural, manufacturing and financial sectors result in the inability of the bourgeois class as a whole to govern as a united force, thus allowing the state to assume control.[18]

This was acutely evident in the France of Louis Bonaparte's day, where the petit bourgeoisie was still a very numerous and powerful class, and capable of defending its interests against the grande bourgeoisie as well as the emerging industrial proletariat. Marx argues that in order for the bourgeois elite to regain a certain measure of unity in such cases, it must sometimes relinquish a considerable part of its political power. In return, it gains from the state a pledge to intervene in an attempt to restore the social conditions necessary for the processes of accumulation and investment to resume 'normally'. Marx goes on to focus his attention on the theoretical dimensions of those conditions in somewhat greater abstraction from actual historical events in his great works of political economy, such as the *Grundrisse* and *Capital*.[19] In the *Eighteenth Brumaire*, however, he demonstrates his ability as an historian to draw out the theoretical significance of socioeconomic and political struggles. He points out that at particular historical junctures of the evolution of capitalism in specific countries, the grande bourgeoisie is likely to assent to a loss in political power if necessary, since by character and interest it is not a politically minded class. According to his analysis, it is a class that in many respects is fundamentally apolitical and almost entirely concerned with production and accumulation. As a consequence, it fails to see political crises coming, or at any rate does not to manage to perceive them before it is too late.[20]

Marx argues that the bourgeoisie can be coaxed or forced to relinquish its political power because its *raison d'être* is social and economic power and control. But civil society is a battle within and between classes, and the market is in reality not comparable to Adam Smith's invisible hand which spontaneously co-ordinates supply and demand. Hence the bourgeois elite occasionally needs a decidedly political state so that it can go on being apolitical. Marx summarises his analysis of Bonapartism by remarking that 'thus the French bourgeoisie was compelled, by its class position to annihilate, on the one hand, the vital conditions of all parliamentary power, including its own, and to render resistible, on the other hand, the executive power hostile to it.'[21] Marx has obviously come quite some distance from any simple conception of the state as a tool of the bourgeoisie. It follows that the notion of 'winning the battle of democracy' evoked in the *Communist Manifesto* needs to be rethought in light of the empirical and historical evidence that what one designates as the state is usually a complex network of fluid socio-economic and political relations. It is not a reified object that can be seized or smashed, or an executive committee that can be simply replaced with a new set of members. In fact, Marx's analysis in the *Eighteenth Brumaire* anticipates some of the ideas of the Western Marxist Antonio Gramsci (1891–1937, see Chapter 2), for whom the state can be understood as a flow of forces and interests that continually transgress the boundaries of state and civil society or base and superstructure. Marx, and later Gramsci, argue that power can be understood as something many-sided and protean, though not, crucially, as something ontological or obscure that is not controlled or influenced and is wielded by any subject at all. For thinkers on the left associated with the labour movement, such as Marx and Gramsci, there is no conflict between a sophisticated view of the relations obtaining between economy, state and society on the one hand, and the political desideratum of a communist revolution on the other. The link between careful analysis and a clear path towards revolution becomes more tenuous in later years, in light of the authoritarian turn of the Russian Revolution and the stabilisation of capitalism through the welfare state after World War II. This point will be taken up again in later chapters, particularly in Chapter 6.

In his writings after the *Communist Manifesto*, Marx presents a highly nuanced and nonreductionist view of the state. He insists on viewing the state as a set of relations, and yet he warns observers of history and political activists not to reify or fetishise power. Like Machiavelli (1469–1527), Marx retains the essential element of political agency (i.e. of practice) in his analysis of power and his strategy for change. By jettisoning the view of the state in the *Communist Manifesto*, and by showing how the state can achieve a certain measure of relative autonomy, Marx moves beyond the simple dichotomies suggested by the state/civil society and base/superstructure models, and provides a key for understanding complex changes in forms of state. These will become much-needed tools for Gramsci and Lukács (1885–1971) (another key Western Marxist who will be discussed in Chapter 2) in the search to understand fascism in non-reductionist terms. Marx shows that in its quest to secure the conditions for the accumulation of capital and profitable investment, the bourgeoisie is prepared to sacrifice its political power at crucial junctures in the transition from one state form to another. In these transitional moments, class alliances are forged outside and even against the legislature, and then enforced by the executive of the modern state.

What are the lessons of Bonapartism for Marx's theory of social classes, historical changes in state forms, and of revolution in the period following the events of 1789, 1848, and Bonaparte's coup in 1851? One of the lessons is summed up quite concisely in the preface to the 1872 edition of the *Communist Manifesto*. Here Marx and Engels write, 'One thing especially was proved by the Paris Commune, and that is, the working class cannot simply lay hold of the ready-made state machinery and wield it for its own purposes.'[22] If the working class cannot simply lay hold of the existing state machinery and wield it for more universally legitimate purposes, smashing the state and building a new one on the ruins is also not an option, since the state usually evolves historically over centuries, and can only very rarely be toppled like a house of cards. This brings us to Marx's analysis of the Paris Commune, which, after the experiences of 1848 and Bonapartism, represents a decisive moment in his ideas about possible alternatives to the constitutional monarchy and democratic republic.

When the Prussian army defeated the French in the war of 1871, the Prussians were shocked to find that a great number of the citizens of Paris were not ready to yield to the invading troops. Instead, the people of the city set up their own government based on radically democratic principles of collective self-government. The event fired Marx's imagination and became a central source of inspiration for Lenin's (1870–1924) *State and Revolution*, in which he argues that the role played by the Russian soviets (councils) in 1905 and 1917 had been foreshadowed by the radical democracy institutionalised by Paris Commune. The Commune gives Marx the chance to concretise his ideas about 'winning the battle of democracy'. He argues that the Paris events indicate that the revolution in the offing would not be another instance of transferring state power from one set of oppressors to another. On the contrary, he maintains, the modern state will be dismantled, so that political authority can be wielded by ordinary citizens organised at the regional and local levels in Communes. Hence at this stage of his thinking, winning the battle of democracy becomes synonymous with democratising the relations constituting the state, and not smashing or seizing the state. What Marx glimpses in the Paris Commune is a new collective body capable of mediating people's concerns as workers with their concerns as citizens: that is, an association uniting the citizen and worker instead of separating manifestly unequal workers and capitalists in civil society from formally equal citizens in the state.

For Marx the great merit of the Commune was, however briefly, to have abolished the political realm as an alienated sphere of unaccountable power. This concern with the state and the danger of bureaucratic political power links Marx with the libertarian tradition examined in Chapter 4. That is, libertarians—like anarchists—consistently maintain that an anticapitalist revolution won at the expense of accepting a highly centralised and authoritarian state is in fact a putsch rather than a genuine revolution. The Communards paved the way by setting up a system of recall on demand, so that the representatives of the people could be removed from their posts from the moment a majority of their electors deemed that the representatives' views no longer reflected the views of the represented.

In Marx's estimation, the Communards sought to fuse the executive and legislative functions of government. On the basis of his analysis of Bonapartism he is convinced that popularly elected legislatures will always be undermined by nonaccountable state executives as long as the executive itself is not integrated into a structure of popular control based on recall on demand. He reasons further that as long as the executive and legislative functions are separated, the popular elements in the legislature will inevitably be circumvented by extra-parliamentary alliances between powerful and well-organised interests amongst the large land-owners, bureaucratic elites, the army, industry, police and church (in today's world one would certainly include institutions such as the media and the World Bank). Thus in the France and Germany of Marx's day, and in many contemporary situations in Latin America, South America, Africa and Asia, the work of the legislature is constantly undermined by extra-parliamentary forces, such that the legislature is severely limited in its ability to formulate something even vaguely resembling Rousseau's (1712–78) notion of the General Will. This is an important point, for it reveals that the practice of liberal democratic states generally falls well short of the liberal democratic criteria concerning reason and equality that supposedly underpin them. Despite what the best liberal democratic theorists—from Locke, Kant and Rousseau to the present—say, the liberal democratic state is not founded on a fundamental form of agreement. This is not an indictment of the Enlightenment as such. It is an indictment of what is ideologically heralded to be the *already achieved* aims of the Enlightenment. The project of highlighting the discrepancy between liberal democratic ideology and liberal democratic practice has been a central aim of the left in theory and practice in Europe from Marx to the present. It begins with Marx's critique of Hegel and the distinction between political and human emancipation analysed in this chapter. It has been seen that what starts as a critique of philosophy and knowledge develops into an all-out critique of the economy, society and state. The rest of this book thus analyses a number of the most significant further developments in the articulation and rearticulation of the project to realise a positive conception of political liberty that is not authoritarian.

Marx thinks that the genius of the Communards consists, among other things, of replacing the standing professional army with a citizen's militia, so that the citizen body was now able to make laws, execute them, and defend the political community for which they had risked so much. Recall on demand is a measure of democratic control of primary importance. It ensures that government officials cannot become career politicians, and thereby nullify the aims of the Declaration of Man and Citizen proclaimed during the French Revolution and the founding of the modern state in France and elsewhere. Marx holds the idea of the professional politician in contempt and as incompatible with the principles of democracy—if, that is, these are to be taken seriously. He explains that the existence and perpetuation of just such a professional caste is possible only when alienation has reached a stage where the state is perceived by the citizens as something external and distant from the average citizen.

He concludes in 1870–71 that it is possible for the Commune to become the standard form of government for even the smallest country towns. For Marx it is the ideal political association for the self-government of the producers, or, as he calls it in *The Civil War* in France, 'the political form at last discovered to work out the economic emancipation of labour'. Such an institution transforms the practice of universal suffrage into a far more effective means of giving expression to all of the wills comprising the general will than is ever possible in parliamentary regimes.[23]

The Russian Revolution and Marx's Contested Legacy

The *Communist Manifesto*, the *Eighteenth Brumaire*, and the *Civil War in France*, all of which are extensively cited by Lenin, raise a number of theoretical questions that were to become matters of immense practical difficulty during the years of Bolshevik rule in the former Soviet Union.

While Marx's critique of existing political arrangements is radically democratic, the actual means for abolishing the division between mental and manual labour and reorganising the labour process are not discussed in any detail. Without being unfair to Marx, it is safe to say that he believed that the historical process destined to culminate in human emancipation would resolve theoretical questions of revolutionary consciousness and practical questions of organisation. As will be seen in Chapters 4 and 5, the libertarian, situationist and autonomist traditions in Europe are keenly aware of these problems, especially in the light of Bolshevik authoritarian *étatisme*.

Marx's earlier philosophical concern with human as opposed to merely political emancipation wanes in the more mature historical writings. In the wake of Bonapartism, Marx focuses his critical energies on the manifestly nondemocratic aspects of the modern state. This shift in emphasis subsequently helps Lenin portray Marx to his Russian comrades as a thinker and activist primarily concerned with explaining the necessity to destroy the democratic parliamentary state, and to establish, if need be, a highly authoritarian transition to communism. The tendency towards authoritarianism is exacerbated in Lenin's case by his tendency to regard the economic organisation of communism mainly as consisting in taking over the productive apparatus left by capitalism, and simply socialising it. The idea that socialised nationalisation of the ownership of the forces of production is not the same thing as worker autonomy and self-management is something the Bolshevik leader usually dismisses as syndicalism or anarchism. This is not the case in *State and Revolution*, but it increasingly becomes so in the struggle for power eventually resulting in the construction of a one-party state. While *State and Revolution*, written in 1917, praises the Paris Commune and the Russian soviets, Lenin's writings on workplace democracy after the establishment of the Third International in March 1919 tend to stress the need for rapid industrialisation and forms of management appropriate to that gigantic task. One must also not forget that the war against reactionary right-wing forces was still raging into the early 1920s, and that the conditions for workplace democracy and laying the foundations of human emancipation were not available. Nonetheless, a couple of observations are relevant in this context.[24]

Lenin interprets Marx and Engels as meaning that since the working class cannot lay hold of the ready-made state machinery and wield it for its own purposes, the working class, hierarchically organised in the Communist Party (which in the Russian conditions of the day had to operate in secrecy and in exile for much of the time leading up to the February Revolution of 1917), must smash the state, including the popular power represented in the legislature. Thus from the anarchist and syndicalist perspectives to be explored in Chapter 4, Lenin and the Bolsheviks were merely continuing the work of Robespierre (1758–94) and the Jacobins rather than reversing the centralist tendencies of modern states. The link between the Paris Commune and the role of the soviets in the 1905 revolution and the revolutions of February and October 1917 began to fade, as the Communist Party became the sole source of political authority. Lenin, and others attempting to understand and update Marx, continually come back to two key points in the *Civil War in France*. First, the existing state machinery had to be transformed into a network of communes. Second, production had to be reorganised by transforming private property into social, publicly owned property. This raises the question: how can a federation of radically democratic and decentralised communes be reconciled with a gigantic and highly centralised productive planning apparatus?

The Communist Party could preside over the centralised direction of the economy. But to this extent, however, the party would then constitute a major obstacle to the radical form of decentralised democratic accountability between representatives and represented suggested by the practice of the Paris Commune, and later by the Russian soviets. In *State and Revolution*, Lenin clumsily attempts to balance the respective roles of the party, unions and soviets so that the imperatives of political leadership are reconciled with demands for direct participation on the factory floor, army regiment and city district (not to mention the enormous questions raised by the role of the peasants). Although the conspiratorial organisational model suggested by Lenin's *What is to be Done?* (1902) seems by 1917 to have given way to a more council-based vision of the revolution, the post-1917 writings seem to shift back to a party-based model.[25] It is extremely difficult to ascertain with certainty whether the ravages of the civil war compelled Lenin to take these steps towards the institutionalisation of discipline and hierarchy against his will. It is also very difficult to determine whether the foundations of the cult of personality and the power of the secret police were already laid in the period of Lenin's leadership of the Bolsheviks, or whether Stalin (1879–1953) managed to do this singlehandedly. What is clear is that after Lenin's death in 1924 a power struggle ensued, which eventually led to Stalin's control of the Communist Party of the Soviet Union and the bureaucratic and authoritarian degeneration of the Russian Revolution. With the failure of the revolution in Russia to offer a desirable alternative to capitalism and parliamentary democracy, and the looming threat of fascism in Italy (1922) and later Germany (1933) and Spain (1936–37), a number of thinkers and revolutionaries broadly affiliated with a current called Western Marxism began to see that it was necessary to go back and reinvestigate Marx's ideas on the base and superstructure as well as the Hegelian bases of Marxist thought. Chapter 2 turns to the most important thinkers and movements connected with Western Marxism.

Suggestions for Further Reading

Avinieri, Schlomo. *The Social and Political Thought of Karl Marx*, Cambridge, CUP, 1968.

Elster, Jon. *An Introduction to Karl Marx*, Cambridge, CUP, 1986.

Furner, James. 'Base and Superstructure in Marx', DPhil thesis, University of Sussex, 2008.

Henry, Michel. *Marx, A Philosophy of Human Reality*, Bloomington, University of Indiana Press, 1983.

Hunt, R. N. *The Political Ideas of Marx and Engels*, 2 Volumes, Pittsburgh, University of Pittsburgh Press, 1974.

McLellan, David. *The Thought of Karl Marx: An Introduction*, London, Macmillan, 1971.

Negri, Antonio. *Marx Beyond Marx: Lessons on the Grundrisse*, London, Pluto, 1983.

Schmidt, Alfred. *The Concept of Nature in Marx*, Cambridge, Polity, 1985.

Notes

1 Kant, *Critique of Pure Reason*, pp. 45–62. For an explanation of Kant's categories of the understanding, see Caygill, *A Kant Dictionary*, pp. 102–6. For a more general exposition of Kant's main ideas on epistemology, see Pippin, *Kant's Theory of Form*, and Allison, *Kant's Transcendental Idealism*.

2 Hegel, *Grundlinien der Philosophie des Rechts* [*Philosophy of Right*], pp. 11–28.

3 Ibid., Section 3.

4 Ibid., paras 250–56.

5 Feuerbach, *Das Wesen des Christentums* [*The Essence of Christianity*], Chapter 6, pp. 115–22.

6 'Kritik der Hegelschen Philosophie' ['Critique of Hegel's Philosophy'] (1839), in *Ludwig Feuerbach: Philosophische Kritiken und Gegensätze, 1839–1846*, pp. 27–28.

7 See in particular Marx's concise *Theses on Feuerbach* in *The German Ideology* (ed. Arthur), pp. 121–23. *Theses on Feuerbach* will be included in any good compilation of Marx's early work.

8 Marx, *Zur Kritik der Hegelschen Rechtsphilosophie* [*Critique of Hegel's Philosophy of Right*] (1843), in Fetscher (ed.), *Karl Marx und Friedrich Engels*, vol. 1, p. 21. There are many good compilations of Marx's early writings in English that contain his writings on Hegel, *On the Jewish Question*, the *1844 Manuscripts* and the *Theses on Feuerbach*. See for example Colletti, *Marx: Early Writings* and Tucker, *The Marx-Engels Reader*.

9 Marx, introduction to *Zur Kritik der Hegelschen Rechtsphilosophie* [*Critique of Hegel's Philosophy of Right*], pp. 32–33.

10 The Young Hegelians were a group of radical students and activists who saw the radical potential of Hegel's philosophy, though, like Marx, without subscribing to the rather conservative implications of the Hegelian doctrine of the state. Marx and Bauer were affiliated, as was the anarchist Max Stirner. For an

elucidating analysis of the theoretical and political positions of the group, see McLellan, *Karl Marx and the Young Hegelians*.

11 Marx, *Zur Judenfrage* [*On the Jewish Question*] (1843), in Fetscher (ed.), *Karl Marx und Friedrich Engels*, Vol. I, pp. 39–40.

12 Ibid., p. 54.

13 Marx, *Zur Kritik der Hegelschen Rechtsphilosophie* [*Critique of Hegel's Philosophy of Right*] (1843), in Landshut (ed.), *Marx: Frühe Schriften*, p. 50. This particular paragraph is not included in the Fetscher edition of the early writings. It is an important one, for it is here that Marx observes the state as an abstract power appearing for the first time in the modern industrial era.

14 Marx, *Zur Judenfrage* [*On the Jewish Question*], p. 55.

15 Marx and Engels, *Communist Manifesto* (1848), in Tucker, *The Marx-Engels Reader*, pp. 253–54.

16 Ibid., p. 261.

17 Magraw, *France 1815–1914*, Chapter 4, and Eyck, *The Revolutions of 1848–49*, Chapters 1–4.

18 Marx, *Der achtzehnte Brumaire des Louis Bonaparte* [*The Eighteenth Brumaire of Louis Bonaparte*] (1852) in Fetscher, *Karl Marx und Friedrich Engels*, Vol. IV, pp. 74–6. Marx's *Eighteenth Brumaire* will be contained in any good edited collection of his political writings, such as Tucker's.

19 It is in the *Grundrisse* and *Capital* that Marx systematically develops his ideas on surplus value, accumulation and consumption crises, the tendency of the rate of profit to fall, the transformation of money into capital and back into money, etc. It is also in these later works that Marx writes more in terms of the base and superstructure rather than the state and civil society. In opposition to the concepts and categories of bourgeois political economy such as laissez-faire, the supposed spontaneous capacity of the market to co-ordinate supply and demand, etc., Marx develops an alternative conceptual vocabulary. Liberal political economists such as Adam Smith (1723–90) and Jeremy Bentham (1748–1832) regard the processes of accumulation and exchange to be consensually mediated by freely chosen contractual obligations. Marx deploys the categories of capital, money, surplus value, profit, accumulation and credit in his own way to explain that capitalist relations of production and capitalist society in general are deeply antagonistic and politicised rather than consensual and neutral. For reasons of space and for thematic reasons explained at the beginning of this chapter, the analysis of Marx offered here concentrates on his philosophical and political writings rather than on his writings on political economy. The latter are nonetheless extremely illuminating. Interested readers should consult the works of Michel Henry, Antonio Negri and Alfred Schmidt listed in the bibliography.

20 Marx, *Der achtzehnte Brumaire des Louis Bonaparte* [*The Eighteenth Brumaire of Louis Bonaparte*], pp. 90–91.

21 Ibid., p. 116.

22 Marx and Engels, Preface to the 1872 edition of the *Communist Manifesto*, in *Selected Works in 1 Volume*, p. 32.

23 Marx, *Der Bürgerkrieg in Frankreich* [*The Civil War in France*] (1871), in *Karl Marx und Friedrich Engels: Studienausgabe*, Vol. IV, p. 212. *The Civil War in France* will be contained in any good edited collection of Marx's political writings, such as Tucker's.

24 Lenin, *State and Revolution,* in *Collected Works,* Vol. 25, p. 429.
25 Perhaps the most famous example is Lenin's *Left-Wing Communism, an Infantile Disorder.* In this pamphlet he ridicules anarchist, syndicalist and council communist challenges to the consolidation of one-party rule as an 'infantile disorder'. For an illuminating look at the historical background to the writing of *What is to be Done?* and the subsequent development of the Russian Revolution from 1905 to the two revolutions of 1917, see Acton, *Rethinking the Russian Revolution,* pp. 5–27.

2
Western Marxism

It was suggested at the end of Chapter 1 that Marx's legacy continues to be somewhat ambiguous because of the association of his name with the former USSR and with manifestly nondemocratic forms of state socialism elsewhere in the world. On the one hand Marxism can still reasonably claim to offer the most systematic explanation available of the mechanisms of capitalist exploitation and the circumvention of democratic political norms by organised private interests. On the other hand, Marxism in power has almost always been far less liberal and less democratic than the liberal democratic systems Marx criticises for being insufficiently emancipated from arbitrary power relations. Hence the ambiguity alluded to refers to the incongruent relation between Marxist theory and actual communist practice. The Bolshevik interpretation of Marxism that eventually triumphed in Russia, and which contributed to the lurch of the Russian Revolution in an authoritarian direction, seemed to many observers at the time to be a plausible translation of Marxist theory into revolutionary practice. While it is clear that Marx would have had very little sympathy for the Bolshevik dictatorship, it is also evident that there are unresolved issues in Marx's account of historical materialism, dialectics and history, which complicate any analysis of the relation between Marxist theory and communist practice.

Marx is reputed to have rejected all over-schematic models of his theories and even to have quipped that he was so opposed to such endeavours that he was 'not a Marxist'. Against all notions of mechanical causality implied by the base-superstructure model, Marx and Engels consistently maintain that the economic base is only the determining factor shaping the legal, political, ideological and cultural superstructure 'in the last instance'. Yet, as Perry Anderson remarks, there is a tension, if not a contradiction, in Marx's historical materialism. This is a tension between a theory of history with scientific aspirations as expressed in the *Preface and Introduction to a Contribution to a Critique of Political Economy* (1859), and a conception of history based on class struggle and political strategy as expressed in the *Communist Manifesto* (1848). In a frequently quoted passage from the *Preface and Introduction* of 1859, Marx maintains that:

> In the social production of their existence, men enter into definite, necessary relations, which are independent of their will, namely, relations of production corresponding to a determinate stage of development of their material forces of production. The totality of these relations of production constitutes the economic structure of society, the real foundation on which there arises a legal and political superstructure and to which correspond definite forms of social consciousness. The mode of production of material life conditions the social, political, and intellectual life-process in general. It is not the consciousness of men that determines their being, but on the contrary it is their social being that determines their consciousness. At a certain stage of their development, the material productive forces of society come into conflict with the existing relations of production—or what is merely a legal expression for the same thing—with the property relations within the framework in which they have hitherto operated. From forms of development of the productive forces these relations turn into their fetters. At that point an era of social revolution begins. With the change in the economic foundation the whole immense superstructure is more slowly or more rapidly transformed. In considering such transformations it is always necessary to distinguish between the material transformation of the economic conditions of production, which can be determined with the precision of *natural science*, and the legal, political, religious, artistic or philosophic, in short, *ideological*, forms in which men become conscious of this conflict and fight it out.[1]

If the scientific dimension in Marx's thought strives for *objectivity* and exhibits certain affinities with structuralist explanations, which tend to abstract from the dynamics of individual motivations and collective action, the transformative dimension focuses on *subjectivity*, consciousness and concrete questions concerning institutions and organisation. Hence the epistemological issues discussed in the first section of Chapter 1 addressing the philosophical mediation between humanity (subject) and nature (object) are of central relevance for an understanding of the political mediation between (a) theory and practice; and (b) nature and history. Following Hegel, Marx always stresses that the relations between subject and object, base and superstructure, and history and nature are dialectical rather than evolutionary, mechanical or one-sidedly linear. The authoritarian turn of the Russian Revolution and the evident lack of revolutionary consciousness on the part of the majority of the Western

European working class compelled the theorists considered in this chapter to consider these questions anew. The outbreak of World War I was a painful reminder that, apart from relatively isolated groups of workers, what one might call a communist consciousness was mainly prevalent amongst avant-garde intellectuals. After the 1914–18 War, the usurpation of revolutionary politics by the Bolsheviks in Russia and elsewhere raised the question of the role of the intellectual in the revolution. Indeed, one of the chief concerns of Western Marxism is to rearticulate the role of intellectuals, politics and culture in such a way that a revolutionary consciousness ceases to be the domain of a highly unrepresentative elite, which can then evolve into a bureaucratic caste of authoritarian rulers, as happened in Russia, China, Cuba and elsewhere. Hence a central aim among Western Marxists is to highlight questions of politics and culture without jettisoning the primacy of the economy suggested by historical materialism.[2]

In the case of Marx, it is possible to regard the tension between objectivity and subjectivity as a potentially fruitful one. But the majority of theorists active in the years between Marx's death in 1883 and the collapse of the Second International Workingman's Association in 1914 were palpably less successful in rearticulating the relationship between philosophical rigour and political practice. Second International Marxism is known for being particularly indebted to a mechanical vision of history predicated on a fatalistic understanding of the inevitable crisis of capitalism and the equally inevitable coming of communist consciousness and an emancipated society. That is to say that in the years leading up to the great catastrophe of 1914–18, the dialectical tension between subjectivity/practice and objectivity/knowledge is resolved one-sidedly in favour of the latter, resulting in the elaboration of a wide variety of evolutionary and positivist models of scientific socialism. Whereas Marx attempts to build on Kant's discovery that all objectivity is mediated by subjectivity as well as Hegel's demonstration of the converse, Second International Marxism tends to neglect the key role of subjectivity and consciousness in the constitution of the objective world and the transformation of the world in creative labour and social struggle. The obvious corollary of ideological scientism at the theoretical level is the bureaucratisation of the institutions of the workers' movement at the practical level, i.e. theoretical as well as practical sclerosis, in which epistemological pseudo-objectivity and political passivity seem perfectly to complement each other.

This chapter focuses on the attempts by a group of original and influential theorists to reinvigorate dialectical thinking and revolutionary practice by rethinking the role of subjective experience, consciousness, culture and other aspects of society and politics that are usually associated with the superstructure in Marxist thought. In hindsight, it appears that this corrective became necessary at the theoretical level as a result of the enormous impact of *Capital* and the mature Marx's analysis of what he considers the economic basis of society. His emphasis on the economy as the key instance of mediation between humanity and nature helped contribute to the widespread perception in and outside socialist movements in Europe and the rest of the world that Marxism is a science concerned with the 'laws' of capitalism rather than a philosophy of human emancipation. It also became urgent at the practical level as a result of the militarist fervour accompanying the outbreak of the war and the post-war crises in Italy and Germany. Not only had proletarian internationalism been upstaged by nationalist chauvinism: parliamentary democracy, although in crisis, was ceding to fascism and authoritarian populism rather than libertarian communism.[3]

The general aim common to the diverse theorists of Western Marxism is the attempt to restore the dialectical tension initially promoted by Marx by emphasising the role of subjective and cultural factors in the revolution. In addition to nationalist consciousness and fascist politics, Western Marxists had to grapple with the manifest shortcomings of Russian Marxism and the eventual triumph of Stalinism in the one European country where a communist revolution actually occurred. This of course produced a series of deep divisions within Western Marxism itself concerning the question of whether support for the USSR should be unconditional or conditional, or if support should be qualified by critique. While the critical theorists considered in the next chapter are sceptical about Soviet communism and Russian Marxism, the Western Marxists are loath to abjure the October Revolution of 1917. They are keen to find an alternative to both subjectivist putschism and the political passivity resulting from the fetishism of objectivity characteristic of the writings of Plekhanov (1856–1918) and Bukharin (1888–1938).[4]

Hence the first question is: how much restoration of dialectical tension between base and superstructure could be undertaken within a theoretical and practical framework still recognisable as Marxism?

This question is at the centre of the life and work of the most influential of the Western Marxists, the Italian Antonio Gramsci (1891–1937). It might in fact be argued that Gramsci is the prototypical Western Marxist. He was a renowned theorist as well as a co-founder of the Italian Communist Party (Partito Comunista Italiano, PCI) in 1921. In contrast to the academic bent of some of the critical theorists considered in Chapter 3, and in contrast to the non-Marxist theorists and activists to be considered in later chapters, Gramsci is both a Marxist theorist and political militant. His work demonstrates an acute sensitivity to the particularity of the conditions prevailing in pre-revolutionary Russia, and a simultaneous awareness that revolution in the West would have to be guided by a different theoretical and practical framework from that which worked for the Bolsheviks. This awareness sets him apart from other Western Marxists to be considered here, such as Georg Lukács, (1885–1971) and Louis Althusser (1918–90), so an analysis of Gramsci's Marxism will occupy a central place in this chapter.[5]

The Problem of the Superstructure Reconsidered (I): Gramsci, Hegemony, Civil Society and Intellectuals

While the tendency of Marxism to degenerate into pseudo-science is palpable across the continent during the years of the Second International, it is especially salient in Italy. Achille Loria and Enrico Ferri developed schematic brands of historical materialism simplifying the work of Darwin and Marx into evolutionary dogmas. The reformist and revolutionary wings of the Italian Socialist Party (Partito Socialista Italiano, PSI, founded in Milan in 1892) were guided by fatalistic perspectives which tended to view the revolution as inevitable. For the reformists it would be the inevitable result of a series of reforms destined to transform capitalism into democratic socialism, but for the revolutionaries it would be the result of the cataclysmic breakdown of capitalism, towards which capitalist society was automatically hurtling. The reformist position in Italy and elsewhere was inspired by Eduard Bernstein's *Evolutionary Socialism* (1890), in which the German Social Democrat argues that several of Marx's main theses have to be called into question. In addition to contesting the labour theory of value and the tendency of the rate of profit to fall, Bernstein disputes the idea that capitalist society necessarily polarises into two hostile camps comprising an increasingly small number of monopolists and an increasingly large number of impoverished proletarians. He concludes that the struggle for socialism has to be guided by the evident reality that capitalism is not preordained to self-destruct or spontaneously generate a revolutionary working-class consciousness, and that a socialist consciousness could only result over the course of a slow process of reforms and patient educational work with the masses. Filippo Turati and the PSI's reformist wing applauded the idea that there was an evolutionary road to socialism. Italian socialists hoped that the winning of concessions from industrialists would educate the masses and gradually increase their understanding in the workings of the economy and its possible transformation.

Bernstein's theses helped bring on what subsequently became known as the 'crisis of Marxism' at the turn of the nineteenth and twentieth centuries. Philosophers such as Benedetto Croce (1866–1952) began questioning the epistemological status of historical materialism. He argued that in its endeavour to be objective and materialist, Marxism had turned its back on the idealist demonstration that reality is simultaneously subjective and objective. While rejecting Bernstein's reformism, Georges Sorel (1847–1922) was persuaded that *Evolutionary Socialism* had the great merit of alerting Marxists to the importance of rethinking questions of consciousness and action. In his *Reflections on Violence* of 1908, he maintains that if Bernstein is correct in seeing that capitalism could indeed be reformed, the prospects for revolution depend upon the revolutionary intransigence of the proletariat and its determination to forge a new set of values. Violence, he argues further, is a great catalyst of solidarity and collective action, in that it propels people beyond the strictures of calculation and personal interest which threaten all social movements with integration into existing institutions. According to this theorist of anarcho-syndicalism (see Chapter 4), socialism would cease to constitute an alternative to capitalism if it could not harness the primitive spirit of violence and revolt to the project of overthrowing the capitalist system of production.[6]

The origins of Western Marxism can be located in Italy in the attempts made by Antonio Labriola (1843–1904) to help solve the crisis of Marxism by insisting on the Hegelian, (i.e. philosophical) origins of Marx's thinking about creative labour and Marx's stress on the importance of understanding the historical and social processes mediating between humanity and nature. Without agreeing completely with Croce or Sorel, Labriola acknowledges that Marxism had become positivist in epistemology and reformist in politics. As a consequence, a possible end to the crisis depended on Marxism once again becoming dialectical in epistemology and revolutionary in politics. Labriola clearly anticipates Gramsci by locating the degeneration of Marxism in the pernicious tendency in academic circles as well as in political movements to treat the superstructure as a mechanical product of the economic base, when in fact the superstructures of modern capitalist societies exhibit their own dynamics and offer possibilities for creative political intervention in the workings of the base itself. Labriola suggests that the act of identifying consciousness as the key to this creative political intervention in the economy is not tantamount to siding with Croce and urging a return to Hegel and idealism. In contrast to some of the more schematic pronouncements on historical materialism made by Engels, Labriola regards communism as a possibility and not as an historical inevitability. History and a certain level of development of the productive forces opens up the possibility of a society freed from material necessity and political oppression, but the realisation of that possibility depends on labouring individuals becoming aware of the possibility and acting on it. Although correct in this assessment, Labriola is not really able to show how this call for a reassessment of the relation between theory and practice could actually lead to the transformation of the social world. His ideas nonetheless point beyond the crisis of Marxism in a manner analogous to the way in which Feuerbach's ideas hint at steps beyond philosophical idealism and humanism without actually showing how to get there. Whilst Feuerbach's ideas prove to be a decisive factor in the evolution of Marx's, Labriola sets the stage for Gramsci.

We saw in Chapter 1 that when investigating the phenomenon of Bonapartism, Marx analyses the historical conditions under which the state can emerge as a force in its own right gaining relative autonomy from the dominant economic class. The implication is that there cannot be any automatic corollary between the economic interests of the dominant class or classes on the one hand, and the structure of the state on the other. Gramsci deepens this insight and develops an articulation of what he refers to as the primacy of the ethical-political moment of the class struggle. That is, Gramsci retains class struggle as the materialist basis of his analysis of social power, while insisting—like his compatriot Machiavelli—that politics is a terrain of liberty on which decisive choices between different possible regimes are enacted. Although a given level in the development of the productive forces makes an array of political choices possible, for Gramsci economic forces are not determining or decisive in the last analysis. The increasing capacity of humans to utilise the forces of nature in order to satisfy human needs does not produce any determinate form of state, and indeed, as Gramsci was to experience personally, can culminate in fascism rather than a liberated society.

Gramsci arrives at a theory of the primacy of politics within a Marxist framework on the basis of a careful reading of Machiavelli, Croce and Marx, and also as the result of a career as a political activist which began in his youth as a Sardinian nationalist. In 1911 he left Sardinia for Turin to study linguistics. He joined the PSI and wrote articles for the socialist newspaper *Avanti!*, and in 1919 co-founded the review *Ordine Nuovo* (*New Order*). The review became the theoretical counterpart of the factory occupations that spread throughout Italy in 1919–20. When the occupations failed to result in a communist revolution, Gramsci, with a number of other comrades, left the PSI to set up the PCI in Leghorn in 1921. In the years 1922–4 he worked for the Third International (established in 1919 following the Russian Revolution of 1917) in Vienna and Moscow, and then assumed leadership of the PCI in 1924. In Italy Mussolini (1883–1945) came to power in 1922 and quickly began dismantling the institutions of parliamentary democracy and imprisoning or murdering his political opponents. After the assassination of the PSI deputy Giacomo Matteotti in June 1924 and the subsequent crisis of the Aventine Secession, it was no longer possible politically to co-exist with Mussolini—one had to be either one of his subordinates or an enemy. In November 1926 Gramsci was arrested and sent to prison. Shortly thereafter he began working on his great theoretical contribution to Western Marxism, the *Prison Notebooks*, which he wrote in prison from 1928 until he was physically too ill to read and write, which was around 1935. Thereafter his health quickly deteriorated and he died in 1937, just two weeks after being released.

Gramsci's experience of fascism convinced him that a given level in the development of the forces of production does not guarantee any determinate political outcome. This may seem obvious today, but it was not at the time of the Second (1864–1914) and Third (1919–40) Internationals and the manipulation of Marx's ideas first as Marxism-Leninism and then as a result of the power struggles within the Communist Party of the Soviet Union (CPSU). In the *Prison Notebooks* Gramsci attempts to reconsider the relations between base and superstructure by analysing the ways in which culture, consciousness and politics influence forms of state and the constant negotiation between the forces of labour and capital. The *Notebooks* cover a wide range of topics, including literature, philosophy, Italian history, the role of intellectuals in the class struggle and the related issue of the shortcomings of Second and Third International Marxism. His prodigious work on these topics was smuggled out of Italy to Moscow after his death, and then brought back to Italy after the end of the Second World War by Palmiro Togliatti (1893–1964), Gramsci's successor at the head of the PCI. Togliatti insisted that Gramsci's ideas would guide the strategy of a communist party which by the 1970s was attaining anywhere from 25 percent to 33 percent of the vote in national elections, and which was firmly established in regional governments and urban politics throughout the country.

The *Prison Notebooks* were published in Italy in the early 1950s. Translated versions reached the rest of Europe and North America in the 1960s and 1970s, after which a large body of interpretations came into existence. His work has been commented upon by Togliatti and theorists inside the PCI, as well as by scholars such as Norberto Bobbio, and such intellectuals of the contemporary left in Europe as Ernesto Laclau and Chantal Mouffe.[7] Although the *Notebooks* are open to a number of different interpretations because of their richness and complexity, a number of key themes unite the various topics that Gramsci analyses.[8]

Gramsci carefully studied the history of Italian unification, known as the Risorgimento, as well as hitherto existing forms of radical socialism in Italy and France, most notably syndicalism. He designates the expulsion of Austrian, Spanish and French political authority from the Italian peninsula in 1861 as an incomplete revolution or, in the terminology of the *Prison Notebooks*, a passive revolution. Stated briefly, the idea of a passive revolution is that things must change in order for things to stay the same. Examples might include the New Deal during the depression years in the USA, fascism and even Thatcherism. The concept of passive revolution is linked with Gramsci's understanding of the class structure of modern capitalist economies. He argues that capitalism is a dynamic system in which the different factions of the economically dominant class are in a constant process of fusion, separation, and recomposition, and that oppositional classes are also constantly changing and re-forming on new bases. This compels the dominant classes not only to push the forces of production forward and increase the level of material prosperity, but also constantly to recast the institutional terms according to which the compromise between capital and labour is enacted. This means that if control over the means of production is to be maintained, the political-institutional framework in which the compromise between labour and capital is enacted must change. He stresses that this continual recasting, recomposition and re-formation of institutions is not a mechanical process which can easily be explained in terms of changes in the structure of the economy or 'the state' in the restricted sense of government and law. It affects and is affected by all areas of civil society and culture in the broadest sense, right down to our daily making sense of tradition, codes, monuments, customs and the unwritten rules that hold society together. Following the philosopher Giambattista Vico (1668–1744, author of the *New Science*), Gramsci regards these codes as constituents of *common sense*. He attributes a great deal of importance to common sense in terms of the way individuals and classes interpret social reality and are prepared to accept or not accept given forms of authority as legitimate.[9]

In the particular case of Italian unification, it is clear that in contrast to the successful revolution lead by the Jacobins during the French Revolution, the Italian bourgeoisie that spearheaded the Risorgimento was able merely to bring about a passive revolution which did not change common sense or educate the masses in the duties and obligations of a liberal-bourgeois version of citizenship. The Italian bourgeoisie managed to expel foreign occupiers and unite the country under the leadership of the house of Savoy in Piedmont, but it was not *hegemonic*. More will be said about this key concept below. For now it might be remarked that the new Italian elites who came to power in the period 1848–70 had to rely on a number of strategic compromises with the papacy, the aristocratic landlords of the South, a newly emerging class of industrialists, and the Savoyard monarchy, in order to consolidate their power under the banner of democracy and national unification. In ideal–typical terms, the new state, civil society and common sense should have been characterised by competitive individualism, diversity of opinion and a well-established culture of freedom of assembly, debate and the press. Instead, the post-unification political class was plunged into a desperate attempt to achieve two objectives. In the interests of stability it had to blur the differences between the discourses of liberalism, national unity and popular democracy on the one hand, and on the other it somehow had to cope with the reality of large-scale exclusion of the masses from state institutions as well as the enduring semifeudal structure of the South. In their 'heroic' period, the French and English bourgeoisie were apparently able to overcome aristocratic and popular resistance in order to convert most of society to the principles of the market and a competitive world view, and thus establish their power and authority on a solid foundation that made them hegemonic. Whereas hegemonic classes transform all social relations and establish their power by remodelling the entire social structure, a class that comes to power on the basis of a passive revolution will have to negotiate and renegotiate the socioeconomic and political foundations of its unstable rule.[10]

Passive revolutions can be utilised by a hegemonic class to counter an insurgency on the part of subaltern classes, or they can be symptomatic of the unsuccessful attempt of a class to become hegemonic. In reference to the Italian case, the Risorgimento is a clear example of the second scenario. The bases of bourgeois power had not been established definitively. This meant that a revolutionary alliance of the working class and peasantry could overturn the corrupt parliamentary regime whose legacy is bound up with the name of Giovanni Giolitti and the decidedly illiberal politics of bribery and buying favours that prevailed during his years in office as prime minister.[11] During the factory occupations of 1919–20 Gramsci thought that this historical possibility might become revolutionary practice. His optimism was fuelled by the Russian Revolution just three years before, and what he perceived to be the complementary roles played by political party and workers' council in the events of 1917. In the pages of the journal *Ordine Nuovo* Gramsci and other members of the council communist movement in Italy at the time, such as Togliatti, argue that the lesson of the Paris Commune and the Russian Revolutions of 1905 and 1917 was not only that the working class cannot lay hold of the ready-made state machinery and wield it for its own purposes. The working class had to become hegemonic rather than (temporarily) victorious in a passive revolution, as the Italian bourgeoisie had done in the Risorgimento. This meant it would have to make a decisive break with all institutional and cultural vestiges of parliamentary corruption and behind-the-scenes bargaining for favours and privileges, and strive instead for the construction of an entirely new producers' civilisation.

Prior to the prison writings, Gramsci was influenced by Sorel and syndicalist ideas about revolutionary politics that stressed the need for the proletariat to assert its own values in strict separation from other social strata.[12] Conceived in these terms, the revolution brings about an intellectual and moral reform affecting the producer in every aspect of his or her life. This means going well beyond issues of wages and hours in order to take up questions of creativity in work, democracy in culture, intimacy in friendship and even heroism in death. It is in this profound sense that the revolution entails changing the institutions mediating between humanity and nature, and as such, changing the structure of experience and the content of common sense. It is in this context too that one can understand the battle for hegemony as a political project to establish legitimacy and authority beyond power and domination.

Syndicalists in Italy responded positively to Sorel's notion that the organised working class has to insist on absolute nonparticipation in state institutions. Many of them were of southern origin and were able to perceive that there was no 'winning the battle of democracy' in parliamentary or electoral terms. The newly created Italian state consolidated the extra-parliamentary alliance between northern industrial capital and southern landowners, in fact undermined a truly popular and democratic political culture in Italy. In 1919–20, Gramsci is in broad agreement with Marx and Sorel that the real bases of power in parliamentary regimes are extra-parliamentary. He is also adamant that the trade union, like the political party, is too integrated into the democratic parliamentary state to be a potential source of a new hegemonic order. Like the union, the council has the virtue of operating on the shop floor, where production is organised and a decisive component of common sense is forged. Like the party, however, the council unites workers beyond distinctions. Factory councils were set up by the Italian government during World War I in an effort to propel production forward by increasing flexibility in the outmoded structures of capital-labour relations based on cumbersome unions and intransigent employer organisations. They continued to exist in the post-war period, and soon evolved into vehicles of radical shop-floor democracy with the possibility of transforming defensive worker contestation into worker control and autonomy. This placed the councils on a collision course with the employers and the state as well as the existing socialist parties and unions. The latter correctly perceived that the step from defensive opposition to autonomy would make them redundant.[13]

A wave of factory occupations led by the councils paralysed the Italian economy during 1919–20. In his *Ordine Nuovo* articles at that time Gramsci argues that the council represents a radically democratic alternative of participation and collective decision-making capable of replacing the liberal democratic state. Not only does the council fuse producer functions and citizen function, as Marx claimed the Paris Commune did; in Gramsci's estimation it also changes common sense by providing an institutional framework for the already existing but ultimately powerless forms of solidarity organised by the traditional organs of the socialist movement, such as unions and parties. In addition, the cultural pages of *Ordine Nuovo* attempt to foster a creative and experimental attitude towards the arts, and indeed, during the highpoint of the occupations in September 1920, workers occupying factories throughout Italy performed plays inside the factories. Friends and family supplied the striking workers with food and fresh clothes if and where it was possible to get past the police guards patrolling the factory gates.[14]

By locking themselves into factories, the occupiers set out to demonstrate the workers' determination to lay the foundations of a new proletarian state separate from the liberal democratic state. Within the factory, the council was meant to be the nucleus of an entirely new producers' civilisation with its own ideas about labour, art, ethics, friendship and mortality. The failure of the occupations to bring about the Italian equivalent of the Russian October forced Gramsci to rethink his ideas about the state and revolution. The employers and state simply allowed the workers to occupy the factories, while the PSI stood by and helped sabotage the movement by publicly disparaging it as foolhardy adventurism. With Togliatti and Amadeo Bordiga (1889–1970), Gramsci left the PSI in January 1921 to found the PCI. Shortly before his incarceration in November 1926 he wrote essays entitled 'Notes on the Southern Question' and 'Some Aspects of the Italian Situation', in which some of the themes of the prison writings are clearly anticipated. He argues that in the more advanced capitalist countries in Western Europe, the dominant classes possess political, cultural and institutional resources which they did not have at their disposal in Tsarist Russia. This means that even the most serious economic crises do not necessarily have immediate political repercussions in the realm of the superstructure, or, as he puts it in 'Some Aspects of the Italian Situation', 'politics always lags considerably behind economics'. This raises some of the key dilemmas of Western Marxism. Since the movements of the economic base did not of themselves produce a revolutionary class consciousness, the issue of consciousness needed to be addressed, though without retreating to the idealism of Kant, Hegel and Croce. Could this be done within a Marxist framework, or did the Leninist model have to be somehow suited to Western realities? Since adoption of Leninism seemed increasingly implausible in the 1920s and even more so after World War II, Western Marxists such as Sartre asked: Could Marxism be tempered by incorporating insights from other bodies of thought, such as idealism, psychoanalysis or existentialism?[15]

Gramsci's analysis of the so-called 'Questione Meridionale' ('Southern Question') in 1926 leads him to the conclusion that if politics always lags behind economics, it can be said that the time of the base is different from the time of the superstructure. Moreover, in terms of economic development and expansion of the material forces of production, time is different in the states of the capitalist core, such as England and France, and in the states of the capitalist periphery, such as Spain, Greece, Ireland and Portugal, with Italy and Germany occupying a somewhat contradictory location in between. To complicate the Italian situation even more, the divide between the rapidly industrialising north and the semifeudal agrarian south meant that differential time across national frontiers had to be balanced by the consideration that time within national boundaries could also differ.[16] The victory and consolidation of fascism in the years 1922–25 compelled Gramsci to reread Marx's *Eighteenth Brumaire* in the light of the specificities of Southern Italian underdevelopment, and to see how in peripheral states the battle for the allegiance of intermediate social strata assumes immense significance in the working-class struggle for hegemony. In prison Gramsci seeks to formulate an alternative to Bernstein's reformism, which was likely to lead to social democracy, and Lenin's voluntarism, which was inappropriate for the conditions of Europe. What was needed was the full elaboration of a Marxist theory of politics, which the first theorist of historical materialism never managed to write.

The *Prison Notebooks* are written with the lessons of the failures of 1919–20 in mind. One lesson is that the emphasis on councils and other institutions rooted in the world of labour is correct and remains valid from a Marxist standpoint. Against the syndicalist notion of the necessity of proletarian autonomy, however, the emphasis on factory organisation would have to be combined with a political engagement with all of society. It becomes clear to Gramsci that seeking refuge in economic determinism or ideological purity allows the political representatives of capital and political reaction to reorganise the relations between capital and labour on their own terms and through passive revolutions. This means that political initiatives from key figures and institutions within the superstructure to overhaul the base are every bit as important as developments within the base itself, if not more so. If there is no direct or immediately causal relation between economic crisis and consciousness and revolution, all the appropriate political conditions for revolutionary transformation have to be created autonomously, from a variety of directions, and in a variety of ways. In the context of Italian postunification and beyond, this means that 'winning the battle of democracy' as highlighted by Marx and Engels in the *Communist Manifesto* entails an ideological and cultural battle on several fronts at once. While it is a battle at the level of the base, it is also a battle at the level of the superstructure. Within the superstructure itself, however, Gramsci distinguishes between institutions of direct repression, such as the army, police, intelligence forces and distinct instances of the executive generally on the one hand, and institutions of hegemony, such as the church, universities, schools, press and media on the other. He refers to the sphere of direct repression as political society and the institutions of hegemony as civil society. Here the issue of winning the battle of democracy raised in Chapter 1 finally achieves concrete expression. It means engaging in a successful campaign to transform common sense and traditional modes of thinking in civil society that maintain the political and temporal gulf between economic crisis and political revolution.[17]

In this formulation the state is not a mere executive of the entire bourgeoisie; indeed the implication is that it is not appropriate to speak in terms of the state or superstructure in monolithic terms at all. The state, like capital, is understood in terms of a network of relations which are to be transformed rather than seized or occupied. In Gramsci's estimation a key role in this process of resistance and change is played by intellectuals. Once again, he makes a distinction that marks an original contribution to Western Marxism. He distinguishes between traditional intellectuals from various backgrounds who establish their status by promoting the idea of the intellectual as a member of a free-floating caste operating above the arena of social struggle; and organic intellectuals from the subaltern milieu who politically remain committed to the groups and classes they come from. While traditional intellectuals (such as Croce in the Italian case) protect their own interests as a caste at the same time as serving the existing order, organic intellectuals are in a position to challenge the existing order because of their organic relation with the masses. Hence Gramsci argues that in Italy organic intellectuals like himself must articulate a working-class (though not narrowly sectarian, as in 1919–20) standpoint, in order to (1) win the allegiance of traditional intellectuals and make them see that liberal democracy and capitalism were English institutions imported by a feeble Italian bourgeois class and are inappropriate for Italian realities; and (2) win the peasantry to the cause of communism as the solution to the question of what new institutions should be adopted. He argues further that the Southern peasantry of the day remained under the influence of large land-owning interests because of the enduring influence of intellectuals who did nothing to discourage the deeply anchored belief that existing social relations are somehow natural. They indirectly encouraged deference to the church and local bureaucracy when they should have been fostering critical engagement with the abuse of public authority.[18]

In the prison writings Gramsci reserves especially harsh criticism for Croce and other intellectuals who he believes had a hand in separating the radical Southern intelligentsia from the peasants by encouraging them to adopt superficially cosmopolitan attitudes while neglecting local conditions. Intellectuals in the Gramscian sense, such as local government officials, journalists, lawyers and academics, play a key role in keeping together what Gramsci refers to as the 'historic bloc' of Southern landowners and Northern industrial capital, which ran the country outside and against parliament, and the little that existed in the way of democratic control in the Italy of Giolitti, and in more obvious ways, of Mussolini. The Italian revolution would thus depend on the ability of the communist party and workers' councils to disaggregate the bloc of Southern landowners and Northern industrialists in order for the peasants to organise independently of these forces. This cultural process of disaggregation could not be accomplished without the help of intellectuals like Gaetano Salvemini, Piero Gobetti and Guido Dorso who had championed the cause of the South. Gramsci insists throughout the *Prison Notebooks* that in order to avoid a successful assault on state power followed by leadership struggles and political indecision, the revolution has to be carefully prepared *before* the actual seizure of power, if this is even necessary, in what he calls a *war of position*. The implications clearly go well beyond the Italian context within which Gramsci formulates his ideas. By the time of the prison writings Gramsci realises that if one wants to understand the networks of power in any society, one must never fetishise or reify the ostensibly crucial role of parliaments and constitutions. One must look instead at how a constellation of class and ideological alliances are simultaneously pursued as political strategies at the levels of the economy, civil society and political society. Strategy in this case refers not only to the secure control of the economy. It refers to a much wider conception of leadership implied by the terms hegemony and common sense. Long before Michel Foucault's seminal theoretical and historical research on power undertaken beyond the parameters of Marxism (see Chapter 6), it is clear to Gramsci that power circulates in protean and capillary networks that ignore the methodological distinctions between civil society and state or base and superstructure.[19]

At this stage of the discussion on Gramsci the usage of the term hegemony is coming more sharply into focus. The former 'peoples' democracies' in Eastern Europe supply a clear example of what hegemony is not. The necessity to resort to heavy policing and extensive propaganda is a sure indication that hegemony is absent or breaking down. Thus the necessity of the USSR and Warsaw Pact to use force in 1953 (East Germany), 1956 (Hungary), 1968 (Czechoslovakia) and 1981 (Poland) suggests that the communist parties of the different Eastern Bloc countries had come to power with the help of the advancing Red Army. Although this assured their ascent to power, they were not culturally or politically prepared to transform common sense and the experience of everyday life. Hence hegemony means something distinct from coercion or authoritarian rule. Marx and Engels anticipate Gramsci's theory of hegemony to a certain extent in *The German Ideology* (1845), where they say that ruling class ideas are, in every epoch, the ruling ideas.[20] But in Gramsci's formulation hegemony does not denote simple ideological mystification or fetishising in the sense that Feuerbach or the young Marx might speak of fetishism or reification. There is a distinctly Machiavellian lineage to the concept, insofar as Machiavelli argues that whether or not a new prince is able to stay in power turns fundamentally on how the prince got there in the first place. In a manner analogous to the Italian Risorgimento, where French aid and Austrian demise were more important for independence than a mass movement for unity, the regimes in Eastern Europe came to power on the strength of the Soviet army and the defeat of German National Socialism. In Machiavellian-Gramscian terms, this can be regarded as an excessive reliance on luck (*fortuna*) and a conspicuous failure to construct anew the socioeconomic, cultural and political bases of a new hegemony (*egemonia*)[21]

A nonhegemonic elite will generally attempt to shore up its control of the economy by authoritarian means, as in the case of the Risorgimento, or with repression and terror, as in the case of fascism. These are examples of attempts to increase the scope of direct state intervention in the economy. There are also instances where changes in the economy necessitate a rolling back of direct state intervention for the purpose of introducing more flexible labour market structures, as Gramsci illustrates in the notebook *Americanism and Fordism*. With remarkable prescience he speculates on the consequences of increasingly sophisticated techniques of domination and surveillance in the workplace and how these could lead to a reshuffling in the historic bloc of forces that rule a country at any given time. He notes that the transition from craft production to industrial production to assembly-line production has effects on consumption, culture and even physical appearances. Gramsci thus anticipates Pier Paolo Pasolini's (1922–75) observation that one could walk into an Italian piazza in the 1950s and accurately predict the social origins of a person simply by looking at their face and body. At this stage in the development of post-war capitalism different social classes displayed conspicuously distinct physiological traits and cultural mannerisms. If one goes back into the same piazza in the 1970s, in the aftermath of the so-called 'economic miracle', Pasolini maintains, one is struck by the large-scale disappearance of these differences. In terms of the passive revolution required to establish the cultural and economic transition to a consumer-goods-oriented economy based on low production costs and systematic de-skilling of the workforce, however, the incorrect conclusion to be drawn from this homogenisation process is that society has become more democratic. Instead, the power that the observer could once literally read from faces and bodies has shifted to other sites of struggle. Power is no longer metaphorically transparent to physical typologies, and hegemony is no longer a function of these kinds of differences. Stated in more contemporary terms, the 'traditional' working class might well become less visible due to structural and superstructural changes; in the case of the gradual influx of migrant workers and young women into the workforce, the new sites of struggle attain variegated levels of social visibility.[22]

Gramsci's *Prison Notebooks* clearly indicate the extent to which Marx's ideas need updating, as well as the tremendous suppleness of Marxism and its capacity to assimilate new ideas and expand in different directions. Developing the concepts of hegemony, historic bloc, passive revolution, civil society and political society, Gramsci provides Marxism with a theory of politics and a new theory of superstructures. His ideas on common sense and hegemony provide the bases of an incipient Marxist theory of culture and form the general background for a number of debates within Western Marxism on culture and revolutionary politics to be explored below.[23]

The Problem of the Superstructure Reconsidered (II): Korsch and Lukács

If Gramsci's lasting contribution to the left in Europe is to have substantially enriched historical materialism with a theory of politics as well as a new base and superstructure model, it is Georg Lukács's achievement to have solidified the bases of Marxist epistemology. Hence, along with the *Prison Notebooks*, Lukács's *History and Class Consciousness* (1923) figures among the most important theoretical works of Western Marxism. Lukács deepens and develops a number of themes that appear for the first time in Karl Korsch's *Marxism and Philosophy*, which is another important text published in 1923. *Marxism and Philosophy* takes up where Korsch left off in *Industrial Law for Workers' Councils* of the previous year. Much like Korsch's earlier essay *What is Socialisation?* (1919), *Industrial Law for Workers' Councils* echoes Gramsci's assessment of the radically democratic structure of the council during the Italian *bienno rosso* of 1919–20. Korsch's political convictions are underpinned by a juridical and philosophical interest in the potentially revolutionary implications of a form of legal universality that is authorised to dissolve the power differential between classes by abolishing property and control over the production process as the private right of capital.[24] In the aftermath of World War I and into the early 1920s, Korsch and Gramsci are convinced that the factory council is an ideal institution combining proximity to the work process offered by the trade union with decision-making capacities normally associated with the political party. Hence both thinkers are also associated with the decidedly anti-Leninist implications of council communism (see Chapter 4). In different ways, they share the conviction that the Marxist critique of capitalism is deficient if unaccompanied by an outline of an alternative economy through which working humanity *collectively* controls the mediation processes structuring its relation with nature. The implication is that an economic system in which this control is usurped by a combination of socialist planners and a single political party within the framework of a so-called 'workers' state' is as unacceptable as a system based on private appropriation and accumulation. If the prerogatives of capital are assumed by a new historic bloc of apparatchiks and central planners the revolution could be considered lost.[25]

Korsch, Gramsci and Lukács were all directly involved in the experiments in council democracy that swept central Europe and Italy in 1919–20. One week after its formation in 1918, Lukács joined the Hungarian Communist Party. He served as a commissar for public education in Béla Kun's coalition government until it was overthrown by right-wing forces in the summer of 1919. He then fled to Vienna, where he began developing his ideas on Marxist epistemology and communist aesthetics. After the collapse of the factory occupations and the founding of the PCI, Gramsci worked in Vienna and Moscow before being sentenced to jail. Korsch quickly fell foul of communist orthodoxy by refusing to moderate his demands for worker, as opposed to party, control of the revolution. Following the defeat of council democracy in Italy, Berlin, Munich and Budapest, and the twin processes of capitalist reconsolidation in the 1920s and the rise of Stalin in Russia, all three thinkers were compelled to address the necessity of rethinking the bases of Marxist theory and practice. It has been seen how Gramsci attempts to provide Marx with a theory of politics. It remains to be seen how Korsch and especially Lukács attempt to develop a Marxist epistemology appropriate for the realities of the twentieth century. The turn of the century crisis of Marxism that forms the background to Labriola's and then Gramsci's ideas in Italy is a general phenomenon with consequences for the left all across Europe and informing the work of Korsch and Lukács. What perhaps seemed like a minor dispute between Sorel, Croce, Bernstein and Labriola assumes great importance with the outbreak of World War I and then with the consolidation of Western European capitalism against the challenges of the Russian Revolution and the short-lived council republics. Many of the most incisive commentators on Western Marxism, such as Anderson, Jay and Jameson, note that the isolation of the USSR and the insufficiently revolutionary consciousness of the Western European working classes and peasantry quite clearly threatened to turn communism into the official regime ideology of the USSR rather than the dialectical theory of knowledge and action that it is for Marx.[26]

It is against this background that Korsch writes *Marxism and Philosophy*. He distinguishes between three discernible periods in Marxist theory and practice. The first is 1843–8, the phase from *On the Jewish Question* (1843) to the *Communist Manifesto* (1848). In a second phase dating from 1848 to 1900, the young Marx's stress on the totality constituted by humanity, nature and their mediations starts to give way to the separation of Marxist economics from Marxist politics, and the dispersion of historical materialist enquiry into the fields of sociology, ideology and culture. The suggestion is that although this tendency is most pronounced in positivist interpretations of historical materialism that appeared after the death of its founders, Marx and Engels nonetheless help promote it to the extent that they stress the need to make philosophical enquiry superfluous by realising philosophy in practice.[27] Korsch then warns of the dangers arising from 1900 onwards. He maintains that in this third stage many Marxists abandoned the ideas of dialectics and totality. The consequence is that the movement bifurcated into positive science and voluntarist politics. Korsch argues that Marxists must address the problems of Second International Marxism and the inability of the council system to establish itself as an alternative to the bourgeois parliamentary state.[28] The key to this project entails a careful re-evaluation of Hegel and the philosophical bases of Marxism.[29] It is much to his credit that he urges this epistemological taking stock nine years before Marx's *1844 Manuscripts* were published for the first time in Moscow in 1932. To a number of Western Marxists and critical theorists, these fragmentary notes reveal the young Marx to be first and foremost a dialectician probing the philosophical and synthetic dimensions of reality rather than a scientist in search of the empirical bases of materialism. In Vienna in the early 1920s Lukács came to a similar understanding of the proper relation between Hegel and Marx in the eight essays collected in *History and Class Consciousness.*

The bureaucratic leadership of the Third International had little time for the advocates of a qualified return to Hegel or a reinvigoration of the role of subjectivity and consciousness in left politics. Korsch was expelled from the German Communist Party (KPD) in 1926 and Lukács was bullied into renouncing the views expressed in *History and Class Consciousness.*[30] Yet for both thinkers the issue is not primarily about the unequivocal primacy of mind or matter, since this would constitute a regression to pre-Kantian philosophy. The issue is more centrally concerned with the dialectical relationship between humanity and nature and their mediation in history; that is, with the overcoming of the static dichotomies that characterise reified modes of thinking. This idea is first developed by Hegel in his critique of Kant, and then given a Marxist framework by Lukács in *History and Class Consciousness.* In order to fully understand this central text of Western Marxism, it is first necessary to say a few words about Lukács' ideas prior to 1923.

In addition to the epistemological ideas of Kant and especially Hegel, the sociology of Georg Simmel (1858–1918) and Max Weber (1864–1920), and the existentialism of Kierkegaard (1813–55) and Dostoevsky (1821–81) form the cultural background to the Hungarian philosopher's early development. Lukács left Budapest in 1906 to study in Berlin, where he attended Simmel's lectures, and then moved to Heidelberg in 1912, where he became friends with Weber and Ernst Bloch (1885–1977), author of *The Principle of Hope*, written in American exile during 1938–47 and published in the mid-1950s.[31]

At the risk of simplification, one can say that what one reads in *History and Class Consciousness* is a remarkable synthesis of Hegel on dialectics and totality, Kierkegaard and Simmel on the inevitable discrepancy between individual life and social forms (institutions), Weber on the rise and spread of instrumental reason, and Marx on reification and the political mission of the proletariat. As indicated above, Lukács is not a political cadre determined to invent epistemological positions that match the party line at any given time. He is a political philosopher and aesthetician whose main aim is to demonstrate how it is possible to move beyond the individualist premises of liberalism and the antinomies of bourgeois thought and life (theory/practice, private/public, individual/state, etc.).[32] He attempts to formulate a radicalisation of Hegelian idealism that also eschews the mechanical and positivist materialism of Second International Marxism. It is thus unsurprising that a number of idealist and existentialist motifs about the structure of experience, the limits of knowledge and the conditions of action inform his entire *oeuvre*, despite his continually professed adherence to the principles of Marxist-Leninist materialism and literary realism.[33]

In the essays written between 1907 and 1910 contained in *Soul and Form* (1911), Lukács ponders the chaos of life. He sees a conflict between the necessity of giving form to the chaos for the purposes of making knowledge of life and reality possible, on the one hand, and the danger of stifling living vitality and distorting reality in the very process of form-giving, on the other. In terms highly reminiscent of Nietzsche and Simmel, he suggests that there can be no knowledge or content without form, yet impoverished form will tend to increase the distance between knowing subjects and the objects of cognition.[34] In the *Theory of the Novel* (1916), he gives these ideas a historical foundation by arguing that epistemological form is a function of society and history rather than a static or transcendental aesthetic concept. In what clearly must have had an impact on Adorno's *Negative Dialectics* and *Aesthetic Theory*, in 1916 Lukács suggests that at the core of the coming utopianism is a creative impulse propelled by the desire for the discovery of aesthetic and philosophical form that strives to be form (knowledge, theory) and content (life, practice) at one and the same time. Another way of saying this in more Hegelian terms is that the right form overcomes the dichotomy between form and content: a surplus of quantity eventually results in an increase in quality.

In the *Theory of the Novel* he distinguishes between the era of the Homeric epic, the period of transition toward incipient modernity in the works of Dante (1265–1321), the bourgeois novel, and the intimations of a post-bourgeois literature in the writings of Dostoevsky. Whereas the conflict between form and life is hardly present in Greek art and society, it becomes flagrant by the time of the bourgeois novel and the appearance of bourgeois interiority. Indeed, throughout his life Lukács remains committed to the idea that the retreat to the inner sanctum of the self he sees in experimental and avant-garde writing is symptomatic of the divorce of life and objective reality from aesthetic form and subjective consciousness. When life is imprisoned by form, knowledge of life is mystified. The result is that freedom is thwarted by fearful withdrawal. He remains steadfast in this conviction: no matter how stylistically innovative and ostensibly revolutionary in certain examples of literary and artistic modernism, bourgeois interiority is basically defeatist if not outright reactionary. One glimpses the profundity of Lukács' contribution to Western Marxism by considering the dilemma with which he is confronted. From the foregoing discussion it is clear that the conflict between life and form has a counterpart in Marx's distinction between the base and superstructure. Because of his knowledge of Nietzsche, Simmel and Weber, Lukács is acutely aware that any conflation between life and base is likely to result in epistemological reductionism and political putchism. Yet because of his understanding of Hegel and Marx, he is equally cognisant of the fact that any rigid separation between life and base is likely to give rise to all manner of theories and nationalist and irrational anti-Marxist existentialist and religious movements. It is clear to him that the choice between unequivocal allegiance to the communist party (conflation between life and base) or the academy (rigid separation between life and base) is admittedly a false choice. Faced with the reality of the 1917 revolution in the East (and not in England, as Marx had predicted), it is nonetheless a choice with which Lukács is forced to struggle. He opts for Hegel, Marx, totality and dialectics against Nietzsche, Weber, Simmel, existentialism and ontology.

Key thinkers on the European left after World War II attempt to work out syntheses instead of choosing sides in this debate. Sartre is one such figure, as will be seen below. For now it is safe to say that for the left it is impossible to overestimate the stakes involved in this endeavour to ascertain the correct relationship between life/form, base/superstructure and Marxism/existentialism. If these phenomena cannot be mediated successfully, there exists the possibility of a highly de-politicising celebration of the inevitable difference between theory and practice. This in its turn could lead to the academic isolation of theory and the proliferation of disoriented and largely futile activism. Given that a cursory glance at the left in Europe today suggests that this might be an accurate depiction of the current political situation, it will be useful to return to the issue in the Conclusion of this book.

In the period following the publication of the *Theory of the Novel* and culminating in the publication of *History and Class Consciousness*, Lukács comes to see that the epistemological project of revolutionising thought in the name of knowledge is inseparably bound up with the project of revolutionising reality in the name of freedom. He concludes that only revolutionised thought and reality can guarantee a form of political freedom that can redeem the radical implications suggested by the idea that real freedom, not simply freedom to sell one's labour power or express one's opinion in largely symbolic ways, is freedom from necessity. Freedom from necessity demands social and political institutions that liberate all of humanity—not merely a single class—from forms of labour mediating between humanity and nature that reproduce heteronomy and necessity. In advanced capitalist economies, he argues, heteronomy and necessity assume an institutional profile in social phenomena such as commodity production, a rigid division of mental and manual labour, and control over the conditions of production by nonproducers interested in profit rather than the satisfaction of needs and creativity. Hence freedom from necessity demands revolution. The first step in this conquest of freedom is revolutionising thought by transcending the bourgeois cultural horizon rather than simply dismissing bourgeois thought and life in favour of irrational vitality, a naive return to primitive spontaneity or pseudo-scientific materialism. To achieve this rational transcendence it is necessary to expose the contradictions in the work of the best thinkers of middle-class culture, such as Kant, Hegel and Simmel. Kant and Simmel stand above idiosyncratic and anecdotal forms of spurious objectivity by *systematically* demonstrating that all objectivity is mediated by subjectivity. From the moment it is recognised that there is a subjective dimension to objective knowledge, it is possible to see that it is entirely possible for subjects to create the world in which they live in a nonarbitrary, i.e. truthful, way. On this account, freedom to know the objective world is bound up with freedom to create the socioeconomic and political conditions that make objective knowledge itself possible. Two closely related consequences derive from this analysis. First, knowledge of the objective world cannot exist without a knowing *subject* that knows the world without the constraints of necessity, lest knowledge be confused with something more akin to religion, superstition, myth or some other desperate response to the evident reality that nature does not automatically provide the remedies to necessity. Second, the only knowing subject capable of abolishing these constraints is a *collective subject* that creates the conditions of objectivity freed from necessity, since it is the collective labour of humanity on nature that remedies the fact that nature is not spontaneously generous with its fruits, and that all hitherto existing forms of society and modes of production have been painfully unsuccessful in overcoming necessity for the vast majority of its members. In the proletariat and communism he sees the emancipatory synthesis of epistemological form and sociopolitical content.[35]

What distinguishes advanced industrial capitalism as a social form and a mode of production is that, for the first time in history, the economy ceases to be a marginal activity performed for the sake of more important purposes such as political authority and religious ritual. Lukács is deeply influenced by Weber's thesis that the rise of specifically ascetic forms of Protestantism indicates that the economy has penetrated all spheres of existence, including spiritual life: the Protestant is calculating about the possibility of salvation and throws himself into work in the hope of receiving some kind of sign from God without the intermediary of the church hierarchy.[36]

Combining the insights of Weber on Protestantism and the young Marx on commodity production, Lukács arrives at the conclusion that the long-term consequence of the penetration of the economy into all spheres of life is the transformation of reason from a dialectical mediating instance in Kant and Hegel into a tool divorced from any recognisable ethical or political ends. In a gradual but inexorable process of reification, 'the economy' acquires its own dynamic and laws which confront individual actors as something natural and against which they are powerless to do anything autonomous.[37]

This situation is fundamentally ambiguous. On the one hand capitalism creates unprecedented levels of economic development, which make freedom from necessity an objective possibility rather than wishful thinking. In this sense capitalism furnishes all the elements necessary for a devastating critique of capitalism. On the other hand, the reification and alienation that accompany the growth process threaten to blind its potential opponents to the workings of the system. A number of the critical theorists examined in the next chapter suggest that reification and alienation incapacitate and integrate the working classes to such an extent that a proletarian revolution in the Marxist sense may no longer be possible. By contrast, in 1923 Lukács is confident that the permeation of economic rationality into all the pores of society creates a class of people who are educated and highly politicised by the fact that their entire being is invested by commodity production and consumption. The very existence of this class marks the beginning of the end of antinomies such as is/ought and theory/practice. The proletariat is quite simply the negation of capitalist society and the *Aufhebung* of the discrepancy between equality of citizenship and the manifest inequality between classes.

The unresolved tension in Lukács's *History and Class Consciousness* resides in his declaration at the end of Chapter 4 that communism will be constructed when the collective subjectivity of the workers is moved to action by an awareness of the objective possibilities offered by the mere fact of their de facto communist *Dasein*, of their revolutionary being and the fact that they are both subject and object of the historical process in advanced capitalist societies. He then equivocates by saying that the communist party has a fundamental role in galvanising that process, since workers in capitalism suffer from alienation and reified consciousness.[38] Lukács stresses consciousness and advocates council democracy. Yet he was also prepared to accept the realities of single-party rule in the USSR and the Soviet bloc after World War II. The dilemma between the objective reality of class structure and the facticity of existential choice of political allegiances fuelled the imagination of Jean-Paul Sartre (1905–80), who highlights the contradictions between life (economy) and form (superstructure) in terms of the precedence of existence over essence.

Existentialist Commitment and Structuralist Epistemology: Sartre and Althusser

Sartre attempts to project beyond the limitations of Lukács's position. It has been seen that the latter is somewhat caught between the epistemological imperative not to reduce the complexity of life to class relations and the struggle for survival, on the one hand, and the political imperative to take collective control of life by impressing a communist form on the labour process, on the other. The logic of his argument drives Lukács to the conclusion that where the proletariat appears to be unable to build communism spontaneously through a network of democratic councils, the democratic centralist communist party must assume the leading role in the process.[39] Sartre acknowledges the dilemma of choosing between philosophical rigour in epistemological questions and adopting discipline in political questions, as well as the more general dilemma between the spontaneity of life and the distorting constraints placed on spontaneous life by epistemological form. Marx, Gramsci and Lukács are confident that the liberation of the struggle for survival from class relations and wage labour will transform the labour process into a means of actively creating reality as well as accurately knowing it. By contrast, Sartre believes that humanity is not only alienated from its labour power because of the private appropriation of socially produced wealth. For Sartre, humanity is also alienated from being, and the latter can never be simply reappropriated for ontological reasons that exceed the scope of human action. Although humanity makes contact with being in consciousness and all forms of action (not just labour), there is always a discrepancy between pure being 'in itself' and human being 'for itself'. The 'for itself', he suggests in his early works, yearns for union with the pure being implied by being 'in itself'. Although it can never fully attain this union, humanity is condemned to try to attain it, and is condemned to freedom and ultimately failure. In terms starkly reminiscent of Heidegger's notion of *Geworfenheit* (the human condition of being *thrown* into the world) the author of *Being and Nothingness* (1943) and the *Critique of Dialectical Reason* (1960) argues that the conflict between philosophical rigour and political coherence must be tested in a series of projects, or what he also refers to as engaged situations of *commitment* and *responsibility*. It also means that the tension between life and form is resolved in the concrete reality of *existence* and the latter, he adds in a much celebrated phrase, precedes essence.[40]

Sartre holds that although in subjective terms the individual is condemned to freedom, Marxism nonetheless constitutes the 'unsurpassable horizon of our time', that is, the most accurate measure of objective reality as long as capitalism decisively structures forms of consciousness and sets the terms of socially imposed necessity. To say that necessity is socially imposed is to argue that in modern societies it is not nature that imposes scarcity on humanity. It is the bourgeois ruling class that dominates other classes by imposing its institutions and values while excluding other possible ways of life. The more capitalism breaks the bounds of a definable economic sphere and begins to embrace all areas of life, the more those other possible ways of living are frustrated, thus necessitating a creative political response on economic, political, ethical and aesthetic levels. This situation is complicated by the fact that there are bourgeois liberals, bourgeois communists, proletarian fascists, proletarian liberals, as well as de-politicised bourgeois and proletarians. People choose their commitments in ways that confirm but also conflict with their social origins. The corollary is that each person, regardless of the milieu they stem from, is capable of overcoming the horizons of that milieu. For Sartre, even if Marxism is indispensable for an understanding of our times, its orthodox formulations are badly mistaken in reducing consciousness and political commitments to location in the class structure. Like Gramsci, Sartre is opposed to any mechanical understanding of the relation between economic objectivity and subjective consciousness. To a greater extent than Gramsci and especially Lukács, however, Sartre is prepared to accept the implications of human freedom and the open-ended character of the historical process. For the latter it is clear that Marxism desperately needs a theory of action that does not reduce motivation to class location. It also needs a theory of existence that acknowledges the incommensurability of consciousness and being. That incommensurability will always place the subject at some distance from the object, such that there can be no subject-object of history. A close inspection of history suggests that what one witnesses is not the Hegelian-Lukácsian tendency towards a subject-object *totality*. History is not simply a class struggle, but rather the struggle of conflicting groups to *totalise* subject-object relations in order to bring about their conception of the greatest possible humanisation of being. On this account Marxism explains why the proletariat could potentially realise an unprecedented humanisation of being. But by ignoring individual human freedom and the responsibility to choose, the PCF and other communist parties were turning their backs on Marx. Hence Marxism needed to be enriched and updated with existentialism. He explains why in *The Critique of Dialectical Reason*, which, with the *Prison Notebooks* and *History and Class Consciousness*, is the third of the three key texts of Western Marxism considered in this chapter.[41]

The fact that political allegiances cannot simply be deduced from class location is just one of the consequences of the divergence between the ontological 'in itself' and the anthropological 'for itself'. Like Heidegger, Sartre does not start from the assumption that epistemology rests on an unshakeable human foundation such as consciousness, as expressed for example by Descartes's 'I think therefore I am', or Kant's transcendental ego. Heidegger proceeds from the nonfoundational reality of collective *Dasein* and *Geworfenheit*, i.e. from the view that the world both internal to and external to the individual that s/he shares with other individuals is already there when each person is born. What humanity knows about the world is revealed to humanity by being in a process in which humanity actively participates 'for itself' but does not own or totally control because being 'in itself' is not an attribute of humanity. For both thinkers the world is an ongoing and plural event into which the individual is thrown, and in which they are forced to answer fundamental questions about their relation to being. For Heidegger these questions include: will I ignore the existence of being and forget that it has its own history that shapes my life on earth, or will I 'allow being to be', so to speak, so that it can reveal itself to me in all of its otherness? For Sartre it is not so much a question of the patience of letting be or attempting to manipulate being. In the introductory 'Search for a Method' section of the *Critique of Dialectical Reason*, Sartre explains that that there is a stand-off between Hegel on the objectivity of history and Kierkegaard on the subjectivity of existence that can only be resolved by Marxism. He remarks that Hegel is correct to speak of objective spirit in institutions and the fact that all subjectivity is constituted by sociopolitical and historical objectivity. Insofar it is true to affirm in Hegelian manner that the totality of subjectivity and objectivity is nothing other than reason operative in history. Yet Kierkegaard is also right to emphasise that the totality is fractured by particularity, and that rational history is interrupted by passion and faith in ways that are not immediately reconcilable with Hegelian notions of totality and reason—not without scoffing at human suffering at any rate.[42]

Marxism represents the unsurpassable horizon of our time for Sartre because it unites what is true in Hegel and Kierkegaard by furnishing the bases of a method of research about the modalities of being and the conditions of freedom. Whereas the CPSU had long since transformed Marxism in Russia from a method into a dogma and a series of irrefutable truths, Marx's writings continue to offer the soundest methodology for exploring existence as a concrete totalisation of subjective desires, objective needs and material objects and forces. That is to say that in terms of explaining the mediation of humanity and nature in the institutional structuration of the labour process, Marx is a constant reminder that freedom remains in large measure ideological until it is organised freedom from necessity for all of society. But Sartre adds that an overemphasis on labour in the process of satisfying material scarcity and need will lead to an ignorance of the fact that people need intimacy and solidarity with some of their fellows, whilst needing distance and separation from others. Anticipating the critical sociology of Pierre Bourdieu (1930–2002), Sartre intimates that people grow up in the *habitus* of socioeconomic classes, where their economic needs are met in vastly varying degrees. But they also grow up in families, groups and neighbourhoods where their intellectual and emotional needs for recognition and community are also differentially satisfied. Just as social class can be an advantage or an impediment to the transcendence of necessity, so too can the family, the couple, the city and even the nation be a positive force or a hindrance. Sartre quips that reading the theorists of the PCF gives one the impression that they were born into the condition of wage labour as adults with no past life as children and youths. This is to ignore the fact that it is one thing to buy or sell one's labour whilst simultaneously having a positive attitude toward love and friendship, as well as a critical view of all forms of authority. It is quite another to buy or sell one's labour power and at the same time be continually frustrated in one's attempts to engage in meaningful relations with others, and to crave forms of authority that satisfy deep-seated needs for emotional security. Since bourgeois and Soviet forms of society are eminently capable of producing both kinds of individual, there is far more to bourgeois and Bolshevik rule than a given system of production.[43]

One can say that the reason why one is continually frustrated in one's attempts to engage in meaningful relations with others and why one craves authority is that one has been made that way by nature or manipulated in that direction by the realities of social class. The tendency to explain individual lack of freedom in this way is to indulge in what Sartre refers to as 'bad faith' in his early writings and especially in *Being and Nothingness*.[44] In Sartre's subsequent evolution towards the existentialist Marxism of the *Critique of Dialectical Reason,* he develops an original analysis of mediations, which substantially departs from the typical macro-Marxist themes of humanity/nature or base/superstructure. He concentrates instead on the formulation of a micro-Marxist analysis of personalities, situations and group dynamics. To do this he invents a range of concepts including the practico-inert, the regressive-progressive method, seriality and the materiality of concepts and language. His aim in this invention will be briefly summarised below.

Sartre intentionally discards the Hegelian-Marxist idea of totality and the corresponding notions of reified consciousness, exploitation/reappropriation and the laws of history. He thinks that for all its claims of being materialist, the Hegelian-Marxism of thinkers like Lukács remains wedded to the idealist notion that the essence of humanity consists in its capacity to transform nature through labour power, and that the revolution achieves the reappropriation of that expropriated essence. This is incompatible with the claim that existence precedes essence. Moreover, he adds, it is this understanding that compels Lukács and others to explain the lack of revolutionary consciousness amongst the workers in terms of reified consciousness, which mistakes relations between things for relations between people, and false consciousness, which is simply another way of saying that they do not think like the party leadership. Instead of enriching Marxism with a credible theory of social action, the consequence of this mode of explanation is to entrust the party with the task of leading the revolution. At one level of analysis, this produces the cult of the leader within the party hierarchy and the reduction of the individual party member to a function of the group. At another level it absolves the party of having to transform the relations constituting the world or engage in political projects to create a new one. It is passively assumed that the laws of history will sort themselves out and reschedule the revolution.[45]

For Sartre it is misleading to say that the working class suffers from reified or false consciousness and fails to see its alienated essence in the products of the capitalist labour process. It is true that commodity production introduces a palpable element of opacity into social relations. But the relationship between the working class and the products it manufactures and services it provides is one of interiority as well as exteriority mediated by concepts, words and particular experiences that vary from person to person. To some extent the workers recognise their labour power in the material they produce, and to some extent they do not; some become politicised and others are happy with private pleasures. Just as there are no laws of history, there are no general laws of consciousness and organisation. On Sartre's account, resistance against the deadness of the laboured material, which he calls the practico-inert, takes shape when groups come into being as a result of the sense of commitment and responsibility of concrete individuals. Group action is so varied that it cannot be assimilated under the single category of class. Strikes, occupations, absenteeism, defiance of official ideology on questions of race and colonialism, and disrespect for traditional gender relations are all instances of the ways different groups respond to the modes in which the living energy of labour power and dissent becomes frozen in the inertia of objects, institutions and monuments. Instead of a monolithic class of workers with reified or false consciousness, Sartre observes a network of groups that coalesce, disperse, and re-form on new bases across a wide field of social conflict marked by congruent, overlapping and contrasting allegiances. It has been observed that in many ways this analysis is much more appropriate for the modes of struggle associated with the May events in Paris in 1968 than mechanical versions of historical materialism or Soviet versions of Marxism-Leninism.[46]

If in this context 1968 stands for a revolutionary critique of the existing order, which includes established political parties like the PCF, then it can indeed be said that Sartre offers the bases of a nonorthodox left-wing politics with contemporary relevance. Using what he calls the regressive-progressive method, he attempts to show that individuals in groups understand the sense of their political projects by mentally returning to their point of departure before action rather than appealing to the inexorable forward march of history. After this regression and taking stock is accomplished, it is possible to progress to new projects and new commitments. Sartre rejects the notion of linear time governed by the idea that we all have a certain number of time units that are gradually running out like sand in an hourglass. If time had this structure and the meaning of life consisted in preserving one's units for as long as possible, we would be compelled to accept the liberal idea that freedom is largely a matter of noninfringement and noninterference in the affairs of others. He also rejects the messianic concept of time adopted in different ways by orthodox Marxism, according to which the injustices of earthly existence will eventually be redeemed in a revolution, so that the workers need only wait for the great day. He sees history instead as regressive-progressive, serial, and marked by the intersection of past and present that defies linearity and messianism.[47]

The ideas of the practico-inert and seriality are closely connected. We have seen in this book that for Kant all objectivity is mediated by subjectivity, and that (in different ways) all subjectivity is mediated by objectivity for Hegel, Marx and Lukács. Sartre objects by arguing that while the mediations in the Hegelian-Marxist tradition set great store by an eventual reappropriation of the objective world by a revolutionary collective subject, i.e. Hegelian *Geist* materialised as the proletariat, it is forgotten that it is precisely the world of objects that is opposed to revolutionary practice. For example, there is something fundamentally flawed about the idea of the TV workers seizing control of their TVs, since most people only need one television, and, more to the point, most of the programmes are idiotic! In a manner analogous to Marx's idea that the working class cannot lay hold of the ready-made state machinery and wield it for its own purposes, for Sartre it is mistaken to suppose that the world of objects is there to be seized, as if this would consummate the revolution. It is not merely that objects like commodities acquire a life of their own when they go into commercial circulation. Some workers resist capitalist production relations, but many objects also resists reappropriation because of their practico-inertness: they are loaded with meanings and cultural significations that have a history of their own. Another way of saying this is that they are embedded in a series of other material objects and historical events, as Sartre puts it in the *Critique of Dialectical Reason*. In many capitalist societies what is produced is enmeshed in an ideological and material web of relations. He suggests that it is hopeless to attempt to reappropriate the object by simply fishing it out of the series of relations within which it is embedded and then wielding it for more emancipated aims. This is an example of reification rather than its antidote.[48]

Sartre's legacy is somewhat mixed. To a certain extent existential Marxism may seem to many to be indissolubly linked to the 1950s and 1960s in post-war France and the intellectual circles of the Paris Left Bank that have long since dispersed. Yet Sartre's influence on the work of more recent theorists is unmistakably present both in and outside universities. His notion of the materiality of language is reminiscent of Foucault's *The Words and Things*, and he also deploys a very Foucauldian concept of resistance. Elements of his analysis of fields of power and the cultural significance of material objects clearly anticipate Pierre Bourdieu's ideas on habitus, field and cultural capital. Sartre's belief that there is not 'philosophy' as such, but rather philosophies, which create new concepts that change the nature of social struggle and the state of epistemological inquiry itself, is evocative of the stance adopted by Gilles Deleuze and Félix Guattari in *What is Philosophy?*. He is neither a traditional nor an organic intellectual in Gramsci's sense, for while he does abandon the role of the traditional intellectual to put his ideas in the service of the revolution, he reserves the right to back the party when he wants to, and to criticise it vehemently when he does not. This sets him apart from Brecht's and Lukács's steadfast adherence to the CPSU.[49]

For Louis Althusser, however, Sartre's existentialist Marxism represents a retreat to idealism and humanism. Like Korsch in *Marxism and Philosophy*, Althusser seeks to bypass various interpretations of Marx with the aim of returning to a close reading of Marx's texts. Yet unlike Korsch, who reminds his readers of the Hegelian background to historical materialism, Althusser is convinced that Marx only really assumes a rigorously scientific approach from 1845 onwards. The shift from the early writings on Hegel and Feuerbach to the mature writings on political economy represents what he refers to as an 'epistemological break' in two key works published in 1965, *For Marx* and *Reading Capital*.[50] Althusser's explicit critique of Hegelian Marxism contains an implicit critique of a number of the ideas of Korsch, Gramsci and Sartre about the relationship between consciousness and revolution. While it is possible to regard the latter as three exponents of Western Marxism in the tradition of Feuerbach, Hegel and the radical humanism of the young Marx, it is precisely the young Marx who Althusser dismisses as pre-scientific. His rejection of humanism, empiricism, historicism as well as his qualified rejection of the base and superstructure model must be understood in the light of the rise of structuralist modes of explanation prevalent in post-war France. His work is deeply influenced by the ideas of the anthropologist Claude Lévi-Strauss (born in 1908), the linguist Roman Jacobson (1896–1982) and especially the psychoanalytic method of Jacques Lacan (1901–81).[51]

In some ways Lacan's work prefigures the 'linguistic turn' of social and political thought associated with Jürgen Habermas and Habermas's critique of the philosophy of consciousness directed at the ideas of Kant, Fichte, Hegel and Marx. But in contrast to the humanist bases of Habermas's theory of communicative action, the line of thought from Lacan to Foucault and Althusser leads to structuralist and poststructuralist notions of the end of the traditional epistemological subject inaugurated with the philosophies of Descartes and Kant. It has been seen that Heidegger and Sartre proceed from an analysis of *Dasein* and existence rather than human essence or a 'made–to–know' epistemological subject. Similarly, Lacan argues that the subject is not sovereign, in any significant sense, but on the contrary constituted by forces internal and external to it. Just as Sartre posits an inevitable discrepancy between ontological being in itself and human being for itself, Lacan observes a *lack* at the core of the subject. This is a departure from the modern subject, centred first in consciousness and then in labour and other forms of action, as well as a departure from the more ancient subject, centred in a soul, of the Middle Ages. Lacan distinguishes between the imaginary, symbolic and real levels of existence, and explains the lack determining the experience of the subject in terms of its inability to explain the real with words (symbolic) or images (imaginary). According to a theory with a major influence on Althusser's notion of the role of the economy in scientific Marxism, Lacan holds that the real reveals itself to the subject in terms of its absence rather than as a presence. This means that there is no single centre of the self which determines its peripheral limits. For Lacan the self is *overdetermined* by a protean combination of imaginary, symbolic and real functions. For Althusser, the economy is *overdetermined* by a multiplicity of political and ideological factors that have their own reality in the sense that they are not epiphenomenal illusions created by the base that give rise to false consciousness or bad faith. Hence structrural determination by the economy is only visible as an 'absent cause'. Moreover, the entire idea of consciousness—false or otherwise—should be dispensed with as a relict of idealism and humanism.[52]

Because it does not determine culture or the state in a mono causal fashion but is itself overdetermined, the economy is a *structure in domination* rather than a base that mechanically 'causes' a superstructure. The mechanical understanding of a base causing a political and ideological superstructure is symptomatic of an empiricist methodology that pursues a core of truth 'behind' the veils of illusion surrounding it. For Althusser it is also part of a Hegelian heritage that tends to regard the social whole as an expressive totality in which all observable phenomena can be seen as effects of a central nodal point that invests all instances of institutional mediation between humanity and nature. Althusser is not concerned with adjusting his theoretical understanding between base and superstructure in order to accommodate superstructural phenomena like Bonapartism and fascism. To judge the validity of a methodology in this way is both empiricist and historicist. One should not judge the scientific status of a theory by actual historical events such as world war or fascism, but rather by conceptual rigour. Since the data of science are mediated by concepts, it is much more important that the concepts relate to each other in a rigorous way that yields knowledge in the form of theoretical practice. He casts theoretical practice in opposition to what he regards as the humanist concern with the correct dialectical relation between theory and practice one finds in Hegel, the young Marx, Gramsci and Lukács. He suggests that a humanist conception of Marxism is likely to yield, at worst, Christian pity for the poor, and, at best, some existentialist notion of commitment or sincerity. These are pre-scientific attitudes rather than a scientific position or a *problematic*, as he calls it.[53]

Despite his implicit critique of Gramsci's residual historicist and Hegelian humanism, Althusser builds on Gramsci's enlarged notion of the state as comprising civil society as well as political society. In *Lenin and Philosophy* (1971), Althusser distinguishes between Ideological State Apparatuses (ISAs, broadly corresponding to Gramsci's conception of civil society) and Repressive State Apparatuses (RSAs, corresponding to Gramsci's notion of political society). One of the somewhat puzzling dimensions to his argument is that despite the distinction he makes between science and ideology, he holds that human relations are always engulfed in ideology. Hence one must suppose that in communist society ideology is somehow more transparent or less repressive than it is in other social forms. This would seem to contradict the antihistoricist polemic against evaluating a theory by its ability to become real in practice. In Lacanian terms, Althusser presumably regards the abandonment of a possible substitution of truthful science for ideological domination as the unavoidable consequence of the irreconcilability of the symbolic and imaginary with the real. Hence where historicism tends to relativise truth in history, Althusser's Marxist structuralism tends to relativise truth in the indeterminacy of overdetermined pluri-causality. Since the economic moment of determination is crucial and nonetheless only visible in terms of its absence, it is not even possible to achieve reconciliation between humanity and nature in a communist society. As will be seen in the next chapter, it is this reconciliation that the critical theorists of the Frankfurt School pursue.[54]

This final note of criticism is not intended to detract from Althusser's originality and importance as a critical reader of Marx. While a number of his ideas are contradictory or polemical, his influence extends to theorists such as Nicos Poulantzas in France as well as a number of Marxist historians in Britain, some of whom regard his ideas as important enough to disagree with in the strongest possible terms.[55]

The point already made in relation to Gramsci and some of the other figures in Western Marxism considered in this chapter is twofold. On the one hand there can be no doubt that Marxism needs updating. On the other hand it is also clear that Marxism is capable of entering into a critical dialogue with idealism, existentialism, psychoanalysis and structuralism while remaining committed to the idea that only a society in which all of its members are freed from socioeconomically produced necessity can be characterised as free and genuinely democratic. Lukács may have felt compelled to choose Hegel and Marx against Nietzsche and existentialism, but Sartre shows that one need not choose definite sides in that debate and can nonetheless be an activist, if not a revolutionary in the usual sense implied by the lives of figures such as Che Guevara (Ernesto Guevara de la Serna, 1928–67).

After a chapter on Marx and Western Marxism, this study now proceeds to other currents of thinking and action working toward a more emancipated society. The non-Marxist left continually defines and redefines its position with regard to Marx. But it can never ignore Marxism entirely as long as humanity's relations with nature continue to be mediated by the system Marx so rigorously analysed, i.e. the system that makes the overcoming of socioeconomically produced necessity largely a matter of luck and privilege.

Suggestions for Further Reading

Anderson, Perry. *Considerations on Western Marxism*, London, Verso, 1976.

Anderson, Perry. *In the Tracks of Historical Materialism*, Chicago, University of Chicago Press, 1984.

Arato, Andrew, and Breines, Paul. *The Young Lukács and the Origins of Western Marxism*, New York, Pathfinder, 1979.

Goode, Patrick. *Karl Korsch: A Study in Western Marxism*, London, Verso, 1979.

Jameson, Frederic. *Marxism and Form*, Princeton, PUP, 1971.

Jameson, Frederic (ed.). *Aesthetics and Politics*, London, Verso, 1977.

Jay, Martin. *Marxism and Totality*, Cambridge, Polity, 1984.

Kellner, Douglas (ed.). *Karl Korsch: Revolutionary Theory*, Austin, University of Texas Press, 1977.

Kolakowski, Lesek. *Main Currents of Marxism*, 3 vols, Oxford, OUP, 1978.

McLellan, David. *Marxism After Marx*, Boston, Houghton Mifflin, 1979.

Stedman Jones, Gareth (ed.). *Western Marxism: A Critical Reader*, London, NLR, 1977.

Notes

1 Marx, *Preface and Introduction to a Contribution to the Critique of Political Economy*, pp. 3–4 (my emphases).

2 Anderson, *In the Tracks of Historical Materialism*, p. 34. Anderson locates the heyday of Western Marxism in the five decades from the end of World War I in 1918 the Paris events of 1968 (see Chapter 5), followed by a residual reflux that lasted until Jean-Paul Sartre's death in 1980. In *Considerations on Western Marxism*, he

analyses the contributions to Western Marxism of Gramsci, Lukács, Korsch and others, together with those of Benjamin, Adorno and Marcuse. In this book the last three are treated separately in Chapter 3 on the Frankfurt School and critical theory—the reasons for which will become clear. See Anderson, *Considerations on Western Marxism*, Chapter 2.

3 The attempt to grasp the significance of nationalism within a Marxist framework which incorporates elements of Kant and international relations theory in an unusual and original synthesis is achieved by the somewhat marginal group of figures associated with Austro-Marxism. A number of the key writings of Otto Bauer, Max Adler, Karl Renner and Rudolf Hilferding are included in Bottomore and Goode, *Austro-Marxism*. Their work acquired a certain importance with the rise of Marshal Tito (1892–1980) in Yugoslavia and the evident reality that Marxists could not ignore questions of ethnicity, nationalism, and the geopolitical conflicts of nation states.

4 For an analysis of Plekhanov's main ideas and their influence on the young Lenin, see Anikin, *Russian Thinkers*, Chapter 14. Stephen Cohen's *Bukharin and the Bolshevik Revolution* provides a very good account of the life and ideas of one of Stalin's many victims during the show trials of the 1930s. There are of course a great many exegetical works on the theoretical and practical bases of Leninism. Neil Harding outlines the evolution of the Bolshevik leader's ideas and tactics in admirable detail in *Lenin's Political Thought*. A general overview is provided by Thornton Andersen in *Masters of Russian Marxism*, which includes a chapter on Leon Trotsky (1879–1940). For reasons of space it will not be possible to enter into a discussion of Trotsky's significant theoretical and practical contributions to the revolutionary politics of the left. Trotsky founded the Fourth International and can be seen as a possible bridge between the concerns of Russian and Western Marxism. Interested readers should consult Isaac Deutscher's monumental three-volume study of his life and work, *The Prophet Armed*, *The Prophet Unarmed* and *The Prophet Outcast*, and Baruch Knei-Paz, *The Social and Political Thought of Leon Trotsky*.

5 In addition to Gramsci's importance as a theorist and activist in the 1920s and 1930s, his thought exercised a considerable influence on the theoretical debates and political strategies of the Italian Communist Party, the largest communist party in Western Europe until its eventual split in 1991. At the theoretical level, his work is highly significant in terms of the evolution of the structuralist Marxism of Louis Althusser (1918–90), a major Western Marxist figure, and in terms of the tremendous resonance of the concept of hegemony across a number of academic disciplines. At the practical level, his thought can be regarded as a key component of what became known as 'Eurocommunism', i.e. of the nonsocial democratic reformism of the communist parties in Italy, France, Spain and other countries, including Great Britain, where for years the major division within the communist party (CPGB) was the rift between Eurocommunists and Stalinists.

6 On the crisis of Marxism and its role as a harbinger of Western Marxism, see Bellamy, *Modern Italian Social Theory*, pp. 65–71, and Piccone, *Italian Marxism*, pp. 81–92.

7 See Bobbio, *Ideological Profile of the Twentieth Century*; Mouffe, *Gramsci and Marxist Theory*; Laclau and Mouffe, *Hegemony and Socialist Strategy*.

8 For a general overview of the evolution of Gramsci's thought from his youth in Sardinia to the factory council movement and *Prison Notebooks*, see Bellamy and Schecter, *Gramsci and the Italian State*.

9 Gramsci, *Note sul Machiavelli e sullo stato moderno* [*Notes on Machiavelli and the Modern State*], p. 10. The *Prison Notebooks* are divided by theme. In addition to the *Notes on Machiavelli and the Modern State* cited here, there are notebooks on the *Intellectuals and the Organisation of Culture*, the *Risorgimento*, *Literature and National Life*, *Americanism and Fordism*, *Historical Materialism and the Philosophy of Benedetto Croce*. Lawrence and Wishart and Columbia University Press have published very good English translations of the *Prison Notebooks*.

10 Gramsci, *Il Risorgimento*, pp. 65–67.

11 Bellamy, *Modern Italian Social Theory*, Introduction. Giolitti held office from 1900 to 1914 and then very briefly after World War I in the period immediately preceding the arrival of fascism.

12 Syndicalism, which can be equated with radical trade unionism, will be discussed in Chapter 4. For a theoretical and historical overview of the main ideas of syndicalism in France and Italy, see Schecter, *Radical Theories*, Chapter 1.

13 For a history of the factory council movement in Italy in 1919–20 that draws out the theoretical implications of the events, see Clark, *Antonio Gramsci and the Revolution that Failed*, and Schecter, *Gramsci and the Theory of Industrial Democracy*.

14 Williams, *Proletarian Order*. The factory council movement during the 'biennio rosso', or 'red two years', as it is called, is itself the subject of a dramatic representation: see Ian Trevor's play *Occupations*, Pluto, 1979.

15 'Note sulla Questione Meridionale' ['Notes on the Southern Question'] and 'Alcuni aspetti sulla situazione italiana' ['Some aspects of the Italian Situation'] in *Scritti politici, 1921–26* [*Political Writings, 1921–26*]. Both essays are included in the Lawrence and Wishart edition of *Antonio Gramsci: Political Writings, 1921–26*, and Bellamy, *Gramsci: Pre-Prison Writings*. Bellamy's edition contains a very helpful introductory essay explaining the context and aims of Gramsci's key concerns prior to the prison writings.

16 Hence the obvious appeal of the *Prison Notebooks* to students of international relations. There have been many Gramscian approaches in recent years, such as Gill, *Gramsci's Historical Materialism and International Relations*. For a wide-ranging critique of neo-Gramscian international relations theory, see Shilliam, 'Hegemony and the unfashionable problematic of primitive accumulation'.

17 Gramsci, *Il materialismo storico e la filosofia di Benedetto Croce* [*Historical Materialism and the Philosophy of Benedetto Croce*], pp. 47–48, and *Note sul Machiavelli e sullo stato moderno* [*Notes on Machiavelli and the Modern State*], p. 201.

18 *Gli intellettuali e l'organizazzione della cultura* [*The Intellectuals and the Organisation of Culture*], pp. 180–81, and 'Note sulla Questione Meridionale' ['Notes on the Southern Question'], pp. 76–77.

19 The theoretical counterpart to the war of position in the Notebooks is the war of manoeuvre, that is, the military strategy that was appropriate for Russian conditions in 1917, but inappropriate for the West. (See Bellamy and Schecter, *Gramsci and the Italian State*, Chapters 4–6.) In addition to hegemony, civil society, common sense and the role of the intellectuals, the historic bloc and the war of position are two key concepts Gramsci employs to move beyond a

rigid dichotomy between base and superstructure while remaining within a Marxist framework of analysis and action.

20 'The ideas of the ruling class are in every epoch the ruling ideas, i.e., the class which is the ruling material force of society is at the same time its ruling intellectual force. The class which has the means of material production at its disposal, has control at the same time over the means of mental production, so that thereby, generally speaking, the ideas of those who lack the means of mental production are subject to it. The ruling ideas are nothing more than the ideal expression of the dominant material relationships, the dominant material relationships grasped as ideas; hence of the relationships which make the one class the ruling one, therefore, the ideas of its dominance. The individuals composing the ruling class . . . rule also as thinkers, as producers of ideas, and regulate the production and distribution of the ideas of their age.' (Marx and Engels, *The German Ideology*, p. 64.)

21 Machiavelli, *Il principe* [*The Prince*] (1513), Chapter 11; and Gramsci, *Note sul Machiavelli e sullo stato moderno* [*Notes on Machiavelli and the Modern State*], pp. 242–43.

22 Gramsci, *Americanismo e fordismo* [*Americanism and Fordism*], pp. 142–43, and Pier Paolo Pasolini, *Scritti corsari* [*Pirate Writings*], pp. 81–83.

23 Western Marxism in Italy did not cease with Gramsci's death in 1937. Significant contributions were made by Gaetano della Volpe and Lucio Colletti. See Anderson, *Considerations on Western Marxism*, Chapters 3–4; Bellamy, *Modern Italian Social Theory*, Chapter 8; and Jay, *Marxism and Totality*, Chapter 14.

24 Korsch, *Was ist Sozialisierung?* [*What is Socialisation?*] and *Arbeitsrecht für Betriebsräte* [*Industrial Law for Workers' Councils*].

25 The extent of Gramsci's anti-Leninism is perhaps more ambiguous. On the one hand the central theme of the *Prison Notebooks* is the necessity of developing a Western Marxist strategy for revolution that differs profoundly from the analyses and strategies of Bolshevism. On the other hand Gramsci worked for the Third International in Vienna and Moscow and recognised the immense importance of the October Revolution of 1917. Just prior to his imprisonment in 1926, in one of his last public statements about the authoritarian turn of the Russian Revolution and the disastrous effects of the leadership struggle within the CPSU, he writes an open letter admonishing the Soviet leadership to settle their internal disputes and get on with the task of building communism. The letter is published in Gramsci, *Selections from the Political Writings, 1921–26*. Whereas Korsch was banished from the Third International for his support of council democracy and other positions considered incompatible with Leninism, Gramsci tried to work with the CPSU. The irony of Gramsci's fate is that while on the one hand prison cut short his life and isolated him, it also allowed him to write the *Notebooks* and to retain a considerable measure of autonomy from the gradual Bolshevisation of the international communist movement at the hands of Stalin and his comrades. Gramsci can thus be situated between Korsch's critical distance from the Soviet Union and Lukács's steady adherence to the Soviet leadership, including Stalin. The unresolved question is whether or not Leninism was ever really appropriate as a revolutionary strategy for Italian society or for Western European society in general. See Jay, *Marxism and Totality*, pp. 128–31. Jay's book is very informative about the evolution of the ideas of Lukács and Korsch and contains a wealth of information about the main thinkers of Western Marxism.

26 Anderson, *Considerations on Western Marxism*, pp. 15–21; Jay, *Marxism and Totality*, pp. 6–8; and Jameson, *Marxism and Form*, pp. xvi–xvii and 182–90.

27 Marx and Engels's somewhat ambiguous relation with Hegel and philosophy is taken up years later by Merleau-Ponty in *Les aventures de la dialectique* [*Adventures of the Dialectic*], p. 90.

28 Korsch gradually moved away from his Hegelian-Marxist position in *Marxism and Philosophy* towards a slightly more positivist and juridical conception of historical materialism and political economy in *Die materialistische Geschichtsauffassung* [*The Materialist Conception of History*] (1929) and *Karl Marx* (1938). By 1950 he comes to the conclusion that the project of human emancipation requires the confluence of a number of bodies of thought, and that Marxism could not pretend to offer the solution by itself without turning into a reactionary dogma. To this extent his evolution parallels that of Sartre's defence of Marxism and existentialism and Marcuse's attempt to combine Marxism and psychoanalysis (see Chapter 3). See Goode, *Karl Korsch: A Study in Western Marxism* and Douglas Kellner (ed.), *Karl Korsch: Revolutionary Theory*.

29 It is precisely this call for a return to Hegel and dialectics that is rejected by the poststructuralist left in favour of other thinkers, most notably Nietzsche in the case of Michel Foucault. Poststructuralist ideas are explored in Chapter 6.

30 The background to the repudiation is the leadership struggle in the CPSU and Stalin's attack on Trotsky's Left Opposition. In 1924 Lukács wrote *Lenin* to atone for his deviations and avoid the marginalisation which became Korsch's fate after 1926. But he also wrote a defence of *History and Class Consciousness* entitled *Chvostismus und Dialektik* [*Tailism and the Dialectic*], which remained unpublished until recently. Published in London by Verso in 2000, the English version is translated by Esther Leslie and contains a postface by Slavoj Zizek.

31 Bloch's major contribution to Western Marxism is undoubtedly the concept of being that is 'not yet' but nonetheless tangible as a possible future (das Noch-Nicht-Sein), and the related concept of that of which we are not yet conscious, but which we might well become conscious of (das Noch-Nicht-Bewusste). To this extent he develops an alternative to Martin Heidegger's fundamental ontology as expounded in *Being and Time* (1927) and other writings. See Jameson, *Marxism and Form*, Chapter 2, and Jay, *Marxism and Totality*, Chapter 5.

32 Stating the matter in this way suggests a parallel between *History and Class Consciousness* and Heidegger's project in *Being and Time*. The possibilities of collective action open to the proletariat are broadly comparable to the collective subjectivity of the national community, i.e., *das Volk*. While the proletariat represents the union of theory and practice and the subject-object of history, Heidegger's *Dasein* can be regarded as a theoretical-practical synthesis or what some political philosophers refer to as *praxis*. One could extend the analysis by comparing Lukács's notion of reification with Heidegger's notion of *Seinsvergessenheit* (forgetting of being). Reification and Seinsvergessenheit are different ways of explaining the rift between theory and practice and an ignorance of the totality of being as a result of the dominance of instrumental reason. The relations between the two thinkers have been explored by the Western Marxist and Lukács admirer Lucien Goldmann (1913–70) in *Lukács and Heidegger*. The book looks at the influence of Heidegger's thought on a number of important thinkers on the left, including Sartre. For an analysis of Goldmann and Heidegger's impact on Sartre, see Jay, *Marxism and Totality*, Chapters 10 and 11.

33 Lukács's staunch defence of what he designates as realism and attempts to transcend the bourgeois novel (in mainly Russian nineteenth-century literature such as Dostoevsky and Tolstoy) against avant garde modernism brought him into conflict with Bertolt Brecht (1898–1956), the author of the *Threepenny Opera* and an emblematic figure of the European left who does not really belong to the Western Marxists, critical theorists or libertarians. Against the libertarians and critical theorists he defends many excesses of Stalinst conformism, and was prepared to make hard choices about political allegiances that in principle would have aligned him with Lukács. Yet Lukács's commitment to literary realism clashed with Brecht's avant-gardism. In Brecht's opinion, Lukács remained committed to very traditional Aristotelian notions of dramatic catharsis, whereas Brecht defended the idea of the epic theatre. Brecht reckons that the Aristotelian and realist traditions defended by Lukács suggest that there is a human nature which is identical throughout the ages, when in fact the task of epic theatre is to show that humanity is always a product of very specific historical conditions, taboos and norms that can be called into question by spectators who, while watching a performance, are simultaneously reminded of the arbitrary character of the norms that govern their own age. See Luhn, *Marxism and Modernism*.

34 See Nietzsche, *Die fröhliche Wissenschaft* [*The Gay Science*] (1882); Simmel, *Die Philosophie des Geldes* [*The Philosophy of Money*] (1900); and Simmel, *Soziologie: Untersuchungen über die Formen der Vergesellschaftung* [*Sociology*] (1908), especially Chapter 1 on the conditions of the possibility of society. All of these works have been translated into English and other languages.

35 Lukács, *Geschichte und Klassenbewusstsein* [*History and Class Consciousness*], pp. 106–10.

36 See Weber, *The Protestant Ethic and the Spirit of Capitalism*.

37 Lukács, op. cit., Chapter 4.

38 Lukács, op. cit., Chapters 4 and 8; Jay, *Marxism and Totality*, pp. 112–14; Merleau-Ponty, *Les adventures de la dialectique* [*Adventures of the Dialectic*], pp. 66–74. Merleau-Ponty's chapter on Western Marxism in *Adventures of the Dialectic* is dedicated almost exclusively to an analysis of *History and Class Consciousness* and offers a very useful exposition of the main tenets of the argument.

39 The term 'democratic centralism' refers to the Leninist notion that there must be constant communication between the base and the leadership of the party, and that the leadership must maintain its credibility with the base by unanimously executing decisions, especially where the final decision has been preceded by a vociferous debate and considerable factional division.

40 The idea that existence, with its flux and uncertainty, precedes any stable notion of fixed essence or unchanging human nature, is often used to define existentialism. See Sartre, *L'être et le néant: essai d'ontologie phéneménologique* [*Being and Nothingness*], pp. 59–60. As the subtitle suggests, in this book Sartre outlines a phenomenology of being which is far more indebted to Heidegger than it is to Marx. Sartre's position evolved toward the existentialist Marxism expounded in the *Critique of Dialectical Reason*, for which he is still famous, as a result of several decisive experiences. These include his participation in the French Resistance and co-founding of the influential monthly review *Les Temps Modernes* (with Maurice Merleau-Ponty, Simone de Beauvoir, Raymond Aron

and other key French intellectuals) immediately following the liberation of Paris, and his long and at times troubled relationship with the French Communist Party (PCF). Sartre and his colleagues on the editorial board of *Les Temps Modernes* were amongst the first to defend a consistently anticolonial critique of imperialism in post-war Europe in ways that clearly prefigure contemporary postcolonial theory and practice. By way of his critical engagement with the PCF, he provided Western European communism with an intellectual prestige that the movement was not able to retain very long after his death in 1980.

41 Sartre, *Critique de la raison dialectique, tome I: théorie des ensembles pratiques* [*Critique of Dialectical Reason, Volume I*], pp. 29–30. Sartre never managed to complete the second volume of his magnum opus, which is nonetheless published in English as *The Critique of Dialectical Reason, Volume II: The Intelligibility of History*. The most important ideas are contained in the introductory section of the first critique, entitled 'Search for a Method'. This was published in English in 1963 by Vintage Press in New York, and has appeared in many subsequent editions. Interested readers may wish to consult the 'Search for a Method' before going on to the more daunting enterprise of reading the 750 pages contained in the first critique alone.

42 Ibid., pp. 29–30.

43 Ibid., pp. 47–49.

44 In addition to the ideas developed in his philosophical treatises, many of Sartre's social and political ideas are also given expression in his novels, most notably *La nausée* [*Nausea*] (1938), and plays such as *Les Mouches* [*The Flies*] (1943) and *Huis clos* (*No Exit*] (1945), as well as in his biographical studies of Baudelaire (1947), Flaubert (3 volumes, 1971–2), not to mention his critical essays such as *Qu'est-ce que c'est la littérature?* [*What is literature?*] (1955) and *L'existentialisme est un humanisme* [*Existentialism is a Humanism*] (1946). It is no exaggeration to say that his output and impact have been prodigious. In fact, according to István Mészáros Sartre is probably the most influential and popular intellectual in modern times, and his importance can be compared with Voltaire's in his day. See Mészáros' contribution on Sartre in Bottomore, *A Dictionary of Marxist Thought*, pp. 490–91.

45 Sartre, *Critique de la raison dialectique* [*Critique of Dialectical Reason*], pp. 101–19.

46 Jay, *Marxism and Totality*, pp. 359–60, and Jameson, *Marxism and Form*, pp. 272–74.

47 Sartre, op. cit., pp. 246–47, 252, 301–4, 325 and 567. See too Poster, *Existentialist Marxism in Postwar France*, pp. 58–62, as well as Poster's compendious *Sartre's Marxism*, pp. 25–27 and 64–67.

48 Sartre, op. cit., pp. 230–32.

49 For an analysis of the different reasons why these two thinkers defended the USSR even under Stalin, see Pike, *Lukács and Brecht*.

50 *Pour Marx* [*For Marx*] and *Lire le Capital* [*Reading Capital*] (written with Etienne Balibar, Roger Establet, Pierre Macherey and Jacques Rancière) have both been translated into English and other languages. Althusser insists that one of the consequences of the epistemological break and the theoretical unreliability of Marx's early work is that there can only be what he refers to as *symptomatic* rather than definitive readings of Marx.

51 It is important to bear in mind Lacan's influence for an understanding of Althusser. It is nonetheless arguable that the origins of structuralism across

different disciplines can be traced back to the idea of the arbitrary relation between signifiers (words) and the signified (objects) developed by Ferdinand de Saussure (1857–1913). In his *Course in General Linguistics* published posthumously in 1916, he argues that language is a structure with no identifiable centre or essence. This is a highly suggestive idea for thinkers who are determined to break with what they consider to be Hegel's notion of an expressive totality in which all phenomena can be regarded as emanations of a single determining essence. For Althusser, the lesson to be drawn from Lacan via Saussure and Freud is that the subject is *overdetermined*, i.e. determined and co-determined in several ways at once.

52 Lacan, *Les quatre concepts fondamentaux de la psychanalyse* [*The Four Fundamental Concepts of Psychoanalysis*], Part 4; Althusser, *Pour Marx* [*For Marx*], Chapter 3; Callincos, *Althusser's Marxism*, Chapters 3 and 4; and Simmons, *Contemporary Critical Theorists from Lacan to Said*, Edinburgh, EUP, 2004, chapters 2 and 4.

53 Althusser, *Pour Marx* [*For Marx*], Chapter 3. It is well known that Althusser later modified his views on theoretical practice in various interviews and conferences. He remained adamantly attached to his antihumanist interpretation of Marxism, however. See his *Écrits philosophiques et politiques* [*Philosophical and political writings*], published posthumously, pp. 433–532.

54 Althusser, *Lenin and Philosophy*, pp. 127–86. The volume also contains an important essay on Lacan and Freud (pp. 195–219).

55 Poulantzas, *Political Power and Social Classes* and Edward P. Thompson, *The Poverty of Theory and Other Essays*. The debate between Poulantzas and Ralph Miliband on the role of the state in capitalist society raged on for years amongst British intellectuals and activists in the 1970s and 1980s. On British Marxism and its relationship with Western Marxism, see Lin Chun, *The British New Left*, Part IV, Chapter 2. Lun does an admirable job of bringing together the divergent strands of the British left from 1956 to the fall of the Berlin Wall in 1989.

3

The Frankfurt School and Critical Theory

In an essay written in 1965 entitled 'Subject and object' now published in *Key Words*, T. A. Adorno (1903–69) succinctly expresses one of the central tenets of the Frankfurt School as follows: the critique of knowledge is a critique of the society producing that knowledge and vice versa.[1] In terms of the critical theory developed by the various thinkers broadly associated with the Institute for Social Research founded in Frankfurt in June 1924, the critique of knowledge means above all a critique of instrumental reason and its seemingly inexorable spread to all areas of social life.[2] As mentioned in the discussion of Lukács in Chapter 2, Max Weber's analysis of instrumental reason suggests that one of the objectively revolutionary aspects of modernity and industrialisation is the real possibility of human emancipation from economic scarcity as well as from mythology and irrational belief systems. Yet this revolutionary potential is accompanied by the simultaneous risk of the rise of an increasingly one-dimensional society governed by a form of narrowly strategic reason. Weber intuits that if triumphant, such reason would be unable to address questions of ethics or aesthetics, and would be empowered, at the same time, to undermine the authority of political decision-making bodies to regulate economic processes. This turns out to be a plausible claim when one considers the effects of globalisation and the neo-liberal push for worldwide deregulation. Despite his deep pessimism, however, Weber's ambivalence about the tendency of strategic reason to eclipse other possible modes of reason is tempered by his hope that charismatic leaders might infuse modern polities with ethical and political values not directly related to economic interests.

But Weber, who died in 1920, was not able to foresee the collapse of the Weimar Republic (1918–33) or the rise of Hitler and fascism. Nor could he have theorised the significance of World War II, Auschwitz, Hiroshima, and the rise of mass society in the years of post–World War II economic growth. Marx was confident that just as bourgeois class society had replaced feudal caste society, a communist and classless society would succeed bourgeois society. But the theory of a historical progression from caste to class to classless society did not actually materialise in the West. Meanwhile the resurrected spectre of caste, albeit in modern bureaucratic form, seemed to haunt the USSR and its satellites in the East.[3] Hence one of the Institute's first tasks was to investigate the causes of the endurance of support for capitalism and right-wing authoritarian populism among broad sectors of Western European and North American society, including the working class, and to analyse the appeal of Stalinist populism in Eastern Europe.

These are also major concerns shared by many of the Western Marxists. But if the latter are nonetheless generally confident about the long-term revolutionary capacities of the proletariat, the critical theorists considered in this chapter are far more cautious in this regard. In the post–World War II period, which they witnessed first hand, the working classes, who in Marxist theory were supposed to be abolishing the institutions of bourgeois society, were actually becoming increasingly integrated within it. This marks the beginning of a fissure between a specifically Marxist understanding of the left centred on the workers' movement, on the one hand, and other currents of thought and action on the left in Europe, on the other. Additional dimensions of this fissure will be analysed throughout the rest of this book. For now it is important to emphasise that the founding of the Institute and the development of what has subsequently come to be known as critical theory does not represent an unequivocal divergence between the fight for socialism and other approaches to extending the Enlightenment and completing the project of social and human emancipation initiated by French Revolution. Instead, it registers a tension on the left between the different possible ways of imagining what Marx in his early writings refers to as human emancipation, as opposed to political emancipation signified by the rights of franchise, expression, assembly and representation. It has been seen thus far that the way one understands this issue depends to a considerable extent on the way one approaches the mediation between humanity and nature, while bearing in mind that humanity is part of nature but not reducible to it.

In different ways, most of the Frankfurt School theorists articulate the idea that the complexities implied by the relation between humanity and nature are actually much older than the bourgeois revolutions of the eighteenth and nineteenth centuries and the consolidation of modern capitalism during the Industrial Revolution. They tend to share the related view that the problems posed by instrumental versus other forms of reason are in all likelihood equally ancient. Insofar as they do so, these thinkers are sensitive to Freud's notion that humanity's problematic co-existence with nature go back at least as far as Oedipus and the Greeks.[4] By extension, the issues involved in defining this relation do not stop with institutional questions about representative democracy and formal equality, especially if these are defined narrowly. It is arguable that they go deeper to anthropological and existential questions concerning life-affirming Eros, the secrets of language, the meaning of art, the relation between philosophy and aesthetics and the structure of knowledge. Here the reasons for the possible points of rupture between the claims of critical theory and the strategies of the Marxist left alluded to above become clear. If one examines the earliest essays, articles and books of the Frankfurt School in the 1920s, and traces the evolution of critical theory through the 1930s and 1940s right up to the 1960s and on to Jürgen Habermas's work today, one detects a common thread. This is the attempt to grasp phenomena such as Eros, creative work, language, art and knowledge in ways that pose questions about the conditions of epistemological inquiry and the possibilities of emancipation.[5]

This is in fact the sense of Adorno's claim about knowledge and society stated at the outset of this chapter. In one of the key texts of critical theory, *Negative Dialectics* (1966), he makes a closely related point by arguing that utopia is best conceived of as a *knowledge utopia* in which it is paradoxically possible to make use of concepts to attain access to nonconceptual knowledge such as the sensual knowledge of art and aesthetics as well as other instances of nonconceptual knowledge. Hence a considerable part of the Frankfurt School project consists in a sustained argument for the existence of a plurality of modes of reason. Adorno's notion of aesthetic reason and Habermas's concept of communicative reason are prime examples. Albeit in radically different ways, their interventions aim to counter what one might call the rationalisation of reason in modern capitalist societies first diagnosed by Weber and Lukács. Weber and Lukács examine rationalisation in terms of the reduction of reason to an instrument in the struggle for economic gain and the domination of nature. While Adorno broadens their analysis of this phenomenon by looking at what he calls the fetish character of music in industrial society and the concomitant regression in our ability to listen properly to music, Habermas addresses the evolution of the bourgeois public sphere from an arena of intellectual exchange of information and informed debate to an increasingly commercialised adjunct of the economy in *The Structural Transformation of the Public Sphere*. Along with *Legitimation Crisis* (1973), this work is probably his most important contribution to critical theory.[6]

Given this stress on the link between knowledge and freedom, one can regard critical theory as an attempt to rethink the Enlightenment project rather than a romantic or communitarian rejection of the aims of Enlightenment. The ideal of a rational society free of prejudice, obscurantism and the arbitrary exercise of power is not abandoned and given up for lost. Instead it is reconceptualised in the light of some of the more brutal realities of twentieth-century history and the critique of instrumental reason in the writings of Weber and Lukács. Critical theory attempts to remain alive to the Hegelian analysis of society as a totality of intersecting mediations, though without accepting the implicit conservatism in the Hegelian theory of history, which resolves the dichotomies in Kantian thinking by championing the inexorable march of history towards absolute knowledge and absolute freedom. Hence the goal is to retain the dialectical emphasis on the dynamic and contradictory movement of thought and reality, while jettisoning the idea that the history of thought and reality is inherently rational and progressive. To members of the Institute, this position necessitates a pluri-disciplinary approach to the study of history and society. The aim is to move from traditional theory, which in their view is narrowly empirical and positivist, to critical theory, which is interdisciplinary and emancipatory. This epistemological-political programme is announced in Horkheimer's 'Traditional and critical theory' and Herbert Marcuse's 'Philosophy and critical theory'. Both essays were originally published in the *Journal for Social Research* in 1937. Together with Adorno's *Against Epistemology: A metacritique,* written in the same period and published in 1956, and Walter Benjamin's precocious essay 'On the programme of the coming philosophy' (estimated to have been written around 1914), they constitute the foundations of the early Frankfurt School's twin critique of traditional epistemology and capitalist society.[7]

Towards a Theory of Reconciliation of Humanity and Nature in the Light of the Non-Identity of Thought and Reality

The status of epistemological inquiry on the left has had a somewhat ambiguous status ever since Marx suggested in his early writings that philosophy must be made redundant by realising its claims in practice as revolution. To some observers this appeared to be an almost anti-philosophical attitude implying that issues concerning revolutionary consciousness were subordinate to the laws of history and the practicalities of political organisation. Yet Marx's *1844 Manuscripts,* as well as his critiques of reification, commodity fetishism and the division of labour had an important impact on the development of critical theory. The Frankfurt School thinkers looked at in this chapter are also inspired by Lukács' argument in *History and Class Consciousness* about the limits of knowledge sounded out by Kant's distinction between direct or metaphysical knowledge of nature, which Kant holds to be impossible, and our experience of nature, which he insists is mediated by a priori categories of the understanding. Lukács demonstrates that the epistemological limits implied by this distinction may well have more to do with the entrenchment of the division between mental and manual labour—something politically conditioned and historically contingent—than any 'natural' or eternal limit to cognition.[8] This insight has obvious importance for the project to transform wage labour into creative labour while transforming instrumental reason into aesthetic reason; that is, for the Frankfurt School project of working toward a political utopia which is at the same time also a knowledge utopia. In *Traditional and Critical Theory* Horkheimer draws attention to the fact that there is a significant imbalance at the centre of the theory of knowledge in the *Critique of Pure Reason* between the secondary role of the senses and the active role played by the twelve categories of the understanding, which for Kant are unity, plurality, totality, reality, negation, limitation, inherence, causality, reciprocity, possibility, existence and necessity. Whilst sensuality is reduced to the status of an intuitive faculty registering the presence of phenomena in time and space, the work of cognition is accomplished in the main by the mental ordering of phenomena performed by the categories. Sensible intuition seems to constitute the broad and rather vague (given the immensity of the problems raised rather than solved by the intuition of time and space) framework within which knowledge is intellectual and mental. Intellectual and mental faculties in their turn are understood as largely mechanical processes in which phenomena are identified and appropriately categorised. The charge against Kant is that he more or less internalises the division of labour in society and builds it into his theory of knowledge. According to this interpretation it is no accident that he also champions the economic interests and political values of ascendant liberalism.[9]

Horkheimer, Marcuse, Adorno and Benjamin claim in different ways that Kant's undeniable rigour in the first of his three critiques of reason is secured at the great price of relegating the role of sensuous cognition to that of a passive function. In their view Marx and Nietzsche, who would ordinarily be juxtaposed by most scholars and activists as radically opposed thinkers, had effectively challenged the Kantian view of epistemology, and by extension, undermined the credibility of Kant's implicitly liberal understanding of Enlightenment. The critical theorists deploy an array of arguments explaining why Marx's *1844 Manuscripts* demonstrate how humanity transforms the natural world through the combined forces of sensuous and intellectual work. In this process of intellectual as well as sensual transformation, humanity comes to know the products of production as well as the institutions that shape the production process. Moreover, in Hegelian-Marxist terms shared by Lukács, critical theory affirms that humanity is itself transformed when it labours on nature, since every successive stage of the development of humanity's productive forces results in the creation of a new humanity with greater knowledge than its predecessors, and more sophisticated needs and greater creative potential than previous generations. In this context the Frankfurt School tends to regard the modern industrial organisation of the labour process as a highly ambiguous phenomenon. Modern industry raises levels of productivity to the point of making the abolition of material necessity an objective possibility. But it also separates the mental and sensual aspects of production to such an extent that people are increasingly unable to discuss freedom, potential and need in a critical way that challenges the fundamental assumptions of the industrial system which makes the abolition of scarcity an objective possibility in the first place. Production becomes an end in itself, acquiring a mythological character that sharply undermines the cognitive content of labour. In some of the more sombre writings of the Frankfurt School, one senses that while critical theory accepts the basic outlines of Marx's theory of capitalism, it also doubts that the working class, due to its steady integration within that system, can offer any alternative to it. This diagnosis occasionally prompts thinkers like Marcuse and especially Adorno to come to their notoriously pessimistic analyses of one-dimensional man and the totally administered society.

Ambivalence about modern industry and technology is one of the main points of difference between Lukács and the Frankfurt School theorists. For Lukács the proletariat, democratically organised in the communist party, will eventually attain class consciousness of its role as the subject/object of history and act on its capacity for collective self-government by revolutionising society. For the critical theorists it is irresponsible and implausible to have this sort of Hegelian faith in history and Marxist confidence about the inevitable arrival of revolutionary forms of consciousness.[10] Following Marx, Lukács firmly believes that the communist society to emerge from the dissolution of the existing capitalist society would have the capacity to establish a relation of the greatest possible transparency between the producers and the products of the labour process. Ownership and control of the means of production by the workers who directly use them would enable the working class to become active protagonists of history rather than the passive executors of the plans of private owners and investors. For the Frankfurt School, this kind of revolutionary transformation is not possible without reversing the sensual passivity that is registered at the theoretical level in Kant's philosophy and institutionalised at the practical level in the division of labour in capitalist society. Here as elsewhere Kant, while erroneous, is instructive in that his errors shed light on how the supposedly permanent structure of knowledge and the historically specific exercise of power and exploitation are complicit with one another in ways that are neither accidental nor mechanically causal. His faulty account of epistemology has the sociological significance of illustrating how property relations and the class structure frame human understanding of subject/object dialectics and shape the relations between the citizen and the state in industrial society.[11]

This is another instance where Adorno's statement at the beginning of this chapter can be regarded as emblematic for the project of critical theory in general. As in Hegel, the mediation of humanity and nature is achieved in the form of a dynamic social totality in which epistemology, law, politics, culture and political economy are all related moments. Against more mechanical interpretations of Marxist historical materialism, it is a form of Hegelianism in which each mediating moment is articulated to the others as a constellation and decidedly not in mechanical or mono-causal terms as an economic base giving rise to a legal, political cultural superstructure. In contrast to Hegel, however, it is not a totality in which the process of cancelling and preserving of contradictory forces suggested by the term *Aufhebung* is accomplished by discarding what is marginal and supposedly peripheral and harmoniously reconciling humanity and nature in successively more perfect forms of knowledge and freedom. Hegel's place in critical theory is somewhat ambiguous, since whilst his dialectical method is a salutary antidote to Kant, empiricism and positivism, he seems determined to see reason at work in historical instances where it has clearly become apologetic of domination. While this is not at all obvious with regard to the *Phenomenology of Spirit,* it can certainly be seen in the *Philosophy of Right,* as the young Marx notes. The point is that reason becomes unreasonable and even barbarous when it is subjectively manipulated by philosophers and social scientists who are fearful of nature's spontaneity. That fear prompts them to extirpate all aesthetic, intuitive and sensual dimensions from the knowledge process in the name of objectivity and methodological rigour. Hegel quite obviously knows this, but his version of idealism subsumes all aspects of reality that are not identical to thinking, such as nature and being, within the all-explanatory power of the concept. Critical theory attempts to move beyond Kant's separation of the sensual and intellectual moments of cognition in the *Critique of Pure Reason* by criticising Kant's transcendental idealism, and thus far it relies on Hegel. But it also distances itself from Hegel's historicist model of dialectical *Aufhebung* underpinned by notions of inexorable progress and the cunning of reason, which suggest that instances of barbarism in the present are necessary steps on the way to absolute knowledge and freedom. Hence the question arises: if Kant and Hegel furnish the methodological tools for social transformation but stop just short of revolutionary practice, why can one not find the answers to the questions raised by critical theory in Marx and Western Marxism? Does not Marx make it clear that philosophers have interpreted the world, which is indispensable, but that the time has come to change the world through revolutionary action? Do not the thinkers of Western Marxism indicate how such transformation is possible?[12]

Marx is necessary but not sufficient because there is no automatic mechanism inscribed within the historical process to ensure that passive consciousness and instrumental reason will become active consciousness and substantive reason, and, looking at the Russian experience, it is clearly problematic to entrust questions of epistemology and consciousness to any political party. Critical theory pursues a line of inquiry that borrows from Kant, Hegel, Marx, Nietzsche, Weber and Freud, though without subscribing unreservedly to any of them. Lukács argues that history must be understood in terms of the development of thought from Kant to Hegel to Marx. Insofar he advocates a view of linear progress which cannot push theory or practice beyond the authoritarian states administering the systems of power presiding over Eastern European state socialism and North American and Western European capitalism. Marx seems to think that the class consciousness of the modern industrial proletariat is immediately forged by direct experience of the contradiction between their productive capacities, on the one hand, and on the other the legal and political institutions that channel that creative power according to the systemic imperatives of profit and capital accumulation. In an attempt to update Marx in *History and Class Consciousness*, Lukács suggests that the direct experience of exploitation and political disenfranchisement need only be given organisational form in the party. For Adorno and the other representatives of critical theory, however, the problems raised by the implications of Kant's philosophy are not quite so easily solved within a Marxist framework. While endorsing Lukács' analysis of reification and agreeing with his ideas on the cognitive content of aesthetics, Adorno is also convinced that the imperative of saving the sensual moment of cognition cannot be achieved by writing Kant off as a bourgeois thinker. In other words, one cannot simply force the sensual and intellectual moments of the knowledge process together in the name of positive dialectics and declare them to be thenceforth happily married in practice. This kind of *coerced reconciliation* between sensual and intellectual inquiry cannot be accomplished without manipulating reason, any more than one can declare theory and practice to be successfully unified in the proletariat without applauding a dictatorial regime as a reign of freedom.[13]

The epistemological validity of sensual knowledge has to be recuperated by way of a careful re-reading of Nietzsche, Freud and other thinkers from non-Marxist intellectual traditions. But it must also be recuperated outside the confines of the academy in the individual aesthetic experience of each thinking and acting person. Seen in this light, the Frankfurt programme of interdisciplinarity requires departures from Marx which nonetheless retain and elaborate the Marxist critique of political economy without which any critical theory of society is inadequate. The critique of political economy and alienated labour has to be broadened into a critique of industrial society and alienated experience both within and outside the labour process. This means that, however suggestively powerful, Marx's notion of the primacy of economic factors in terms of explaining the mediation of humanity and nature must give way to a more supple and pluri-directional understanding of that process.[14] Here the break with the materialist Hegelianism informing the Western Marxism of intellectual activists like Lukács and Gramsci becomes clear. Whilst Hegel regards the unity of subject/object and nature/humanity to be achieved in *Geist*, Lukács and Gramsci see this synthesis in the labour power of the proletariat and its organisational forms of action. This is how they interpret Marx's dictum that Hegel must be 'stood on his head' in order to extract the rational kernel of the dialectic from the idealist shell within which it is lodged, and thereby facilitate scientific epistemological inquiry as well as revolutionary political practice. Bearing in mind the real differences between its individual theorists, Western Marxism tends on the whole to rely on a notion of individual subjectivity as a direct reflection of social relations, as well as an idea of collective subjectivity as mastery over nature and suppression of nonsocialist humanity. By contrast, the more advanced theoretical expressions of critical theory in the work of Marcuse, Benjamin and Adorno attempt to retain the dialectical method whilst jettisoning the models of consciousness and subjectivity that Kant, Hegel and finally Marx bequeath to thinkers like Lukács. Especially in Benjamin and Adorno one sees an attempt to move beyond anything resembling a traditional notion of the epistemological subject in an effort to transcend the epistemological content of pragmatic conceptions of understanding and knowledge. Instead of regarding consciousness to be a reflection of social relations, which in turn can be distilled into class relations (or, for that matter, broadened to include race, gender or other social relations), Benjamin and Adorno seek to *recover* a natural or what Adorno sometimes refers to as a 'somatic' moment in thought, which escapes the mechanisms of social integration anchored in daily language and institutions. What is meant by recovering in this context will be discussed in more detail below with regard to the search for a critical hermeneutical (Benjamin) and negative dialectical (Adorno) method. As will be shown in Chapter 6, the attempt to transgress the limits of traditional subjectivity and conventional notions of what constitutes thinking suggest comparisons on the left between certain instances of Frankfurt School thought, on the one hand, and Foucault's ideas on genealogy of power, Derrida's theory of deconstruction as well as Deleuze and Guattari's concept of the anti-Oedipus, on the other. It will be seen that, in different ways, all of these currents of thought attempt to ask questions about philosophy and politics raised by Marx and, to an even greater extent, by Nietzsche.[15]

Nietzsche's appeal to the Frankfurt School consists in his insistence in the *Birth of Tragedy* (1872) and other writings that there is a sensual and intuitive (Dionysian) as well as a rational and intellectual (Appolonian) component to knowledge, of which the Greeks were fully aware, and which the modern industrial world has largely forgotten. He anticipates 'a revolution of all values' which liberates creativity from utilitarian considerations of profit, and transforms the static conception of human nature defended by the bourgeoisie into a pluralist and spontaneous play of Apollonian and Dionysian life-affirming forces. While in the *Destruction of Reason,* Lukács dismisses Nietzsche as a champion of irrationalism, thinkers like Horkheimer and Adorno praise his insight into the truth and knowledge content of aesthetic experience.[16]

Moreover, it is clear to the founders of critical theory that by illustrating the weaknesses of Kantian epistemology, Marx and Nietzsche also manage effectively to criticise Kant's liberal views on negative freedom and the antagonistic premises informing the theoretical and institutional bases of the liberal democratic state. Following Marx and Lukács, Horkheimer notes that an economy based on the division of labour, private property and commodity production does a great deal to sever the links between the transformation of nature in work, on the one hand, and the possibility of cognition that is not shackled to the knowledge-deforming pressures structuring the struggle for self-preservation, on the other. Far from being a particular feature of modernity, this struggle between humanity and nature has been institutionalised throughout human history in the class struggle and different versions of the authoritarian state. Here Horkheimer does not depart substantially from the analyses of Marx and Lukács.

But in *Traditional and Critical Theory* Horkheimer adds that Kant does not manage to prove that the mere fact that there is consciousness guarantees a successful mediation of humanity and nature through reason (though Kant's methodology prompts Nietzsche and Foucault after him to raise questions about the social bases constituting what counts as deficient or even pathological consciousness). By extension, the mere existence of the modern industrial working class and its communist vanguard do not produce conditions sufficient to guarantee a real revolution in epistemology and politics. Horkheimer explicitly states that if the existence of a social class and its interests did happen to offer a sufficient condition of valid knowledge and political freedom, there would be little need for philosophy or for inquiry full stop. Had this been the case, one would have the epistemological luxury of truthful immanence, either in the institutions embodying Hegelian *Geist,* or in the successful union of theory and practice automatically incarnated by the Marxist proletariat.[17] However, the insufficiency of *Geist* or a single class to fulfil the conditions of noninstrumental knowledge and positive freedom beyond the negative liberty of liberal noninfringement does raise one of the key questions of critical social theory. What kind of restructuring of the socioeconomic institutions guiding the labour process would be necessary in order to enable production to abolish scarcity for everybody, whilst transforming work into a source of aesthetic pleasure to the greatest possible extent? With the possible exceptions of Franz Neumann (1900–54) and Otto Kirchheimer (1905–65), this question is never really answered with any clear implications for practical political transformation by any of the members of the Institute. But by asking extremely provocative questions about the feasibility of interdisciplinary methodology and the relation between epistemology and a possible utopian politics of the future, Frankfurt School ideas became a major source of inspiration for activists and radicals on the left throughout the 1960s and beyond. Although incapable of decisively moving political economy beyond the limits explored by Marx, the founders of critical theory embarked on a rigorous interdisciplinary programme of research aimed at establishing a series of tentative philosophical and aesthetic answers broadly related to the question about the transformation of the labour process posed above. These answers are examined in the rest of this chapter.[18]

The idea that the mere existence of the proletariat does not guarantee the attainment of noninstrumental knowledge or the outbreak of revolutionary action is more than a small point of tension between critical theory and Western Marxism. It will be recalled from Chapter 2 that in the *German Ideology* Marx and Engels claim that the ruling ideas are, in every époque, ruling class ideas, and that Gramsci regards this power over ideas to be one of the key factors explaining how the hegemonic classes are able to establish the legitimacy of their ways of thinking and acting for society as a whole. Gramsci does not question the analysis provided by Marx and Engels as such, but wants the working class to become the ruling class so that working-class ideas can become the ruling ideas. It is also clear to him that the strategy that worked for the Bolsheviks in Russia is not appropriate in central and Western Europe, where intellectuals and the institutions of civil society mediate between the economy and the more openly repressive organs of state violence, such that the class struggle in the economy is also a battle of ideas in civil society. In comparison with the Russian case, the army and police play a relatively minor role in the physiognomy of bourgeois hegemony in the West. Whilst the Bolsheviks did not need to worry too much about civil society and could make a direct assault on the Winter Palace in St Petersburg, Western Marxism needed to find an alternative, more consensual route to power. Hence, while Marx and the exponents of Western Marxism ask how working class ideas can become the hegemonic ideas, critical theorists such as Benjamin and Adorno ask a different set of questions. These include: in what kind of society would ideas cease to be defence mechanisms against nature's lack of spontaneous generosity with its fruits, and, in what kind of society would thought and language open up the secrets of objects instead of being tools for their manipulation? In their work this leads to an implicit distinction between the *real* (the actual, which presents itself at face value as 'the ways things are') and the *true* (the marginalised, which is often incompatible with the way things happen to be), and the related development of a methodology of critical hermeneutics and negative dialectics.[19]

Critical hermeneutics and negative dialectics are deployed against the traditional idealism of Kant and Hegel, Husserl's phenomenology, and Heidegger's ontology. Adorno cites the philosophies of Bergson (1859–1941), Husserl, and Husserl's pupil Heidegger as the most important of the many failed attempts to re-establish the epistemological foundations of the bourgeois order in the face of the challenges posed by Marx and the gradual democratisation of political representation. For Adorno these projects are as flawed as the attempt in Western Marxism to assume that the problems of individual epistemological subjectivity are redundant in the supposedly postbourgeois era of collective subjectivity announced in different ways by the philosophies of Lukács and Heidegger.[20] For the authors of *History and Class Consciousness* and *Being and Time,* the proletariat and *Das Volk* (the people) spontaneously overcome the liberal dichotomies separating subject, theory and ethics from object, practice and politics. In theory, the philosophical bases of the liberal democratic *Rechtsstaat* are transcended in a way that points to the possibility of more thoroughly legitimate political forms of authority than parliamentary democracy and its cumbersome system of petty deals and endless compromises. Proletarian action and the *Dasein* of national communities realise a modern unity of theory and practice reminiscent of Aristotle's concept of *Phronesis,* i.e. a kind of spontaneous knowledge which is simultaneously both theoretical and practical.

Adorno does not directly pronounce on the problems raised by Aristotle's notion of the unity of theory and practice, nor does he in any way intend to defend liberalism. For all of the problems in Kant and liberalism generally, however, Adorno regards the supposed unity of subject/theory and object/practice in Lukács and Heidegger to be coerced, and in significant ways as a step back to pre-Kantian and pre-Hegelian positions. One must bear in mind that the philosophies of Kant and Hegel are the most mature theoretical expressions of the philosophy of an ascendant social class which is demonstrably progressive vis-à-vis its aristocratic predecessor. As such, their ideas bear a moment of objectivity in the Hegelian sense of objective spirit: they say something true about a world that is false, i.e. about a form of existence that is not yet liberated from domination and to that extent still falsely represented in a philosophy that is nonetheless as truthful as thought possibly can be at that particular historical juncture.

However much they might disagree on other issues in an imaginary dialogue with one another, it is clear to Marx and Adorno that philosophical error in Kant and Hegel is not mystified. Error here indicates the direction in which theory and practice should move in order for philosophy to be eventually able to say something true about a world in which humanity and nature are reconciled in a harmonious totality mediated by noninstrumental reason and knowledge, that is, where domination has been overcome in a genuinely pluralist community of nonidentical equals rather than in patently false forms of state-manipulated consensus and nationalist bigotry. Another way of saying this is that the idealism of Kant and Hegel expresses something real, not just ideological, about knowledge and politics, and it does so at a precise historical moment when class relations and a given level of development of the productive forces makes determinate modes of consciousness and actual forms of freedom possible. It is Adorno's contention that, despite their repeated claims to the contrary, thinkers like Lukács and Heidegger remain trapped within idealism. But by this later historical point idealism sheds its progressive character because it has not managed to realise its claims about knowledge and freedom in practice. Philosophical idealism fails to redeem the promise implicit in its own errors and lacunae by not following the path that would have possibly led to a reconciled world. Hence its latter-day representatives have to deny they are idealist in order to present themselves as the radical successors to idealist thought, offering something bold and new, and tend to end up working in the service of the interests of political power, desperately trying to hang on to something that in reality is old and in the process of decomposition. In the case of Lukács and Heidegger it is a mystified kind of idealism resolving the tension between subject and object in the spurious instances of *Aufhebung* afforded by the rhetoric of positive dialectics and the history of being. At first glance they seem to radicalise the positions of Hegelian Marxism (Lukács) and Husserl's phenomenology (Heidegger). But in both cases, however differently, they offer an untruthful radicalism which unsurprisingly aligns itself with party dictatorships. In theory, philosophical and historical development should have run from Kant and Hegel to Marx, and from there to a libertarian communist revolution. In practice, this path of development has been blocked (but not cancelled and preserved in Hegel's sense) by actual events. In the opening lines of *Negative Dialectics* Adorno explains that philosophy which seems outdated remains alive because the historical moment of its realisation has been missed. In this fundamental text of critical theory he develops a critique of Kant, Hegel and Heidegger, and systematises some of Benjamin's more intuitive and cryptic ideas on law and history of the 1920s and 1930s.[21]

The historical moment which has been missed cannot be reproduced because circumstances change, but the truth content of the lost moment can be recovered and redeemed against the seemingly inexorable forward march of history and the apparent inaccessibility of the past. This is what is suggested by the terms 'negative dialectics' and 'critical hermeneutical inquiry'. Hegel and Marx see truth and reason working dialectically in history, and are implicitly prepared to accept feudal violence and capitalist exploitation as necessary stages in humanity's struggle to overcome alienation from nature in an emancipated society. By contrast, Benjamin and Adorno regard history as a catastrophic succession of blueprints designed to master nature, which boomerang in the guise of oppressive social and political institutions. This is the consequence of thinking as mastery. Thinking as mastery results in the eternal return of different forms of mythology, and mythology culminates in destruction as a prelude to the flourishing of new myths. Particularly in Benjamin's usage of the term, a catastrophe, as opposed to a systemic crisis, is indicative of a condition that cannot be patched up with some good management and diligent engineering. If one wants to understand why the Enlightenment becomes another instance of mythology, one has to surpass mythological thinking, i.e. thinking in the service of domination. Part of what this entails is transcending the standpoint of the traditional epistemological subject, though not in the ways suggested by Lukács and Heidegger. In Benjamin's mature work the task is to make the ruins of destruction visible before they actually become ruins, so that humanity can finally change the course of history instead of remaining within the spell of catastrophe by seeking to reverse or accelerate it.[22] The possibility of dismantling rather than assuming control of the ruling dialectic of mastery-mythology-destruction-new mastery turns on the chance of recovering a buried truth about so-called historical progress that is so true it can break the continuum of successive catastrophes. Critical hermeneutics and negative dialectics attempt simultaneously to work backwards in time (though not as a conservative attempt to salvage tradition and culture from the ravages of capitalism), and to work forwards in time (but not according to some specious and dangerous notion of progress). They reject conservative and superficially radical conceptions of hermeneutics and historicism that do not go to the root of the problem, which remains the relation between epistemology and human emancipation.[23]

From Mimetic and Constellational Thinking to the Theories of Structural Transformation and Communicative Action

From the perspective of critical theory, the epistemological foundations of the bourgeois conceptions of state and society have been quaking ever since Hegel's deconstruction of Kant's first critique of reason. In the *Critique of Pure Reason* Kant is keen to map out an experience-based theory of knowledge that is distinct from the dogmas of pure reason and other notions of unmediated essence. In so doing he argues that thinking and experience are not the same, since thinking can stray into pure reason and thereby transgress the limits of possible experience and the objective knowledge it yields. What is left of experience and objectivity once they have been 'purged' of sensual knowledge and imaginative thought, however, is capable of rendering a rather ahistorical model of subjectivity and a model of cognition that seems to be significantly indebted to the methodology of the natural sciences. From this perspective, the road from Kantian reason to Weberian rationalisation is relatively easy to retrace. Kant's victory over pure reason and metaphysics is obtained by limiting the claims of reason to the verification of a series of mechanical mental operations which seem to steer thinking away from freedom and autonomy in the direction of predictability and efficiency. More will be said about this below. For now it might also be mentioned that on a Frankfurt School reading, Kant's political writings also seem to transform the limits of what we can know into the limits of what we are permitted to hope. The epistemological argument about the possible existence but ultimately unknowable noumenal world is translated into a series of arguments about the *theoretical* compatibility of individual happiness and legal universality, in pure reason, but the *actual impossibility* of anything more substantive than negative freedom and punitive justice in practice.[24]

While in the *Phenomenology of Spirit* Hegel demonstrates that the Kantian distinction between thinking and experience is not really tenable, Marx and later Georg Simmel show that 'normal' experience of everyday life in industrial capitalist regimes has become fragmented, reified and traumatic. Marx concentrates on reification, alienation and the division of labour; Simmel's work both confirms and challenges Marx in fundamental ways. He agrees with Marx that labour power in the broadest sense of mental and manual creation mediates between humanity and nature. But he adds that once individual and collective creations assume social form in objects and institutions, they acquire a life of their own—a third term, between humanity and nature, belonging to neither—which cannot be simply reappropriated by humanity in the way suggested by Marx in the *1844 Manuscripts*. Hegel speaks of objective spirit as being constantly created and reappropriated and created anew, but Marx thinks the working class can collectively reappropriate its political essence from the liberal democratic state in the same stroke that it reappropriates its productive essence by assuming control of the economy it creates but does not yet run. Hence revolution and reappropriation of alienated essence are twin concepts for Marx. Even if the working class were to constitute the overwhelming majority of the population, Simmel regards reappropriation in this sense as impossible because of the irreducibility of social form to the will of individual and collective social actors. Due to the division of labour and what Simmel refers to as the growing gap between objective and subjective culture, social institutional form in modern society is particularly elastic and resistant to attempts at direct political control by individuals, classes and groups.[25]

The crisis of epistemology resulting from the division of labour and the elasticity of institutional form is also a crisis of radical political agency. Agency is unproblematic in Marx's writings on Hegel and Feuerbach, i.e. where revolution is conjured up as the simple reappropriation of the alienated essence of a unified collective subject. What remains of radical *subjective* agency once the reality of *objective* form is confirmed? For Simmel agency remains possible as a reciprocal interaction between subjective actors and objective institutions, but it is a kind of agency that is always mediated by a social dimension of objective reality that is not the property of an individual or collective agent. Mediation of this kind drastically reduces what individuals can know about society, and drastically limits the extent to which society can be changed by radical politics. As a result, individuals are increasingly thrown back on their own resources and inclined to formulate individualistic and arbitrary explanations of the structure of social action. The implications of the twin crises of epistemology and agency diagnosed in different ways by Marx and Simmel are clear. One witnesses a decline in the depth of individual experience, as well as increasing levels of social integration and conformity: where knowledge of social structure and social action becomes obscured, people tend to look to their neighbours for orientation rather than relying on their own impulses and judgements. In terms of a critical reconstruction of history since the Industrial Revolution, the end of integral experience heralded by fragmentation and mass trauma is twofold. First, institutionalised forms of reason are for the most part reduced to an instrumental dimension capable of addressing technical and administrative problems only. Whereas in theory reason elucidates the contours of political freedom and a public conception of autonomy for an Enlightenment thinker like Rousseau, in the course of industrialisation reason in practice is increasingly embedded within the contractual negotiations regulating conflicting economic interests. According to this interpretation, the privatisation of reason and the corresponding utilitarian exercise of autonomy contribute to a Weberian rationalisation of politics and its assimilation to various modes of economic conduct. The consequence is that political action is measured in terms of means and ends (subject to highly subjective criteria of efficiency), rather than evaluated in terms of its quality (subject to publicly debated criteria of judgement).

Second, it is no longer possible to write symphonies and operas in the manner of Beethoven and Wagner in which the totality and fullness of the 'ordered chaos' of life are captured in art. The corollary is that it is also not possible, except in reactionary terms, to deny the reality of fragmentation and abjure modern art in the name of realism, as Lukács does. His particular theory of realism can be seen as symptomatic of trauma concerning what he perceives to be the destruction of reason, the real causes of which are not addressed if one resorts to flight and denial. The same holds for Heidegger's determination to re-establish the integrity of some source or origin which has been obscured by a supposed forgetting of being and its history. In short, Lukács's diatribe against modernism disregards his own analysis of the fragmentary effects of the division of labour and is ultimately futile. Heidegger's notion of ontological forgetting offers a very inadequate alternative to the Marxist theory of reification. Theory that is critical in the sense of the Frankfurt School insists on facing the staggering challenges posed by the historical end of integral experience in the modern industrial world as well as the reactionary implications of folkloristic projects for a 'homecoming' to some point of unmediated origin and pristine tradition.[26]

The end of the particularly rich forms of experience that inform the philosophy of Hegel, the music of Beethoven, the many-sided creativity of Goethe, the revolutionary imagination of Marx and Nietzsche, etc., does not signify the end of experience full stop or the permanent demise of creativity or radical change. Theory and practice can certainly be relaunched on new bases, but this entails confronting the conditions that contribute to (a) the reification of thought, (b) the rationalisation of reason, and (c) the increasing complexity of social form. It is simply inadequate to suggest that decisive agency by the party solves the problem, or that individual and national 'authenticity' can catapult humanity beyond thinking institutionalised as mastery and domination. Critical theory rearticulated from a more contemporary perspective might add that it also means confronting the conditions that make thought reified and reason instrumental rather than appealing to already existing agents and spheres such as 'the multitude', communicative action, civil society, 'the political', etc.

Somewhat surprisingly, given the implicitly disparaging tone of some of the preceding discussions about the problems with Kantian philosophy, Kant actually offers an apposite starting point for addressing the conditions of instrumentality and reification. In Kant's third critique, the *Critique of Judgement* (1790), he intimates that one can say that a landscape is beautiful. But one can also say that a landscape painting is beautiful, and in so doing, humanity becomes aware that there is more to beauty and aesthetic experience than what is beautiful in nature, even though that 'more' resists easy conceptual or linguistic definition. This insight combines the idealist point that humanity is part of nature but not reducible to nature with the aesthetic notion that works of art always exceed what one can articulate about them. Moreover, the individual steps involved in the creation of a work of art can be thought of in terms of intersections rather than mono-directional linearity. Hence the artwork reveals something about subject and object relations and about temporality as well. In *Counter-Revolution and Revolt,* Marcuse points out that this symmetry of beauty in art and nature is not merely an analogy. It points to aesthetics as a form of noninstrumental cognition and the existence of possible bridges between conceptual and nonconceptual modes of knowing.

This idea can be explained as follows. For Hegel and the conservative idealist philosopher Schelling (1775–1854), nature and consciousness are ultimately one and the same; for Kant in the *Critique of Pure Reason,* nature represents the limit to what consciousness can know. The analysis in Kant's third critique suggests that there may be a way beyond a rigid dichotomisation of subject/object, past/present and humanity/nature which would point beyond traditional idealism without adopting the inadequate solutions to the problems of idealism offered by thinkers like Husserl, Bergson, Lukács and Heidegger. The subject can attempt to absorb object or external nature in the manner of Hegel and Schelling. The subject can also confront the external world as an intractable limit and a hostile alien force in the way instrumental reason faces nature. Indeed, traditional subjectivity tends to operate in either or both of these ways. But the *Critique of Judgement* implies that it might be possible to articulate the truthful moments of subjectivity to the truthful moments of objectivity. This happens when we formulate judgements that are neither arbitrarily subjective nor dogmatically objective, i.e. when we realise that the truth or falsity of our judgements about art are not true or false according to the usual dictates of logic, where by definition what is true cannot also be false. Depending on the quality of the artistic form as well as the social relations embedded in which the work of art is, there can be truth in falsity as well as falsity in truth, and an implicit desire to make truth even 'more true' that it is in any given present. Adorno maintains something somewhat similar when he writes that subject is never completely subject (because of the Hegelian argument that all subjectivity is mediated by social and historical objectivity), and object is never completely object (because of the Kantian argument that all objectivity is mediated by subjectivity). Although Kant does not explicitly speak in such terms, Marcuse and Adorno read Kant in the light of their knowledge of Hegel and dialectics in order to formulate the idea that in great works of art one has a constellation of the subjective, objective as well as temporal moments of reality. This signals a qualitatively different way of knowing than identity thinking positing an *Aufhebung* of subject (thesis) and object (antithesis) in an authoritarian and falsely manufactured unity (synthesis as coerced reconciliation).[27]

It has been seen that, according to the Frankfurt School critique of Hegel and Lukács, falsely manufactured unity at the epistemological level unfolds in the institutions of a coercive totality based on fabricated unity and mass conformity at the level of society. There is thus a utopian dimension to this project of thinking, which can avoid rigid dualisms, as well as practical implications entailed in eschewing the coerced reconciliation of the individual terms of the dualism in question. If the truthful moments in the subject can be articulated to the truthful moments in the object, it may be possible to get beyond thinking as mastery and move on to the epistemological-political breakthrough mentioned at the outset of this chapter. It may be objected that it is far from obvious how subjectivity and objectivity might be experienced in terms of a constellation of moments rather than as a predatory conquest by thinking of what is non-identical to thought. It might be asked: if instrumental reason is generally a defensive construction of barriers against the unpredictability and spontaneity of nature, how does one break through to a noninstrumental dimension of thought which is nonetheless rigorous? Adorno and the mature Marcuse look to modernist aesthetics. Benjamin believes he may be on the right track by questioning the juxtaposition of past and present, the separation of means and ends, and a number of other dichotomies typical of reified thought. He interrogates the conditions necessary for a transition from *dualisms,* which appear to be locked in permanent opposition, to *paradoxes* that can be solved in a revolution.[28]

In *The Work of Art in the Age of Mechanical Reproduction* (1935), Benjamin suggests that the end of the particularly rich forms of experience that inform the work of Goethe, Marx etc., actually signifies the possible advent of revolutionary radical political change. This is because in the age of mechanical reproduction works of art do not need to be performed live or experienced as unique and original. The work loses what Benjamin refers to as its 'aura'. This changes the mode of reception of art, the relation between the masses and the cultural elite, and in the process transforms the dialectic of tradition-revolution. He suggests that once freed from the weight of tradition, the artificial foundations preserving various social hierarchies can be undermined. Experience in the widest sense then becomes shock. But rather than being a shock that incapacitates people with passivity and trauma, as Simmel and Freud at times seem to suggest in different ways, for Benjamin it is a shock accompanied by the realisation that humanity has entered into a phase where hierarchy is no longer the necessary price of survival. When it becomes clear that past generations have borne the weight of hierarchy and oppression to make a life without want a real material possibility, it dawns on everyone that this possibility is indeed an objective reality rather than an exercise in the wishful thinking normally accompanying the fetishised consumption of commodities in capitalist society. The extent to which regimes that perpetuate hierarchy and oppression are no longer legitimate becomes glaringly obvious. This realisation comes in a flash of collective insight that

Benjamin calls a profane illumination. Profane illuminations often come when the continuum of past and present is broken in a 'nowtime' of intergenerational transparency and solidarity in which the prevailing limits on thought and action are suspended. If one analyses the themes in the 'Critique of violence', the *Paris Arcades Project* and *The Work of Art in the Age of Mechanical Reproduction* in conjunction with Benjamin's 'Theses on the philosophy of history', it becomes apparent that he rejects what he considers historicist notions of linear time in favour of a messianic vision of time in which moments of truth from the past, present and future are distilled and intersect. In the past artistic creation could reconcile humanity and nature, and contribute to the preservation of forms of society in which culture in the traditional sense flourished. In advanced capitalism, by contrast, tradition is undermined. Instead of bemoaning this situation in the conservative manner of Lukács and Heidegger, however, Benjamin argues that works of art can lift the oppressed social classes of society out of their dreamlike slumber induced by the production and circulation of commodities. He is convinced that, on waking, they will rise to the task of ending oppression and exploitation. The legal system masking hierarchy is then destroyed and replaced by justice, where justice, for Benjamin, is synonymous with truth.[29]

Benjamin's acute sensitivity to the political possibilities offered in periods of historical transition is a central theme in the work of a number of the other members of the Institute as well. In 'State capitalism: its possibilities and limitations' (1941), Friedrich Pollock (1894–1970) attempts to show that just as the negotiation and renegotiation of the relations between church and state is one of the defining characteristics of modernity, so too is the constant renegotiation between the forces of labour and the representatives of capital. He intimates that it is the hallmark of this constant readjustment that forms of state vary over time in accordance with changes in the structure of the economy. In Chapter 1 we saw that in the *Eighteenth Brumaire* Marx explains how the state can assume relative autonomy from the dominant classes in civil society if the latter are locked in a struggle in which no single class is hegemonic enough to dictate the terms of political compromise. Pollock attempts to develop Marx's ideas further by outlining a theory capable of explaining how recurring crises in capital accumulation produce predictable political crises. These are typically crises concerned with co-ordinating the degree of planning capitalism needs in order to function without actually introducing so much planning that the prerogatives of private property are fundamentally challenged. He formulates a theory of state capitalism which situates the phenomenon of state capitalism as the necessary successor stage to 'free' market capitalism. Despite some of the ambiguities in the term state capitalism, Pollock thinks that it captures four essential aspects related to the transition from free market to late capitalism: (1)

the structural problems of market capitalism (co-ordinating supply and demand without planning) lay the bases for the move to state capitalism; (2) at a certain stage in the evolution of capitalism state intervention becomes a systemic necessity; (3) capital accumulation and profit continue to be the driving forces of the economy; and (4) state capitalism introduces planning, though without thereby becoming a system of production based on the satisfaction of human need and the desire for creative forms of work. In other words, state capitalism is not state socialism on the Soviet model and certainly not libertarian socialism as Marx had envisaged it in broad outline when discussing human as opposed to political emancipation.[30]

Pollock's ideas on the correlations between determinate stages in the evolution of capitalism with structural changes in forms of law and state are developed with striking clarity by the legal theorists connected with the Institute, Otto Kirchheimer and Franz Neumann. In 'Changes in the structure of political compromise' (1941) Kirchheimer shows that in the transition from free market to state capitalism, the executive of the capitalist state is restructured in order to enable it to perform key planning functions. This occurs because of a *subjective* factor concerning class consciousness and class culture (also analysed by a number of Western Marxists), on the one hand, and an *objective* factor concerning the systemic features of capitalist production in each stage of its unfolding journey towards permanent and irresolvable crisis (first analysed in terms of systemic logic and structural tendencies by Marx), on the other. While the subjective factor contributes to the stalemate of class forces alluded to above, the objective factor results in Keynesianism and a variety of other attempts to patch up capitalism without really going to the root of the problem: *socially* and co-operatively produced wealth continues to be *privately* appropriated. That is to say, the root of the problem and its solution is subjective and objective, i.e., dialectical, such that subjective revolutionary will and organisation by itself would have as little chance of producing real social transformation as a supposedly materialist science of history without an active and conscious agent of change. While subjectivist intransigence might be 'successful' in military terms reminiscent of the party-based movements of Lenin, Mao and Castro, it is also likely to produce authoritarian and hierarchical societies as well as leadership cults. Similarly, theoretical objectivist materialism is likely to dry up in academic sterility.[31]

Though planning and state restructuring introduce decidedly public and political criteria into the mode of production, the representatives of capital and private accumulation retain the private right to decide what is to be produced in determinate quantities for which markets. Kirchheimer notes that the reinforcement and expansion of the role of the executive is secured at the expense of the legislature. Two implications of this development are clear. First, the undermining of the legislature is the first step toward the undermining of the popular bases of the state and the transition towards more and less authoritarian state forms such as fascism and corporatism. This is a development that marks the transition from a juridical epistemology in which the claims of reason and the practice of law mutually complement one another, to an authoritarian-populist epistemology in which law sheds its rational character and assumes the character of something which is more like a command or decree than a rational law. Second, the introduction of large-scale planning under the auspices of private ownership of the means of production and exchange blurs the distinctions between private/civil society and public/state to such an extent that one can reasonably speak of a totalitarian, or as Adorno puts it, totally administered society. Kirchheimer's analysis foreshadows Hannah Arendt's (1906–75) notion that totalitarianism is marked by the rise of social, administrative and instrumental reason to the detriment of political judgement and political action. For her this is a consequence of the rise of ubiquitous sociality accompanying the demise of the public/private distinction and the concomitant disappearance of the public sphere. It also anticipates the young Habermas's notion that the dismantling of the public-private distinction marks the end of the liberal democratic phase of capitalism. During the 1960s and 1970s he articulates the view that the colonisation of communication in the life-world of interacting citizens by technical criteria tends to supplant communicative reason directed to understanding and an interest in emancipation with instrumental reason directed towards competition and an interest in strategic advantage. In *Legitimation Crisis* (1973) Habermas argues that systemic erosion of the structures of the life-world casts considerable doubt on the long-term prospects of capitalist states to generate the requisite degree of legitimacy necessary to secure social stability. Seen within this theoretical framework, the introduction of capitalist planning will either generate a consensus for the implementation of the legal institutions necessary for consistent planning, i.e. some form of socialist planning, or it will perpetuate the highly unstable combination of state intervention and private prerogative which produces and reproduces the periodic legitimacy deficits in modern industrial societies. The neo-liberal offensive of the 1980s and 1990s indicates that the latter possibility has prevailed to date, thus making the presentation of a socioeconomic and political alternative to capitalism one of the contemporary left's main theoretical and practical priorities.[32]

The question of legitimacy is at the centre of the political ideas of Kirchheimer, Neumann and Habermas. In 'Remarks on Carl Schmitt's *Legality and Legitimacy*', Kirchheimer reminds readers that although one is apt to say 'liberal democracy' when speaking about the governments of advanced capitalist societies, the term itself connotes a potentially volatile combination of ideas about legality ('liberal') and legitimacy ('democracy'). Commenting on the legal theory of Carl Schmitt (1888–1985) and his book *Legality and Legitimacy* of 1932, Kirchheimer observes that, despite his National Socialist affiliations in the 1930s, Schmitt's work draws attention to one of the most basic contradictions in liberal democratic states. Liberal democracy champions *individual liberty* and the sanctity of contractually mediated private interests within a legal framework that is said to derive its legitimacy from *collective liberty* based on a non-contractual foundation—popular sovereignty. Individuals are free to enter into and terminate contractual agreements when buying and selling labour power and other commodities, but they cannot sell their political rights of citizenship. The latter are non-negotiable attributes that are said to belong to the sovereign people in the manner of a precontractual, nonalienable and unitary source. On this account, the legitimacy of the legal state resides in its ability to restore the original unity, which is fragmented and strained as a result of the processes of economic competition and class conflict. In liberal democratic theory, socioeconomic inequality and stratification in civil society is overridden by a more fundamental unity and political equality in the state. Kirchheimer shows that the plausibility of this argument is undermined as soon as the bases of suffrage are widened without a corresponding reform of property rights and the relations of production. He points out that the evolution of European states in the period from 1848 to the National Socialist assault on the Weimar Republic in 1933 is characterised by increasing political enfranchisement, though without a decisive transition to social ownership. The result is that political equality becomes a lever to pursue social equality, which runs up against the structural limit imposed by private ownership of the means of production. Each country is then faced with the choice of either socialising private socioeconomic rights in order to secure democratic legitimacy, or of enforcing liberal legality by protecting the rights of property and capital from egalitarian political infringement. Kirchheimer convincingly shows that any state that opts to consolidate the prerogatives of property and capital cannot indefinitely withstand democratic pressures for change without curtailing or eventually even abolishing democratic rights of citizenship. This is precisely what occurs in fascism, where trade unions are forcibly integrated into the state and opposition parties are repressed or banned outright.[33]

The hypothesis that a transition from a rational juridical epistemology to an authoritarian-populist epistemology corresponds to the structural transformation of legal reason into authoritarian decree also informs the work of Franz Neumann. Like Kirchheimer's 'Changes in the structure of political compromise', Neumann's 'The change in the function of law in modern society' (published in the *Journal for Social Research* in 1937) is a key text of critical theory, exploring the modalities of political transformation in relation to changes in the capitalist economy and society. Whilst adopting a broadly Marxist framework of analysis, neither thinker really relies on a base-superstructure model of explanation. Changes in legal argument and practice are not analysed as mere reflections of economic centralisation and monopoly formation. Without explicitly referring to Hegel in any detail, both authors retain the Hegelian idea that there can be no valid contract—and hence no modern forms of economic exchange—without a sovereign state that validates contract in the first place. Hence law and the state are neither conceived of as by-products of economic change, as in schematic Marxism, nor posited as autonomous from the economy, as in much liberal democratic theory and structural and functionalist analyses. In the foreword to a collection of Neumann's most important essays, Marcuse remarks that Neumann seeks to develop an overarching theory of politics and a political theory of freedom combining history, sociology, political economy and legal theory.[34]

In attempting to formulate an explicitly political theory of freedom, Neumann knows that there is no easy way back to Machiavellian or other versions of republicanism in light of the questions raised by Marx and Weber. In this context one must bear in mind that just as Marxism is not meant to be a dogma or pseudo-science, Weber's ideas are not synonymous with the inevitability of rationalisation, the disenchantment of the world and the end of politics. Marx and Weber force the student of politics to interrogate the conditions under which republican citizenship could flourish in the modern world of advanced industry, and this, Neumann suggests, is not possible without a radical reorganisation of the economy and property relations. One cannot simply exhort the citizenry to virtuous political participation as if one were still in the Greek polis or Renaissance city state. Marx indicates that to all intents and purposes the modern state is a vehicle for enforcing contracts and collecting taxes. This means that key political questions become the possible ways of financing state operations rather than giving expression to the general will (Rousseau) while respecting the autonomy of individual citizens (Kant). For Neumann it is not that Machiavelli, Kant, Rousseau and Hegel have become irrelevant. The point is rather that it is reactionary to simply invoke a hallowed canon of thinkers without acknowledging the caesura with political tradition represented by Marx. To do this is symptomatic of the conservative tendency to bemoan the degradation of individual experience without addressing the economic bases of this degradation. Marx is the first to furnish a systematic account of the periodic structural transformations in state, society and economy accompanying modernisation understood in terms of increasing industrialisation, secularisation and urbanisation. Weber rounds out the picture by showing what becomes of the notion of reason in the wake of these developments.[35]

In *The Change in the Function of Law in Modern Society* Neumann suggests that the idea that the law is an example of the expression of the rational will of the citizenry rather than arbitrary whim or force is bound up with a particular account of the origins and sources of the authority of the law. It is his contention that the sources of the authority of the law change over time in conjunction with changes in church/state and state/civil society relations. He adds that the specificity of national context must be borne in mind when considering these changes. In England, for example, in contrast to Germany, the bourgeoisie relied on parliament to a great degree to express its will in its dealings with the Crown and other sectors of English society. This meant that the transition from feudalism to more modern social and political arrangements in England was decidedly smoother than in Germany, where the bourgeoisie was more likely to deal with the army and landed aristocracy in extra-parliamentary alliances. The precariousness of the German situation attained unparalleled clarity during the Weimar Republic. The extra-parliamentary power of the workers in the factories and their demands for socialised property came into conflict with the extra-parliamentary demands of the industrialists and their demands that the state guarantee propitious conditions for growth and accumulation.

This turned out to be an irresolvable problem within the framework of the German version of the liberal democratic state form, especially since the Weimar Constitution made considerable concessions to working-class interests concerning equality and rights of industrial consultation, and at the same time made concessions to capitalist interests concerning industrial discipline and securing the institutional conditions for the generation of private profit. For Neumann one of the important lessons of that period in German history is that if democracy in practice is to be a form of state with real rather than merely symbolic content, it must be borne in mind that democracy *presupposes* a significant degree of social harmony and minimal levels of conflict between social classes. Democracy will not automatically *produce* harmony and, indeed, democratic states will be structurally barred from doing so if their economies are continually reorganised according to the antagonistic premises inherent in the capitalist conception of contract and unquestioned disposal over labour power. This means that the relation between democracy and freedom is fundamentally misconstrued by liberals who believe that the role of the state is to create a legal framework regulating the competitive pursuit of private economic and personal interests. For Neumann freedom and democracy are terms referring to the rights of citizens to make collective decisions and participate in public life as equals. That equality is undermined, and freedom and democracy along with it, when one tries to counter the expansion of franchise by restructuring economic processes so that capital is reallocated the privilege to control the labour process on new bases. Seen in this light, the importance of the question of legitimacy comes into clear focus. On the one hand legitimacy can be secured by the rationally discursive content of collective decisions made by an informed citizenry actively constructing its representative institutions. In this case it is possible to talk about political freedom. On the other hand legitimacy can be manipulated by charismatic leaders allied with powerful extra-parliamentary private interests seeking to transform the citizenry into a mobilised and frightened mass. In the latter case one is observing passive obedience.[36]

The discursive content of political legitimacy is a central theme in *The Structural Transformation of the Public Sphere* (1962) by Jürgen Habermas. In this early work Habermas takes up and elaborates the conception of the public sphere evoked in Kant's essay 'What is enlightenment?' (1784). In that work Kant argues that the sphere of morally autonomous private individuals can be linked to the political community of public citizens through the mediation process actualised in public debate. He quips that although it is extremely difficult for an individual to transcend their state of ignorance by themselves, a critical public can successfully achieve this by openly exchanging views, provided that this happens in a public sphere rather than in the workplace or at home. This is because the latter are examples of contexts where hierarchy serves as a means for maximising efficiency, and the individuals in question are clearly not equal. By contrast, among the members of an assembly of equals, reason and speech can potentially function as ends in themselves, projecting subjective discussion toward objective understanding with cognitive content. Kant maintains that violent civil disobedience is never justified—only public discussion can be used to mediate between what he understands to be the natural rights of private individuals and the positive laws of public authority. Seen in this light, Kant's position would appear to founder on the reality of government power by enjoining the participants of public sphere debate to suffer in nonsilence whilst the sovereign state carries on monopolising legitimate authority. As a tentative response to this problem he suggests that just as all maxims resulting from the deliberations of the critical public *should* strive to be in accordance with existing law, existing law *should* try to conform to the moral and ethical standard set by disinterested discussion aiming at truth rather than power or interest. By stressing that this ought to be the case he concedes that there is always likely to be a discrepancy between the claims of order and authority, and the claims of discursive rationality and understanding. In one sense this discrepancy is regrettable in that it implies that the law may never fully transcend authoritarian paternalism. In another sense, however, it is necessary. Anticipating Adorno's concept of coerced reconciliation, Kant intimates that the declared fusion of ethics and politics would dissolve the ethical as a vantage point from which political reality can be criticised.

Kant's hope is that if the claims of the public are redeemed in open discussion, and if they acquire a universal validity as a result of the forms of agreement that ensue in the course of this process, then the maxims formulated by the public acquire a discursive truth content which legitimate lawmakers simply cannot ignore.[37]

In *The Structural Transformation of the Public Sphere* Habermas analyses the Kantian model of the public sphere as a possible source of norms for legitimating political authority. He indicates that the marked differences between democratic and undemocratic polities can be compared by ascertaining whether authority is legitimated in terms of reason and free discussion, according to the stated goals of the Enlightenment, or if authority is legitimated as a result of the rather more arbitrary play of powerful interests in search of strategic compromise, in keeping with the practice of despotisms throughout the ages. Habermas warns that the promise of Enlightenment as democratic politics is threatened by the technological and administrative forces behind industrialisation if the latter are allowed to fundamentally structure the conditions of political compromise and determine the parameters of collective decision-making. Modern forms of economic organisation tend to do precisely this in a series of processes to which he refers as the colonisation of institutions like the public sphere by the systemic imperatives of economic growth. This argument is rearticulated in *Knowledge and Human Interests* (1968), *Legitimation Crisis* (1973), and in considerably modified form in *Between the Facts and the Norms* (1992). Whether he is theorising about the public sphere, the life-world, or civil society, Habermas emphasises the idea that legitimate forms of democracy cannot be attained through strategic compromise alone. This is the traumatic lesson of Weimar that needs to be borne in mind especially in periods of economic growth, when the economy seems to be able to legitimise the polity, since it is really the other way round—the polity must legitimise the economy in a democratic state. The norms of efficient means, inequality and hierarchical command have their place in a sphere of activity where people pursue technical interests. However, these interests cannot be allowed to colonise the norms of discursive ends, equality and mutual understanding and recognition that people have in a sphere where people pursue communicative and emancipatory interests.[38]

Habermas is one of contemporary Europe's best-known living theorists, a man with an illustrious career who knew and worked with a number of the first generation of Frankfurt School critical theorists. There is no space here to evaluate his role as the key thinker of the second generation of critical theorists, or to analyse his evolution from critical theory to communicative action marked by the two-volume *Theory of Communicative Action* (1981). The aim of concluding this chapter with a brief word on some of his ideas about the public sphere and political legitimacy is to illustrate the immensity of issues taken up by the Frankfurt School from its earliest days in the 1920s to today. In addition to the rich patrimony of ideas bequeathed to present and coming generations of militants on the left, the Frankfurt School and critical theory remain highly instructive about the possibilities as well as the great difficulties of translating theory into revolutionary action. It has been seen that they regard interdisciplinary research as a key component in the project to mediate theory and practice. Chapters 4 and 5 will show how this mediation has also been and continues to be conceived in more direct terms by other approaches to creative social transformation.

Suggestions for Further Reading

Arato, Andrew, and Gebhardt, Eike (eds). *The Essential Frankfurt School Reader,* London and New York, Continuum, 1982.

Caygill, Howard. *Walter Benjamin: The Colour of Experience,* Oxford, Basil Blackwell, 1988.

Geoghegan, Vincent. *Reason and Eros: The Social Theory of Herbert Marcuse,* London, Pluto, 1981.

Held, David. *Introduction to Critical Theory: Horkheimer to Habermas,* Berkeley, University of California Press, 1980.

Jarvis, Simon. *Adorno: A Critical Introduction,* Cambridge, Polity, 1998.

Jay, Martin. *The Dialectical Imagination: The Frankfurt School and the Institute for Social Research,* Boston, Little, Brown, 1973.

Scheuerman, William E. *Between the Norm and the Exception: The Frankfurt School and the Rule of Law,* Cambridge, MIT Press, 1994.

Scheuerman, William E. (ed.). *The Rule of Law under Siege: Selected Essays by Franz Neumann and Otto Kirchheimer,* Berkeley, University of California Press, 1996.

Stirk, Peter M. *Max Horkheimer: A New Interpretation,* Hertfordshire, Harvester Wheatsheaf, 1992.

Thomson, Alex. *Adorno: A Guide for the Perplexed,* London and New York, Continuum, 2006.

Wiggershaus, Rolf. *The Frankfurt School,* Cambridge, MIT Press, 1999.

Notes

1 Adorno, *Stichworte: Kritische Modelle 2* [*Critical Models*], Frankfurt, Suhrkamp, 1969, p. 158.

2 For a history of the Institute, which also offers a fine analysis of the ideas of its members, see Rolf Wiggershaus, *Die Frankfurter Schule: Geschichte, theoretische Entwicklung, politische Bedeuung,* published in English as *The Frankfurt School.* Martin Jay provides a very insightful theoretical overview in *The Dialectical Imagination.* With the financial backing of Felix Weil, the Institute was initially directed by Carl Grünberg until he suffered a stroke in January 1928. After a brief interim period Max Horkheimer (1895–1973) assumed direction of the Institute in October 1930. He continued its direction during the National Socialist Years in Germany, when the Institute was forced to move to Geneva and then New York. The Institute reopened in Frankfurt in 1950, one year after

Horkheimer's return from the United States, and was then headed by Adorno from 1958. It continues to exist today under the direction of Axel Honneth. For a selection of critical theory texts supplemented by excellent introductory commentary, see Arato and Gebhardt, *The Essential Frankfurt School Reader*, London and New York, Continuum, 1982.

3 It is probably inappropriate to describe the communist leadership clique in the former Eastern Bloc in either caste or class terms. The very rapid collapse of state socialist power shortly after 1989 suggests that they were not nearly entrenched enough to be hegemonic class regimes of the kind found in Western Europe and North America. It is also clear that they were not caste systems in the traditional sense. For an attempt at theoretical clarification of the bases of state socialism in the former USSR and Eastern Europe, see Konrad and Szelényi, *The Intellectuals on the Road to Class Power,* and Djilas, *The New Class: An Analysis of the Communist System.*

4 Erich Fromm (1900–80) shows that Freud uses the myth of Oedipus to explain that regardless of social class, the (male) child in Western societies directs his sexual wishes towards his mother. This brings him into conflict with his father, who oppresses him by frustrating his desires and threatening him with punishment. The male child experiences feelings of animosity towards the father mixed with a sense of resignation in the face of the father's superior force. The result of these feelings of hostility and helplessness is a sensation of fear, which in its turn induces the child to abandon his own desires and, in a larger sense, to renounce his own projects. The child submits to paternal authority and even identifies with the figure of the father. In genealogical terms, what begins as desire is converted into guilt, fear and submission in a series of stages. On becoming a man, the male adult either remains imprisoned by his feelings of powerlessness and his need for authority, or he becomes rational, independent and stoical about the severe limits imposed on his erotic impulses. Fromm points out that Freud neglects to explore how the authoritarian structures of the bourgeois-paternal family link up with the broader mechanisms of oppression and control in capitalist societies. He convincingly shows that Freud assumes the latter to be timeless and natural, when in fact it is the task of critical theory to show that they are socially conditioned. See Fromm's essay 'Die Determiniertheit der psychischen Struktur durch die Gesellschaft' ['The Social determination of psychic structure'] (1937), now in *Die Gesellschaft als Gegenstand der Psychoanalyse* [*Society as an Object of Psychoanalysis*], pp. 158–60. Fromm was a member of the Institute throughout the 1930s, after which he found it impossible to work with Horkheimer and Adorno, and subsequently went his own way. In 1940 he became an American citizen and began writing in English. His most famous works are *Fear of Freedom* (1941), *The Greatness and Limitations of Freud's Thought* (1979), and *To Have or to Be?* (1976). Whatever else may have divided Fromm from Horkheimer and Adorno, all three are in agreement that instrumental reason and sensual oppression have a much older history than capitalism.

5 Many of the articles were originally published in the *Zeitschrift für Sozialforschung* [*Journal for Social Research*], and have been translated into English. A number of the people affiliated with the Institute for Social Research who wrote articles for the *Journal for Social Research* also published articles in *Die Gesellschaft* [*Society*]. Although less renowned than the journal directly linked

to the Institute, *Society* contains some very original contributions to social theory in the tumultuous period spanning the last years of the Weimar Republic and the first years of National Socialism.

6 Adorno, 'On the fetish character in music and the regression in listening' in Arato and Gebhardt, *The Frankfurt School Reader*; Habermas, *The Structural Transformation of the Public Sphere* and *Legitimation Crisis*. For an extremely useful guide to Adorno's main ideas, see Thomson, *Adorno: A Guide for the Perplexed*, and Jarvis, *Adorno: A Critical Introduction*. For an introduction to Habermas's ideas and an explanation of his evolution from the critical theory informing *The Structural Transformation of the Public Sphere* and *Legitimation Crisis* towards the theory of communicative reason and action of his mature writings, see Thornhill, *Political Theory in Modern Germany: An Introduction*, Chapter 4, and Gordon Finlayson, *Habermas: A Very Short Introduction*. It is debatable whether his work after *The Theory of Communicative Action* (1981) can be characterised as critical theory. The issue is made more complicated by the fact that there is no single definition of critical theory that would permit a conclusive view of the matter. Those interested in forming their own judgement should read *The Theory of Communicative Action* and *Between the Facts and the Norms*.

7 The German title of Adorno's *Zur Metakritik der Erkenntnistheorie* would normally be translated as *On the Meta-critique of Epistemology*. The 'Against' in the English translation (Cambridge, MIT Press, 1992) is therefore somewhat misleading, since the aim of Adorno's critique of the philosophy of Edmund Husserl (1859–1938) in the book is to relaunch epistemological theory in post-idealist terms. Marcuse (1898–1979) is probably best known as the social theorist of the American New Left and the author of *Reason and Revolution* (1941, on Hegel), *Eros and Civilisation* (1955, on Freud) and perhaps most famously *One-Dimensional Man* (1964, on the impoverishment of experience in industrial society). He fled Germany in 1934, and wrote many of his most important works in English. For a sympathetic overview, see Geoghegan, *Reason and Eros*. In addition to his prodigious output as a literary critic, Benjamin (1892–1940) is known as the author of *Das Passagen-Werk* (translated as *The Paris Arcades Project*), in which he examines the relations between architecture, politics, commodities, myth and modes of thought in nineteenth-century Paris. Although a somewhat peripheral member of the Frankfurt School due to his isolation in Paris after 1933, the *Arcades Project* is one of the most important texts of critical theory. Frisby's *Fragments of Modernity* offers a brilliant examination of Benjamin's ideas situated within a broad analysis of culture in modern capitalist societies.

8 Lukács, *History and Class Consciousness*, Chapter 4. The impact of the division of labour and commodity production on consciousness and epistemology is a constant theme in the work of a marginal but very original 'fellow-traveller' of the Frankfurt School, Alfred Sohn-Rethel (1899–1990), whose work influenced Adorno, Benjamin and Marcuse. See Sohn-Rethel's *Soziologische Theorie der Erkenntnis* [*The Sociological Theory of Knowledge*], which can be read as critical theory's response to the sociology of knowledge developed by Karl Mannheim (1893–1947).

9 Horkheimer, *Traditionelle und Kritische Theorie: Fünf Aufsätze* [*Traditional and Critical Theory: Five Essays*], pp. 219–21. In addition to the essay 'Traditional

and critical theory', this edition contains four others, the most important of which is 'Reason and Self-Preservation' (1942). There are several good collections of Horkheimer's work in English. In addition to the articles in Arato and Gebhardt, see Horkheimer's *Critical Theory: Selected Essays* and *The Critique of Instrumental Reason*. Some of his more important essays are also included in Bronner and Kellner, *Critical Theory and Society: A Reader*.

10 This rift between Lukács and the Frankfurt School subsequently became unbridgeable with the publication of Benjamin's *Paris Arcades Project* and Horkheimer and Adorno's *Dialectic of Enlightenment*. While the idea that the modern productive apparatus casts a kind of mythological spell on its participants is developed in the former, the thesis that this mythology is older than capitalism and even more difficult to overcome than suggested by Benjamin is defended in the latter.

11 Adorno's lectures at the University of Frankfurt on negative dialectics and freedom repeatedly make this point in relation to Kant (see also note 14 below). He shows that while there can be no epistemological inquiry that completely abstracts from sociology after the discoveries of Hegel and Marx about the social and historical foundations of knowledge, it is also impossible to rely on Hegel and Marx's progressive view of the historical process. See Adorno, *Vorlesung über negative Dialektik* [*Lectures on Negative Dialectics*], pp. 170–71. The volume, which contains 25 lectures, is currently being translated into English and other languages.

12 Adorno, *Drei Studien zu Hegel* [*Hegel: Three Studies*]; Marcuse, 'A note on the dialectic', in Arato and Gebhardt, *The Essential Frankfurt School Reader*, pp. 444–51, and Marx, 'Theses on Feuerbach' , in Marx and Engels, *The German Ideology*, pp. 121–23.

13 Adorno, 'Erpresste Versöhnung' (usually translated as 'Reconciliation under duress') in *Noten zur Literatur* [*Notes on Literature*], pp. 251–80. Any attempt to reconstruct the history of the left since Marx will have difficulties coming to any definitive conclusion on the relative merits of the practical political positions adopted by the theorists and political militants of Western Marxism and those taken up by the Frankfurt School from 1920 until Adorno's death in 1969. The periodic support of Stalinism on the part of figures like Lukács (as well as Bloch, Brecht, Sartre and others) seems to be as problematic as the occasional academic aloofness of the Institute for Social Research. Some people may find Adorno's radio broadcasts in the 1950s and 1960s, which are rich in pedagogical and political suggestions for political policy innovation, to offer a potential way out of the impasse. These can be obtained from the Frankfurter Rundfunk (radio) archives. See Wil Kuo, 'Adorno and Habermas as public figures'.

14 Marcuse, 'Philosophie und kritische Theorie' ['Philosophy and critical theory'] in *Kultur und Gesellschaft I* [*Culture and Society*], Frankfurt, Suhrkamp, 1965, pp. 112–16, and *Konterrevolution und Revolte* [*Counter-revolution and Revolt*], Frankfurt, Suhrkamp, 1972, pp. 87–89. See also Benjamin, 'Über das Programm der kommenden Philosophie' ['On the coming philosophy'] (1918) in *Angelus Novus* [*Reflections*], pp. 27–36. While Marcuse and Benjamin suggest that it is not a rejection of Kant that is needed, but rather a radicalisation of idealism that points towards Marx and revolution, Adorno is more interested in Kant's notion that all knowledge is mediated and conditioned. The implication is that there can be no credible philosophy of origins or essences, which in political

terms implies that there can be no 'pure' sources of culture or the state. See Adorno's ideas on idealism in the concluding pages of *Zur Metakritik der Erkentntnistheorie: Studien über Husserl und die phänomenologischen Antinomien* [*Against Epistemology*], written in exile in Oxford during 1934–37 and dedicated to Max Horkheimer), pp. 234–35 and Adorno's lectures on Kant contained in *Kant's Critique of Pure Reason*. It should be mentioned in this context that right from the outset Adorno was undoubtedly more pessimistic than most of the other members of the Institute about the revolutionary potential of the working class. In contrast to Horkheimer, however, who in the 1950s and 1960s became an exponent of traditional values, Adorno never became a conservative thinker.

15 Attempts to transgress the limits of subjectivity and conventional notions of what constitutes thinking are rarely found amongst conservative and right-wing thinkers. The great exception is of course Heidegger's critique of Western subjectivity and metaphysics, and many people have argued that Heidegger actually paves the way for thinkers like Sartre and Derrida. A considerable portion of *Negative Dialectics* is concerned with taking up and refuting Heidegger's solution to the problems of idealism and phenomenology. See *Negative Dialectics*, Part I.

16 Adorno is probably the most sympathetic to Nietzsche's aesthetic epistemology amongst the Institute's members. See his *Ästhetische Theorie* [*Aesthetic Theory*] (published posthumously), pp. 55–56, pp. 198–200, and *Negative Dialektik* [*Negative Dialectics*], pp. 50–51, as well as Horkheimer, 'Zum Begriff der Philosophie' ['On the concept of philosophy'] in Horkheimer, *Gesammelte Schriften*, Vol. 6, pp. 175–82, and Horkheimer's article 'On the problem of truth' in Arato and Gebhardt, *The Essential Frankfurt School Reader*, pp. 424–25. *Aesthetic Theory* is now available in English, published by Continuum, London, 1997. The translator is Robert Hullot-Kentor, who also provides an instructive introduction.

17 The possibility of immanence is rearticulated by the poststructuralist left in the 1960s and 1970s, especially in France. Nietzsche and Spinoza are invoked against Hegel and, by implication, much of Western Marxism, as will be seen in Chapter 6.

18 Horkheimer, *Traditionelle und Kritische Theorie: Fünf Aufsätze* [*Traditional and Critical Theory: Five Essays*], pp. 230–32. Neumann and Kirchheimer are theorists of politics and law connected with the Institute. Their ideas are looked at briefly later in this chapter.

19 Hermeneutics is the practice of interpreting texts. It is often associated with holy and legal texts, where the meaning of God and the legislator is not unequivocal and therefore is in need of interpretive elucidation. The term is also associated with a series of debates about the methodological specificity of historical understanding and the human as opposed to the natural sciences. One might begin to think about critical hermeneutics in terms of a form of inquiry that asks questions about the *absence* of God and the absence of the conditions of noninstrumental knowledge, nonpunitive forms of justice, etc., without necessarily positing the permanent *nonexistence* of such phenomena. That which is nonidentical to what actually exists may be absent and recoverable rather than simply transcended or fictional.

20 Adorno's critique of Bergson and Husserl is found in *Against Epistemology*. The critique of Heidegger is in *Negative Dialectics* and *The Jargon of Authenticity*. That Husserl was himself aware of the stakes involved in this crisis of epistemology

is clear in his last work, *The Crisis of the European Sciences and Transcendental Philosophy* (1938).

21 Adorno, *Negative Dialektik* [*Negative Dialectics*], p. 1. Benjamin expounds a closely related view in the 'Critique of violence' (1921) and his *Theses on the philosophy of history* (1940), where he suggests that humanity will always live in a permanent state of extra-legal exception until the day legal norms cease to legitimise force. Only by transcending forms of law that are expressions of an arbitrary will to power given the semblance of juridical objectivity might it be possible to do justice to all of the victims, dead and alive, of legally mediated violence. If the feudal-aristocratic order at least has the virtue of being transparently hierarchical, modern law is particularly insidious in that it legislates as if people with radically different lives, such as capitalists and workers, are equal and must be treated identically. This is an example of how what Adorno refers to as identity thinking is translated into oppressive social, political and economic institutions. See Benjamin, 'The critique of violence' in *Reflections*, and his 'Theses on the philosophy of history' in *Illuminations*. The possibility that there is a critical hermeneutic which recovers what is nonidentical to what actually exists is an idea that runs throughout Adorno's *Negative Dialectics* and *Aesthetic Theory*.

22 The *Paris Arcades Project* can be seen as Benjamin's most systematic attempt to demonstrate how it might be possible to make ruins visible before they actually become ruins, which can be likened to his dictum that what he wants to do is to read and make readable what has never been written. Benjamin suggests that Freud makes readable what has never been written in his *Interpretation of Dreams* (1900), by analysing a dream and giving it a written form. In the *Arcades Project* Benjamin examines the sudden appearance of the commercial centres lodged in covered passages during Haussmann's rationalisation of the structure of Paris. Without being written phenomena as such, one can 'read' the passages allegorically as a text about the inevitable fate of an immense apparatus of production designed to perpetuate scarcity and myth rather than eliminate need and put an end to mythological explanations of human suffering.

23 There are generally two ways in which the term 'historicism' is used. One suggests that there is something specific about each historical époque and its forms of knowledge. The other posits that historical process is shaped by patterns and processes which in the natural sciences one might call laws, bearing in mind that the word law might be implicitly too mechanical to be applied to history.

24 See Benjamin's 'Über das Programm der kommenden Philosophie' ['On the coming philosophy'] and 'The critique of violence', and Adorno's *Kant's Critique of Pure Reason*.

25 Freud certainly provides added evidence of the traumatic character of modern experience, though his contribution to a critical theory of society is somewhat limited by the fact that he tends to assume a static individual human nature that *inevitably* conflicts with the hierarchical and bureaucratic demands of social organisation, regardless of the relations of production and the level of development of the productive forces. From this perspective Simmel's work is of potentially greater interest. In *The Philosophy of Money* (1900) and other works he follows Marx in illustrating what is qualitatively new about experience in

modern industrial societies, and remains open to the possibility that the structure of experience can and does change. See also Frisby, *Fragments of Modernity*, Chapter 2.

26 Each member of the Institute proposes different ways of facing those challenges. For example, Fromm is confident that a creative reinterpretation of Marx and Freud can provide the bases of a humanist response to Soviet state socialism and American consumer capitalism. Marcuse thinks that new social subjects such as women and ethnic minorities will reinvigorate the political life of advanced western societies. Benjamin suggests that the end of integral experience opens up the possibility of galvanising popular revolutionary energies which have been lulled into submission by the oppressive weight of the aura of traditional forms of art (see below). In the music of the Viennese composer Arnold Schönberg (1874–1951) Adorno intuits the possibility of a new musical culture beyond the framework of tonality and, with it, new vistas in aesthetic experience. Habermas argues that colonisation of noninstrumental communication by the economy and the systems of political and administrative control can be held in check and perhaps even reversed by defending the prerogatives of the public sphere in civil society. These details must be borne in mind when discussing the famous pessimism of the Frankfurt School.

27 Marcuse, *Konterrevolution und Revolte* [*Counter-Revolution and Revolt*], pp. 84–89; Adorno, *Kants Kritik der reinen Vernunft* [*Kant's Critique of Pure Reason*], pp. 313–20, and 'Zu Subjekt und Objekt' ['On subject and object'] in *Stichworte: Kritische Modelle 2* [*Critical Models*], pp. 151–68, also contained in Arato and Gebhardt, *The Frankfurt School Reader*.

28 *The Paris Arcades Project* addresses the possibility of making ruins visible before they become ruins, 'reading' the city as a text, i.e. reading something that has never been written. The 'Theses on the philosophy of history' (1940) discuss the possibility of a tiger's leap into the past, as well as 'nowtime' (Jetztzeit), a moment where different dimensions of time are united and freeze in a moment of messianic visibility. There are a number of interpretations of his work that admirably elucidate these issues. See Caygill, *Walter Benjamin* and Jacobson, *Metaphysics of the Profane*, as well as Hollis, 'Walter Benjamin'.

29 Benjamin, 'The work of art in the age of mechanical reproduction', in *Illuminations*. For Benjamin truth is synonymous with the word of God expressed in a meta-language in which the arbitrary relation between signifier and signified is transcended. In his work this transcendence is articulated in a unique synthesis of Marxist materialism and messianic theology in which revolution is also a restoration of the truthful, i.e., divine, relation between words and things.

30 Friedrich Pollock, 'State capitalism: its possibilities and limitations', in Arato and Gebhardt, *The Essential Frankfurt School Reader*, pp. 71–72.

31 Here one clearly sees the political relevance of the discussion of epistemology in Chapters 1 and 2 as well as the political importance of subject/object relations in Kant, Hegel, Marx, Marcuse and Adorno. See Kirchheimer, 'Changes in the structure of political compromise' in Arato and Gebhardt, *The Essential Frankfurt School Reader*, pp. 52–57. One can analyse new social movements as an attempt to create organisational forms pointing beyond Leninist militarism and academic abstraction. This issue will be taken up in Chapter 6.

32 Kirchheimer, 'Changes in the structure of political compromise', pp. 63–65; Arendt, *The Human Condition*, Section 3; Habermas, *Legitimation Crisis*.

33 Otto Kirchheimer, 'Bemerkungen zu Carl Schmitts *Legalität und Legitimität*' (`Remarks on Carl Schmitt's Legality and Legitimacy'), in Wolfgang Luthardt (ed.), *Von der Weimarer Republik zum Faschismus* [*From the Weimar Republic to Fascism*], pp. 113–25. Kirchheimer's essay is contained in Scheuerman, *The Rule of Law under Siege*. Kirchheimer and Neumann's main ideas are very well explained in Scheuerman, *Between the Norm and the Exception*, and Thornhill, *Political Theory in Modern Germany*, Chapter 3. Both books also deal with the complex issue of Kirchheimer and Neumann's relation with Schmitt's ideas on law, sovereignty and the state of exception. For an analysis of German fascism see Neumann, *Behemoth*.

34 Marcuse, Foreword to Pross, *Franz Neumann, Demokratischer und autoritärer Staat* [*Franz Neumann, The Democratic and Authoritarian State*], pp. 5–8. English versions of Neumann's most important essays in political theory are included in Scheuerman, *The Rule of Law under Siege*.

35 Neumann, 'Der Funktionswandel des Gesetzes im Recht der bürgerlichen Gesellschaft' ['The change in the function of law in modern society'] in Pross, *Franz Neumann, Demokratischer und autoritärer Staat*, pp. 31–32.

36 Ibid., pp. 52–57. Another key essay is Neumann's 'The concept of political freedom' (1953), now in William Scheuerman (ed.), *The Rule of Law under Siege*, pp. 195–230.

37 Kant, 'Beantwortung der Frage: Was ist Aufklärung?' ['In answer to the question: what is enlightenment?'] in Weischedel, *Immanuel Kant*, p. 54, and 'Zum ewigen Frieden' ['Perpetual Peace'] in the same volume, p. 241. Both essays are contained in Reiss, *Kant: Political Writings*.

38 Habermas, *The Structural Transformation of the Public Sphere*, Part IV, *Knowledge and Human Interests*, pp. 25–35, and *Between the Facts and the Norms*, pp. 350–60.

4
Building Networks Instead of Pyramids: Syndicalism, Council Communism, Libertarian Socialism and Anarchism

Common to the various theories and movements considered in this chapter is the conviction that the ideal of democracy as self-government is thwarted in equal measure by capitalism and the sovereign state. This view distinguishes the militants associated with syndicalism, council communism, libertarian socialism and anarchism from liberal democrats, social democrats and other supporters of parliamentary democracy. But it also sets them apart from the Bolsheviks and others who are at times willing to underwrite excesses of state power and restrictions on freedom of expression and assembly in the defence of a supposedly legitimate socialist state against which protest is by definition counter-revolutionary. The libertarian currents examined in this chapter set great store by the implicit anarchism of the young Marx. In various ways they share his intuition that the answer to the riddle of overcoming capitalism is somehow linked with the project of establishing more thoroughly democratic forms of political community than parliamentary democracy. The ideal of workers' self-government, or *autogestion,* as it is referred to in French, expresses the aspiration to take the liberal notion of individual autonomy and extend it to a much wider array of collective social action than merely officially recognised political institutions. In the first instance this usually means the factory, field or office, in other words, the workplace understood in the widest sense as the site where humanity transforms nature in order to solve its needs as well as to create the bases of political freedom by overcoming natural necessity. It is in this respect too that the movements considered here share the young Marx's conviction that in order correctly to diagnose social oppression and to launch a libertarian movement of resistance against oppressive social relations, one must be radical in the precise Latin sense of going to the root of the matter. In general theoretical terms, being radical means addressing the question of the economy and the legal relations of ownership that stamp a particular character on the human transformation of nature in the labour process operative in a given epoch. In specific historical terms, it means resisting capitalist exploitation in ways that point beyond social democratic reformism and Bolshevik authoritarianism. For the theoretical orientation of many of the thinkers looked at in this chapter Marx is clearly a central point of reference. Yet these thinkers are also aware that Marx is not always directly relevant in terms of specific historical struggles directed against capitalism, liberalism and fascism on the one hand, and against the manipulation of the revolutionary workers' movement by the forces of social democracy and Bolshevism on the other.[1]

The main problem with social democracy is that with its emphasis on redistribution it is not radical enough. Although social democratic traditions vary a great deal from country to country, social democracy everywhere is constantly confronted with the problem that when the capitalist economy slows, redistributive measures are considered to be luxuries that have to be limited. Bolshevism is radical, by contrast, but by concentrating power in the communist party and the party's control of the state apparatus and economy, it wins a largely pyrrhic victory over capitalist exploitation. Replacing the prerogatives of capitalist managers with the prerogatives of communist central planners turns out to be a highly inadequate way of challenging the power of private capital over social labour.[2] Hence a central issue in libertarian politics is ascertaining ways of overcoming the problems of social democratic reformism and redistribution without relying on a centralised; hierarchical and authoritarian political party like the one the CPSU became after Lenin's death in 1924. In this search for an alternative to the parliamentary state and the communist party, a variety of institutions and organisations have been tested. These include the syndicalist and anarcho-syndicalist trade union, the anarchist and republican commune, the communist factory council, and the guild, to name but a few.[3]

By way of introduction to the central themes of Chapter 4, one can quickly summarise the trajectory of this book so far as follows. With his ideas on human emancipation, political economy, and history, Marx lays the theoretical foundations of the revolutionary left in Europe. Albeit in very different ways, Western Marxists and the critical theorists of the Frankfurt school respond to the problems of historical materialism, Soviet authoritarianism, fascism and the planned capitalism of post-war Western Europe by turning their attention to questions of consciousness, epistemology and culture not directly or not adequately addressed by Marx. In Chapters 2 and 3 it is seen that Marx's theories, however profound and wide-ranging, leave a number of important questions unanswered. Foremost among these is the proper relation between theory and practice. Moreover, apart from some rather cursory pronouncements in favour of the Paris Commune, there is relatively little in Marx concerning concrete practical alternatives to capitalism and the parliamentary state. Rather than continuing the work on consciousness and culture characteristic of Western Marxism and critical theory, the libertarians looked at in this chapter take up the issues of resistance and institutional organisation first raised by trade unions, social democratic parties and the Bolsheviks. As will be seen, they do this in markedly antisocial-democratic and anti-Bolshevik terms. While the Jacobins and later the Bolsheviks prove that the political party can be a very effective means of seizing power, social democracy establishes the efficacy of the party as a reformist tool for moderate redistribution and change. But while social democracy is usually forced to become a 'responsible' party of discipline and austerity in periods of economic stagnation, Jacobinism, Bolshevism and related movements tend to concentrate authority in the organs of a political party whose *raison d'être* becomes the consolidation of its own power rather than the democratisation of society. Beginning with syndicalism, this chapter focuses on theories and movements that seek to translate Marx's critique of capitalism into practice by enhancing Marxism with a critique of the party as a form of collective action as well as enriching it with a critique of the state as an instance of coerced reconciliation between citizens.

Moving Democracy into the Workplace: Syndicalism and Council Communism

Syndicalism attempts to transform the trade union from a defensive institution concentrating on the protection of wages and hours into a vehicle for the expansion of democracy beyond a disembodied parliamentary political sphere removed from the realities of production. Although the process of industrialisation produced syndicalist movements throughout Europe, including England, Scotland and Ireland, syndicalism has tended to be strongest in France, Italy and Spain.[4] In France the movement was born as a revolt against the French Socialist Party (PSF). Like other socialist parties in Europe at this time, such as the Labour Party in England, the SPD in Germany, the PSI in Italy and so on, the PSF can be seen as a precursor of modern social democracy. The French revolutionary syndicalists rejected the reformist policies of the PSF leaders Jean Jaurès (1859–1914), Jules Guesde (1845–1922) and Alexandre Millerand (1859–1943), who at the beginning of the twentieth century argue that there should be a parliamentary victory in the battle of democracy alluded to by Marx in the *Communist Manifesto* of 1848. Jaurès suggests that the working class can win the battle of democracy through proper education and social legislation aimed at the gradual erosion of the extra-parliamentary power of the bourgeoisie. He maintains that if the aims of Enlightenment required a revolution in 1789, they now require a lucid and consistent political programme based on extension of the franchise, redistribution of wealth, and parliamentary control of the state executive. To many militants in the French labour movement this gradualist approach seemed to constitute an abandonment of what Marx refers to as human emancipation in his early writings, and is challenged with particular vigour by Fernand Pelloutier (1867–1901) and Georges Sorel (1847–1922).

Pelloutier opposed the PSF conception of socialism as being attainable as a result of a series of state-sponsored reforms. He evolves from republicanism to Marxism, and from there to the view that revolutionary syndicalism is the correct doctrine of working-class emancipation. His most effective theoretical interventions came in the form of articles written in the journal *L'ouvrier des deux mondes* (*The Worker of the Two Worlds*) between February 1897 and June 1899. This journalistic activity complemented his active participation in the *Bourses du Travail* (most approximately translated as Labour Exchange). His defence of the *Bourses* stems from the belief that if workers try to protect their interests in political parties seeking to push for legislative concessions from a largely bourgeois parliament, they will lose their revolutionary élan to the very extent that they are successful. In order to safeguard its autonomy from the bourgeois social classes, as well as the state that mediates between the bourgeoisie and other classes in the interests of the former, the working class needs its own economic, cultural and educational institutions.

Pelloutier regards the *Bourses* as the germ cell of a new proletarian civilisation. They were created in 1892 as a workers' educational and informational institution providing services ranging from setting up libraries, to running museums of labour history, to founding technical colleges and schools for the education of workers' children. Under his leadership the *Bourses* assumed additional functions, including the provision of information about finding employment, how to gain membership in the *syndicats* (unions) and consumer co-operatives, as well as how to battle employers in strike situations where one could not count on state neutrality. Where possible the *Bourses* attempted to publish their own newspapers and disseminate information about the labour market, employment opportunities and possible access to money set aside for strikers.[5]

In Pelloutier's view the *Bourses* strive to make the workers independent and dynamic. They help construct a new centre of authority outside and in opposition to the existing 'democratic' parliamentary state of the day. He thinks that workers schooled in the *Bourses* represent the image of the future socialist—the emancipated producer—which the social democratic socialists had abandoned in their search to integrate the working class into the mainstream of society. He hopes that once educated in their own institutions, the producers will forge a new system of values that have nothing in common with what he perceives to be the bourgeois obsession with calculability, utility, comfort and personal gain. If it were somehow possible to create maximum autonomy from what Gramsci refers to as the exercise of hegemony, then technical skills, discipline and the spirit of sacrifice could be used to forge the political institutions for the social emancipation of labour. The leaders of the producing classes might then generate a political elite capable of educating the whole of society in the duties demanded by the rigours of a producers' civilisation able to dispense with party systems, personality cults and oppressive state bureaucracies. The *Bourses* were thus meant to mediate between state and civil society in a democratic and participatory fashion capable of catapulting humanity beyond the twin poles of liberal bourgeois atomism on the one hand, and the already anticipated problems of a collectivist, i.e. state socialist, remedy to capitalism on the other.[6]

Pelloutier maintains that although the trade unions and the *Bourses* are indispensable for the realisation of the self-government of the producers, in his estimation they are distinct institutions with separate functions. The unions have the task of establishing the material basis of a democratic civil society. In addition to co-ordinating production within a given sector of the economy, it is the job of the unions to send representatives to the *Bourses*. The *Bourses* in their turn have the task of co-ordinating efforts between different sectors of production, and function in the manner of decentralised planning bodies. In contrast to corporatist arrangements introducing an element of planning to co-ordinate production and consumption within a capitalist framework geared towards private profit and immediate accumulation, however, planning here is accomplished in the spirit of egalitarian harmonisation of technical knowledge, individual and collective need, and long-term capacity for growth and development. The failure of the French syndicalists to produce their own equivalent of Marx's *Capital* is not such a problem as it might seem, since they always stress that action (practice) rather than analysis (theory) would bring down capitalism and parliamentarianism. The movement bequeathed its clearest statement of principles and aims in the Charter of Amiens, drawn up in accordance with the resolutions of the Amiens Congress of 1906. At this meeting they declare their hostility towards parliamentary reform, socialist politicians, and anything that departs from the goals of the revolutionary trade union movement. The following excerpt from the text of the charter is of particular importance for a general understanding of syndicalism:

In the daily fight, syndicalism pursues the co-ordination of workers' struggles, and the increase of working class welfare through the achievement of immediate reforms such as decrease in the hours of the working day, increased salaries, etc. . . . But this task is only one aspect of syndicalism, which also prepares the ground for complete emancipation. This can only be realised by the expropriation of the capitalists through the General Strike. The trade union, which today is a defensive institution, will be, in the future, the basis of production, distribution, and the reorganisation of society.[7]

The General Strike, understood as the immediate unity of theory and practise, is also a salient feature of the social and political ideas of Georges Sorel.[8] A civil engineer by training, his first major foray into political theory came near the beginning of the twentieth century, when he participated in the debates on the crisis of Marxism with Benedetto Croce, Antonio Labriola and Eduard Bernstein. The apparent discrepancy between Marxism's aspiration to offer a scientific theory of history and society and the failure of its most important predictions sparked a raging controversy throughout Europe (see Chapter 2). In the course of these debates Sorel argued that Marxism's scientific rigour must be complemented with a theory of socialist intransigence and revolutionary ethics appropriate for the era of the Industrial Revolution, increasing urbanisation and secularisation. This emphasis on action is not articulated in anticipation of Lukács's theory of reification, Sartre's notion of authenticity or Adorno's theory of reconciliation. Sorel wishes to retain Marx's emphasis on materialism and science, but he is also convinced that social action is the result of a complex network of drives, emotions and collective projections fuelled by the imagination rather than class interest. In fact, he maintains that if class interest were to become the basis of Marxist politics, socialism would surely degenerate into the business of a reformist or spuriously 'revolutionary' party of professional politicians removed from the real site of history—the workplace and production. In 1896 he began contributing to the journal *Le Devenir Social* (*The Social Process*). During the months of October to December of that year he wrote his 'Study of Vico', in which he attempts to supplement historical materialism with his interpretation of Vico's conception of history as a cyclical process in which dominant and subaltern groups struggle to impose their way of life and values on all of society. For Sorel this imposition is not realised or thwarted exclusively on the basis of force or interest. He argues that symbolic rituals and mythical representations are more powerful spurs to sacrifice and heroic deeds than economic calculations of interest.[9]

As Sorel became increasingly doubtful about the scientific status of Marxism, the labour theory of value, and the theory of causality suggested by the base and superstructure model of historical explanation, he insisted that the working class must abandon rational-legal approaches to the struggle for socialism in favour of a mythical-poetic approach. As in the example of Christianity, the birth of new civilisations is seen to come about as a result of revolutions in values. Replacing liberal bourgeois parliamentary representatives with the likes of Jaurès or Guesde or Millerand was insufficient to achieve the scope of change Sorel and other revolutionary syndicalists had in mind. The future revolution would have to be an intellectual and moral reform affecting the daily existence of each individual producer. This entails not only the transformation of political and economic macro-structures and institutions; it involves new ways of looking at art and creating, conceiving of friendship and understanding death. In Sorel's estimation the proletarian revolution will change our most basic understanding of the world and experience, and as such, in order to prepare the ground the working class must remain strictly separate from the bourgeoisie and all its corrupt institutions. In the journal *L'humanité nouvelle* (*The New Humanity*) at the beginning of the twentieth century Sorel wrote a series of articles entitled 'The socialist future of the unions', in which he asserted that the key to the foundation of a proletarian civilisation lay in a return to the healthy spirit of primitive humanity, which had not yet learned to see the world in terms of profit and self-interest. The right institutions and myths could recreate this primordial vitality. He argues that the working class needs its own myth—the General Strike—to return humanity to its recurrent instinctual and intuitive understanding of reality. For Sorel and his followers in France, Italy, Spain and elsewhere, the General Strike represents the purest expression of the proletariat's determination irrevocably to break with the bourgeois social order in order to establish its own autonomous system of law and ethics.[10]

In 'The socialist future of the unions' and other essays and books, Sorel stresses that proletarian ethics of solidarity and collective action cannot simply be produced by taking control of the means of production—especially if this is by nationalisation or other forms of state ownership. He shares Marx's view that there can be no real equality where people can be represented abstractly as equal citizens in a sphere designated as political, while in their life as producers they are exploited in a supposedly private sphere designated as socioeconomic. The democratic parliamentary state aggregates a sum total of individual votes, as if society is comprised of separate atoms, each with its own interest. In principle, there is nothing essentially capitalist about parliamentary democracy: majorities can decide to legislate major changes in the economic system and the class structure. Yet in Sorel's view the syndicalist should insist that social classes are the constituent element of a given mode of production. Marx points out that the mode of production provides the key to understanding forms of political representation, social structure, ideology and aesthetics, i.e. what he refers to as the totality of social relations constituted by humanity's interaction with nature. Reformists like Kautsky and Jaurès ignore Marx's theory of totality as well as his analysis of the Paris Commune by suggesting that one can really change society by occupying positions of power within the existing state apparatus. Even an overwhelming socialist parliamentary majority could do relatively little to change the relations of production and the power of capital decisively to shape the labour process, since the state was created to preserve the power relations particular to a given mode of production in the first place. Thus even if in principle there is nothing essentially capitalist about the democratic parliamentary state, in reality one must change the economy and the state in one swoop, so to speak, rather than trying in vain to superimpose political changes on existing forms of economy. From a contemporary syndicalist perspective on French politics, one could say that this is the crucial limitation of social democracy from Jaurès and Millerand to Mitterand (1916–96). In the eyes of its supporters yesterday and today, syndicalism is revolutionary because it steadfastly refuses to divorce questions of political reform from strategies for worker control of the economy.

Syndicalists in Italy studied Sorel carefully and found that his ideas had direct application to Italian realities. Like the PSF, the PSI (Italian Socialist Party) hoped that the battle of democracy could be won by reforming capitalism in a socialist direction and, like the PSF, the PSI seemed to suppose that there is an invisible but real continuum between increasing political democratisation and the establishment of a socialised economy. Although neither the French nor the Italian syndicalists ever made reference to Alexis de Tocqueville, they could easily have made good use of Tocqueville's *Democracy in America* (1843), in which he shows that the culture of democracy is more likely to foster social conformism and a striving for private material welfare than a concern for the public good or *autogestion*. The Italian syndicalists challenged this continuum theory and approved of Sorel's thesis that, together with co-operative societies and credit associations, the trade union contains within it the embryonic bases of a new society. They agree that wrestling with the state for reform of the existing socioeconomic system is bound to produce passivity amongst the working classes. But with the formation of the Italian Confederation of Trade Unions (CGL, the parallel organisation to the French CGT and the Spanish CFT) in 1906 and its formal separation from the PSI, Italian socialism in practice amounted to CGL demands for reform of capitalism's excesses, which the PSI would then seek to enact in the form of parliamentary legislation. This strategy is subjected to a cogent critique by Arturo Labriola (1873–1959) in *The History of Ten Years: 1899–1909*.[12]

Labriola's book illustrates how the South of Italy became a virtual colony for the raw material and manpower needs of the industrial north of the country. He explains that the south was assailed by four chronic problems: illiteracy; poor communication and transport links between the cities and the countryside; the perennial existence of a mass of poor peasants; and the power of the large southern landowners over the southern peasants. Rather than helping to solve these problems, the Italian state passed measures to alleviate southern misery, but never challenged the right of the landowners to exploit the peasants. The prime minister of the time, Giovanni Giolitti (1842–1928) had correctly guessed that if workers' wages in the north could be kept artificially high through selective tariff protection, the revolutionary demands of the industrial working class could be co-opted within the decidedly nonrevolutionary parliamentary channels of the PSI. The fact that such tariffs made it difficult for the southern peasants to export their products was not a problem for the Italian political class as long as Giolitti made sure that landowner profit levels remained high. Political leaders from various parties thus made deals on legislation which carefully subordinated northern labour to the needs of northern capital, whilst at the same time ensuring that southern labour was marginalised to the benefit of southern land-owning interests. It was thus abundantly clear to Labriola and other Italian syndicalists that Marx's analysis in the *Eighteeth Brumaire* offered a reliable theoretical barometer for measuring extra-parliamentary power. Just as in the France of Louis Bonaparte, the real political questions in Giolitti's Italy were being negotiated by nonelected actors; by the time the questions were formally voted on in parliament they were already largely settled in actual practice. This manifest reality made any notion of a parliamentary road to socialism in Italy seem naive, if not outright hopeless.[13]

Syndicalists in Italy were thus not attracted to the PSI version of reformist socialism, nor were they in favour of any kind of full-scale state socialist management of industry, as the Bolsheviks were to propose after 1917 in Russia and elsewhere. They were far more interested in a synthesis of Marx on the Paris Commune and Sorel on the revolutionary potential of the trade union. The political form for the economic emancipation of labour was the Commune, as Marx had argued. In opposition to Marx's scattered proposals for a planned economy, however, the economic content of a repoliticised civil society was to be realised in the union, as Sorel had vehemently argued. In *Syndicalism and Reformism* (1905), Labriola expresses his misgivings about state socialism in the following terms:

> . . . the substitution of state ownership for private ownership does not abolish the capitalist system of production. This system is distinguished by the separation of owners of the means of production and wage owners. Instead, syndicalism seeks to create an autonomous and worker-controlled system of production which eliminates the distinctions between producers and owners of the means of production. With the passage of private industry to the state, the state bureaucracy replaces the capitalist, and the worker remains a wage-earner.[14]

Labriola and others believed that if the new socialist economy were organised by self-managed firms on a trade union basis, local communes could tend to the political needs of the community. These communes would have little in common with existing government bodies, since for the most part social life would be centred on the trade union, sport, and other decentralised but collective activities rather than the family, individual consumption and private enterprise. Like Pelloutier and Sorel in France, Italian and Spanish syndicalists think that once the state is abolished, society can re-absorb most of the political functions of the central state. At the same time, they argue that the unions will cease to perform the defensive tasks that they do in capitalism, in order to become affirmative centres of education, technical training and the cultivation of new forms of art and friendship. For a series of reasons which will be explained below, a different group of militants also in support of *autogestion* argue that the factory council is an institution much better suited than the union to assume a positive role in the fight against capitalist oppression.[15]

Interest in the council as an alternative to the union and the party goes all the way back to the Paris Commune and Marx's discussion of it in *The Civil War in France*. This interest was renewed in 1905 with 'the first Russian Revolution', as it was called, in which workers' and soldiers' *soviets* (councils) played a major role in challenging the legitimacy of the increasingly fragile Tsarist autocracy. The revolution forced the autocracy to acknowledge the principle of parliamentary representation, and as a result, to recognise the first Duma (parliament) in 1906. In Germany, the Jena Conference of the SPD took place amidst the great excitement aroused by the Russian events. The conference participants celebrated the resurgence of the council as what they considered the paradigmatic institution of direct democracy. For the first time in the history of German social democracy the reformist positions of the trade unions came in for harsh criticism. In her contribution to the conference debates, Rosa Luxemburg combined an incisive critique of the unions with a cogent argument explaining why the SPD itself could only play a limited role in a truly democratic revolutionary movement. In 'The mass strike, the party and the trade unions' she expresses her admiration for the militancy of the relatively young and inexperienced Russian working class and criticises the conservative tendencies inherent in the German trade union and party bureaucracies. Although Luxemburg never outlined a detailed theory of council democracy, she articulated the premise that was to become a central tenet for all council communists: the revolution would not succeed until the working classes created their own institutional forms of radical democracy in which they were not subjected to the bureaucratic prerogatives of professional intellectuals in unions, parties and universities.

In other words, they had to learn the art of self-government and collective autonomy by practising it themselves.[16]

Luxemburg argues that the unions and party bureaucracies had become patrons of reformist socialist officialdom. In virtually all advanced capitalist economies these relatively privileged members of the working class develop an interest in maintaining the social order and the advantages of secure employment and comparatively high wages it offers them. In opposition to the tendency of the union and the party to act as a break on revolutionary activity, she advocates the mass strike, which can be regarded as the council communist equivalent of the syndicalist General Strike. She is not opposed to political parties in principle, and she accepts the continuing necessity for a party that provides a certain amount of ideological guidance to the struggle for human emancipation. But she strongly opposes the views of Kautsky, Jaurès and Turati which, she argues, encourage workers of Germany, France, Italy and elsewhere to believe that the revolution can be won through a succession of parliamentary reforms. In her estimation the Russian developments of 1905 indicate that working-class spontaneity can overcome the lethargic politics of European social democracy. Hence the immediate task of the left entering the twentieth century is to spread support for the mass strike and the cultural and political consciousness necessary for council democracy. In fact the choice was stark: prepare for revolution, or face a tremendous reaction on the part of the propertied classes. Why was this reaction foreseeable long before Mussolini's March on Rome in Italy and the demise of the Weimar Republic in Germany? A brief word below about the council communist theory of structural transformation illustrates the radical and prescient character of council communist analysis in these years.[17]

The debate between Luxemburg and Kautsky was fought out in the most important theoretical journal of the SPD, the *Neue Zeit* (*New Age*), in the years following 1905, until the Dutch Marxist Anton Pannekoek wrote *Marxist Theory and Revolutionary Tactics* and *Mass Action and Revolution* in 1912. In opposition to Kautsky's call for steady but gradual reform, Pannekoek argues that in the age of nationalist colonialism and militaristic capitalist imperialism, industrial workers struggle to find more radical forms of organisational solidarity than the party or union. Institutions like the council are more radical precisely because they are potentially capable of accelerating the revolutionary process towards complete self-management in the workplace. The leitmotiv of Pannekoek's work is that it is imperative to accelerate this drive toward *autogestion* in the era of imperialism, lest the antistatist movement for industrial democracy be absorbed within the parties and unions of the existing state. Pannekoek thus anticipates Kirchheimer's view that following the Industrial Revolution there is a structural transformation from free market capitalism regulated by the 'minimal' state, to planned capitalism armoured by an interventionist state at home and an expansionist state abroad. The transformation occurs at different rates and with different intensity depending on the country in question. Since Germany and Italy were largely excluded from the imperialist quest for colonies at this time, the contradictions inherent in this structural transformation were particularly acute. As a result, the response was all the more radical, both in terms of council offensive in the workplace as well as capitalist affirmation of the right to direct the labour process.[18]

World War I marked a profound crisis in European society and a catastrophic moment for the European left in the twentieth century. Two details are highly significant. First, with the exception of the PSI, social democratic parties supported their respective governments, thus opting for national chauvinism rather than international solidarity. Second, the social democratic failure to adopt an internationalist perspective helped pave the way for a three-way split between social democrats, libertarians, and Bolshevik-style communists. The Zimmerwald Conference forms the background to this split. In 1916 a group of Italian and Swiss socialists called for a meeting of all socialists remaining intransigently opposed to the war. The conference was attended by Lenin, among others, and was held in the Swiss mountain village of Zimmerwald from 8 to 15 September of that year. The result was the formation of what became known as the 'Zimmerwald Left'. The group declared its commitment to world revolution and its intentions to draft a programme capable of guiding mass action and avoiding the reformist mistakes of the past, which they believed had contributed to widespread popular support for the war effort. In January 1917 an antiwar faction within the SPD was expelled from the party. It subsequently reformed in Bremen in April 1917 with Pannekoek's participation and was initially known as the 'Bremen Left'. In the same month strikes broke out all over Germany, and a workers' council formed in Leipzig which assumed the task of uniting the efforts of striking workers in different industries. In order to combat the efforts of the SPD and reformist trade unions to oppose such initiatives, a network of factory committees with workers of all trades sprang into existence; this network subsequently became the co-ordinating basis of the council movement that took Germany by storm in 1918.[19]

After the abdication of the German Kaiser and the proclamation of a republic in November 1918, the conflict between the new reformist social-democratic government and the left wing of the revolutionary movement centered on the alternative of a constituent assembly and parliamentary system versus a council republic.[20] In March of the following year the Communist Third International (also known as the Comintern) was set up with the explicit purpose of co-ordinating the communist movement on an international scale from what the Bolsheviks hoped would be its new centre—Moscow. Organisational as well as strategic tensions between Soviet Marxism and Western Marxism can be traced in part to the centralising role that Lenin and his comrades wanted to confer upon the Comintern. During the months following March 1919 communication between east and west was impeded by the imperialist blockade of the USSR and the destruction of transport networks caused by the war. These difficulties necessitated the creation of Western European bureaux of the Comintern in Berlin and Amsterdam. The Amsterdam office held its first public conference in 1920 with the express purpose of articulating the future orientation of communists in Western Europe. Although the conference was badly organised and disrupted by the police, the resulting manifesto emphasised the importance of workers' councils in any future victory over capitalism, parliamentary socialism and reformist trade unionism. This programmatic statement of intent came precisely at a time when the Bolsheviks began curbing workplace democracy and insisting on the leading role of the party in the projecting of building communist society. This conflict between Western Marxist and Comintern conceptions was to surface time and again, as will be seen with the example of the Spanish Civil War discussed later in this chapter.[21]

In August 1919, as the factory council movement in Italy began heading for a frontal collision with the PSI and the Italian government, the Bremen Left called for a federation of syndicalist-style (industry-wide) 'workers' unions', which was to co-ordinate its efforts with the German Communist Party (Communist Party of Germany, KPD, founded in January 1918) and the Comintern. The stated aim was the creation of a *Räterepublik* (council republic) in Germany as a preliminary step towards an international federation of councils. The basic unit of each republic would be a council comprising workers of various trades, so that each council represented the greatest possible number of total trades involved in the production process. All of the councils within a city were called upon to federate in local networks, which would in turn send representatives to regional and national level producers' councils. In an article in the Bremen-based *Der Kommunist* (*The Communist*), Pannekoek argues that while traditional trade unions are dominated by a bureaucratic caste, workers' unions challenge the wage system by rejecting the very principle of differential wages for different trades. It is against this background that KPD leader Paul Levi, head of the party since the assassination of Luxemburg and Karl Liebknecht (1871–1919) in January 1919, defended the leading role of the party as a communist vanguard. Levi's stance provoked the formation of the breakaway KAPD (German Communist Workers' Party), which announced a programme of uncompromising opposition to party domination and complacent union officialdom. The party programme of 1920 states:

The Factory committee is the economic precondition for the construction of a communist community. The political form of organisation for a communist community is the council system. The factory committees defend the idea that all power must be exercised by the Executive Committee of the councils.[22]

In the period following the First World War and moving into the early 1920s, Pannekoek's and Gramsci's arguments for council democracy were echoed in the writings of Otto Bauer, Max Adler, Karl Korsch and many others.[23] Co-founding KAPD member Otto Rühle (1874–1943) argues that although the council system witnessed its initial spread and development with the Russian soviets, the movement for radical democracy in Russia was being suppressed by the CPSU. Conflicts between the CPSU and movements for council democracy continued after World War II, most notably in Hungary in 1956. It seems perhaps ironic that council action should be taken against a socialist state. But in reality this illustrates the determination of council activists to reject the political straitjacket represented by having to settle for social democracy as the best possible compromise between state socialism and liberal democracy.[24]

In October 1956 a demonstration against Soviet interference in Poland's internal politics was organised by a group of Hungarian students and intellectuals in the Petöfi circle (named after lyric poet and Hungarian patriot Sandor Petöfi, 1823–49). The demonstration was initially banned, and then permitted at the last minute by the government of Imre Nagy (1896–1958, condemned and eventually executed for his supposed complicity in the events of 1956). In a show of solidarity there ensued a mass walk-out by factory and office workers, many of whom formed committees to express their views on the Russian military presence in Poland and Hungary. In the city of Miskole a council was elected consisting of delegates from the various factories in the city. The delegates held a variety of political viewpoints but were nonetheless united in their intention to launch a General Strike affecting all sectors of the economy except transport, energy and health. On 25 October several delegates of the Miskole council travelled to Budapest to confer with similarly formed councils in the Hungarian capital. A joint statement was issued demanding four reforms: (1) the immediate withdrawal of Soviet troops from Poland and Hungary; (2) the formation of a new government in Hungary; (3) recognition of the right to strike; and (4) amnesty for all arrested in antigovernment demonstrations. The resolution of the Miskole council called for international working-class solidarity and refusal to submit to any form of subordination to the military strategies of the USSR.[25]

The council continued provisionally to support the Nagy government, but rather than complying with the government's request to down arms and return to work, it organised the formation of workers' militias reminiscent of those temporarily set up during the Paris Commune. The Miskole council pushed for the continuation of the General Strike as well as the spread of a network of committees and groups capable of holding the Hungarian Communist Party accountable for its policies. On 26 October Radio Miskole made an appeal to workers of all the surrounding cities to take similar measures and co-ordinate their efforts in a single, powerful movement. In Gyoer and Pecs similar councils sprung into existence. These attempted to follow the Miskole appeal by uniting economic activity with political and military functions. The vacillation of the Nagy government prompted a Soviet invasion in which the councils were disbanded, militias were disarmed, and Nagy was replaced with János Kádár (1912–89). Though Soviet troops were able to put down the Hungarian councils, they could not extinguish the democratic imagination and the aspiration to *collective self-government* that animated them, as the events in former Czechoslovakia (1968), Poland (1981) and former East Germany (1988–9) were to show. The idea that collective self-government might be able to assert itself against state socialist collectivism in the East (populist legitimacy without much genuine legality) and liberal democratic hegemony in the West (authoritarian legality propped up by largely symbolic forms of legitimacy) continues to inspire libertarian socialists, anarchists, and broad sectors of the antiglobalisation movement today. While syndicalists and council communists were not always successful in articulating a convincing account of how political decentralisation could be co-ordinated with socialised property and democratic control of the means of production, this project is central to libertarian socialist and anarchist visions of *autogestion*.[26]

Co-ordinating Workplace Democracy with Pluralist Decentralisation: Libertarian Socialism and Anarchism

Libertarian socialism, or guild socialism as it was originally called in England, traces its roots to a confluence of ideas in early British socialism and the romanticism of figures such as Thomas Carlyle (1795–1881), John Ruskin (1819–1900) and William Morris (1834–96). Their ideas on the alienating consequences of the division of labour and the disintegration of individual experience under the weight of capitalist rhythms of production found a receptive audience among the numerous members of the co-operative movement. Carlyle, Ruskin and Morris exerted an immense influence on the group of architects, artists and intellectuals who contributed to the journal *New Age* between 1907 and 1920. Those who sought more left-wing alternatives to Labour Party orthodoxy on questions of economic organisation, political representation and aesthetic expression looked to *New Age* with hopes of radicalising British political culture. Prior to the publication of the *New Statesman* in 1913, no other English journal could boast such a diverse range of contributors, who included Hilaire Belloc and Ezra Pound. The journal's editor was Alfred R. Orage, a gifted orator and synthesiser of other people's ideas. He came to *New Age* at a time when large-scale dissatisfaction with the Labour Party made an alternative with mass appeal seem possible to many people.

In a series of *New Age* articles entitled 'National guilds', S. G. Hobson argued that the practice of selling labour as a commodity like any other is incompatible with the essential role of creative work in any individual's life. British advocates of state socialism such as the Fabians, as well as Labour Party politicians, had not grasped the point that the social reward given to the labour force must be liberated from the shackles of the capitalist wage system. Failure to liberate work from the pressure to produce for someone else's private gain would surely transform it into a commodity with which other commodities could be bought. That is, in a society of *genuinely autonomous* individuals of the kind liberalism *claims* to defend, work is an end in itself as well as a source of creativity and pleasure. Demands for higher wages and shorter hours distract attention from the more fundamental goal of making work a process of experimentation and innovation instead of a routinised mechanism designed to produce banal products at a lower cost than the competitors'.[27]

In terms reminiscent of Pannekoek's call for the formation of industrial unions in order to overcome the divisions caused by the proliferation of craft unions, Hobson proposes the amalgamation of unions into a fellowship of all those employed in a given industry. In terms that today might seem antiquated and even medieval, Hobson refers to such an association of autonomous workers as a *guild* and, indeed, what is referred to in the rest of this chapter as libertarian socialism was originally called guild socialism.[28] As in Germany and Italy, various plans for worker control of industry were proposed immediately after the end of World War I. Many workers returning from the front who had risked their lives for their nation were unwilling to return to the previous authoritarian system of industrial relations, in which capitalist control of the labour process was accepted as the unconditional prerogative of the factory owners. Government-sponsored initiatives such as the Whitley Report called on major industrialists to adopt some form of worker participation in shop-floor decision-making. While these reforms were greeted with enthusiasm by many trade union leaders, Hobson and the editorial board of *New Age* regarded the report as an unacceptable compromise with the wage system and the principles of private control of the means of production. In fact, they were much more interested in the militancy of the shop steward movement than the Whitley proposals.[29]

In contrast to the union bureaucracy, shop stewards at this time were union representatives who usually worked alongside the rank and file on the shop floor. Stewards often had close contact with workers and union leaders of various trades; they attempted to restore unity to a working class that was being fragmented by task specialisation and the introduction of assembly lines. In *National Guilds and the State* (1920) Hobson argues that the qualitative increase in shop steward militancy after World War I opened up the possibility of establishing a genuinely labour-controlled economy. Stewards' demands for the amalgamation of industrial unions into large federations capable of managing the entire labour process seemed to provide ample evidence for transition from theory to practice. In contrast to the syndicalists, who put their hopes in the unions, the stewards more closely resembled council communists in the sense that they hoped to make the workshop the basic unit of industrial democracy and thereby cut across traditional trade lines. For Hobson the workshop is a potent source of spontaneity and direct democracy and is capable of much swifter action than the trade union. While trade unions are primarily concerned with the protection of the integrity of the trades of their respective members, the workshop unites workers across trades in a spirit of collective industrial autonomy. Along with Orage, Hobson and other *New Age* contributors, A. J. Penty proposed to fuse all trade unions involved in a given industry into powerful national bodies. After recruiting all workers in a trade—including the unskilled—these bodies would be able to organise themselves as a solid united front capable of dictating the price of labour to capital rather than the other way round. This was planned as the first step towards total worker control of the economy. Penty advocated use of the General Strike in the event that the representatives of capital refused to acknowledge the legality of these bodies.

The real visionary of the guild socialist movement, however, was G. D. H. Cole (1889–1959), who by the age of 24 had already fashioned an original synthesis of Fabian, syndicalist and *New Age* ideas.[30]

The almost total absence of consideration of aggregating consumer demands beyond plan or market in the writings of Gramsci in 1919–20, Pannekoek and other council communists is rectified in Cole's theory of libertarian socialism. In his book *The World of Labour* (1913) Cole states that:

> It is, on the face of it, improbable that either producer or consumer ought to have absolute control; it is unlikely that either the state or the unions should take the place of the exploiter entirely; for then either the *state* would be in a place to exploit the *worker,* or the worker would be in a position to exploit the *community*—just as the *capitalist* exploits both at present. The solution surely lies in some sort of division of functions, allowing both producer and consumer a say in the control of what is, after all, extremely important to both.[31]

In distinguishing between the workforce, state and community, Cole is keen to point out why liberal democratic capitalism and state socialism, as well as doctrines that over-emphasise worker control of industry, such as syndicalism and council communism, are all fundamentally flawed. In anticipation of the eventually unsolvable problems faced by Bolshevik as well as other versions of state socialism, it is clear that replacing the power of capital with the entrenched power of an unwieldy bureaucracy of state planners does not abolish exploitation and alienation. At the risk of a certain amount of simplification, one could say that capitalist speculation is converted into bureaucratic privilege. It is at any rate not a simplification to say that Marx did not really tackle this issue in sufficient detail anywhere in his work. In an attempt to update Marx without pursuing the paths of Leninism, Western Marxism or critical theory, advocates of syndicalism and council communism argue in different ways that worker control is the most compelling answer to the question of what Marxist theory should look like in institutional practice. The problem is that worker-controlled factories organised on industry-wide syndicalist lines or across trade distinctions in factory councils can destroy the local and national environment with polluted air and other forms of toxic waste, as the quotation above indicates. It is at this point that Cole directly confronts the central plan versus market impasse as well as the producer autonomy versus consumers' interest dilemma. He does this by carefully considering what he refers to as the community interest, which is a prerogative neither of the workforce nor of the state. What emerges is a convincing critique of state sovereignty and a theory of political pluralism with a great deal of actuality and contemporary relevance.[32]

Cole's theory of libertarian socialism is structured by the categories of production, personal and collective consumption, and politics. Politics does not culminate in a state organised on the bases of a party system or a single vanguard party. Instead, it consists in the daily co-ordination of production (organised by guilds) and consumption (preferences are aggregated in consumer councils) at local, national, and eventually international levels. He notes that although it may seem very old-fashioned to speak of guilds, it is important to remember that the guilds flourished at a time when guilds, churches, universities and other associations co-existed with the state. This means that the centralisation of authority in the state and the corresponding demise of what the young Marx refers to as the universal content of civil society are relatively recent phenomena that could still be challenged and reversed. Cole is convinced that the answer to liberal democratic centralisation cannot be socialist centralisation, for this would only confirm Max Weber's suspicion that socialism means more rather than less bureaucratic power for parties, government ministries and economic managers. Weber is influenced in this assessment by his reading of Simmel's *The Philosophy of Money* (1900), in which Simmel explains that modern capitalism is more than an economy in the strict sense of a system of production and distribution. For Simmel it is a social and cultural phenomenon in which money functions as a medium of exchange, but is also a medium of communication of values in a much wider sense. Money creates a social bond capable of substituting for the forms of personal loyalty and domination prevalent in social formations characterised by more and less advanced systems of barter. Hence money and the circulation of commodities attest to the quality of a social bond, which at one level is highly depersonalised vis-à-vis the transparency of feudal hierarchies. At another level it is personalised in the extreme because of the reification and fetishism that enable consumers to impute the commodity with all kinds of subjective aspirations and desires.[33] Readers of Simmel, such as Weber, often conclude that modern society is far too complex and differentiated for there to be anything like widespread *autogestion*.[34] The argument is that modern steering mechanisms such as money are anonymous to such an extent that any attempt at self-government can only result in the reintroduction of the personalised forms of domination that gradually faded with the demise of the feudal system. Without directly referring to Simmel, Cole acknowledges the complexity and differentiation of modern society by showing that the state is a highly inadequate institution precisely because it is too centralised and monolithic to be able to effectively co-ordinate production and consumption in a way that reflects a plurality of values, productive capacities and consumption preferences. The answer to complexity is not money, the capitalist market and the state, as it is in different degrees for liberal and social democrats. Nor is it state socialist central planning, as it is for Fabians and Bolsheviks, which does indeed reintroduce outmoded forms of personal subordination to planners and party officials.[35] For Cole the choice between money-based autonomy versus paternalist management is impoverished. He argues that communication can be instituted between producers and consumers without relying on the anonymous codes of money or imperious command from the socialist state. His proposals are briefly outlined below, beginning with his view of trade unions.

Cole maintains that if unions are at times capable of limiting the power of capital to direct the labour process, their power is largely a negative one limited to the contestation of abuses and excesses. Within the private enterprise system they have little power to make a positive contribution to the organisation of production. The result is often a stalemate between capital and labour with disastrous consequences for the project of liberating humanity from natural scarcity and necessity. Like Orage, Hobson, Penty and others associated with *New Age*, Cole wished to see a reduction of the at that time approximately 1,100 existing craft unions to some 20 industrial guilds. He sees this as the pre-condition for an economy based on guilds, that is, based on the co-operation of all the apprentices, semi-skilled and highly skilled workers in an industry. He does not think that the first step is a General Strike or some other break with legality. Instead, the guilds must unite and demand that the government buy privately owned firms, and then entrust these enterprises to the productive expertise of the workers organised in their respective guilds. He calls this the strategy of encroaching control, which he prefers to social democratic reformism, syndicalism and militarist vanguardism. Cole accepts that large-scale industry is likely to remain the norm in areas, such as the railways and mines, where it is demonstrably more efficient than decentralised models. But wherever possible, he urges a return to small-scale manufacture and the ethic of the production of high-quality goods and services designed to meet the multifaceted requirements of consumers. His view is that this is possible if there can be a constant vertical communication between workers and managers within guilds, as well as constant horizontal communication between guilds and consumers organised in councils at the personal and collective level. Stand-offs between producers and consumers can be settled by the political commune at local, regional and national levels. By replacing the state in this way, the commune 'reinvests' society with a substantial political content, though not in the manner of a party dictatorship or feudal lordship. Citizens are organised in overlapping networks in the framework provided by guilds, consumer councils and communes. Everyone—not just the working class—is involved in at least one of these institutions. In this way the workerist orientation of much of left thought and practice is overcome. Politics becomes integrated into the life of each person rather than a largely symbolic action of voting once every six years or so to determine which member of the ruling elite is allocated 'the right to misrepresent the people in parliament', as Marx quips with regard to parliamentary democracy in *The Civil War in France*.[36]

Cole supports the continued use of markets to safeguard consumer interests. However, the libertarian socialist market was not to be dominated by competing firms selling relatively similar commodities determined to keep wages low and the labour force subservient to the dictates of private fortunes. Like all economists, he had to face the problem of what to do in the event that one producers' guild produces above cost, while others manage to produce at cost or below cost. In other words, how would it be possible to terminate the power of capital over labour without (a) recourse to the bureaucratic socialist state, artificially imposing equality, and (b) having to reintroduce capitalist criteria of price and efficiency in order to guarantee that producers' associations respond to consumer demand, thereby resurrecting inequality? Although he thinks that competition between guilds will persist in the arenas of quality and responsiveness to consumer demand rather than in quantity and keeping down the cost of labour, he accepts the need to outline institutional measures to ensure equality of incomes between guilds. He hopes that the political commune can perform this function, as will be seen presently.[37]

In *Guild Socialism Re-Stated* (1920) Cole divides consumption into personal consumption (including individual preferences in food, clothing and other articles of daily use) on the one hand, and collective consumption (of services such as water and electricity, to be managed by a collective utilities council) on the other. He believes that in a future libertarian society these collective councils will inherit some of the functions performed by local authorities in the existing system. While he envisages joint consultation and constant dialogue between producer and consumer associations at local, regional and national levels, he also proposes citizen councils to represent the consumer in the areas of health and education. In the domain of education he thinks that given the right institutional framework, it is not at all unreasonable to expect students to form councils, confer with teachers on matters of curriculum, grading and discipline, and in general to spread the idea of self-government from the distant parliamentary level into the fabric of daily life, just as producer and consumer councils would do. In addition to health and education councils, there would also be cultural councils in which members of the community could meet to discuss their views on drama, music, painting and sculpture. As in the economy, the idea is to relieve creative individual expression from the homogenising and instrumental tendencies inherent in capitalist production, though without thereby relying on the state to sponsor artists who produce 'socialist' art. Thus in Cole's writings libertarian socialism has a clear answer to the nagging problem of theory and practice. He believes that the inclination to participate in decision-making or passively to submit to authority is fostered or stifled at an early age. He argues that early experience is likely to shape each individual's reaction to authority inside and outside the workplace, and that the spheres outside the workplace deserve as much attention as the workplace itself in any fully democratised society.[38]

The commune is the key mediating institution between civic consumer councils in health, education, culture, collective consumption and personal consumption on the one hand, and the guilds as organisers of production on the other. By limiting the role of political authority to this highly decentralised body and assigning it the role of promoting dialogue between all sectors of society, the commune cannot be confused with the sovereign state in any of its socialist or capitalist variations. Cole reasons that if the one-party state is spectacularly inept at promoting dialogue and notoriously bad at responding to the diversity of abilities and needs of advanced industrial populations, parliamentary multi-party systems do not do a great deal better. The gulf between state and society is enforced in a number of palpable ways, some of which had already been diagnosed by Marx in the *Civil War in France* and other writings. Marx, Cole and other libertarian radicals are in broad agreement with the assessment that the modern parliamentary state is largely a vehicle for collecting taxes and staging plebiscitary forms of democracy. Its legitimacy is based on a volatile juggling of interests rather than anything one might meaningfully refer to as the transparent mediation of different positions. The results are lack of transparency and bureaucratic overload, as well as the proliferation of parliamentary committees and subcommittees issuing documents that are read by very few people. It should be noted that this view is not monopolised by a tiny minority on the far left. It is shared by Weber, Joseph Schumpeter, Carl Schmitt and a host of others situated to the political right of Marx and Cole.[39]

Despite its impressive theoretical coherence, libertarian socialism in England enjoyed a relatively brief period of popularity and influence. By the time of the failure of the General Strike in 1926, Cole concedes that be had been too optimistic about the possibility of amalgamating trade unions into producers' guilds. A crucial blow came with the stock market crash and the world recession of 1929. The labour movement adopted a much more conciliatory stance than the one needed to unify democratic theory and institutional practice in the way envisaged by libertarian socialism. Seen in this perspective, one might regard the social democratic reformism and commitment to the welfare state of the Attlee government in the immediate post-war period as a principled compromise between Cole's libertarian socialism and what has subsequently become the ideology of New Labour today.

New Labour has abandoned the major tenets of reformist leaders such as Attlee and Aneurin Bevan (1897–1960) in its successful bid to become a party of government, though this was not possible before the elimination of its left wing in several of the London boroughs and key cities such as Liverpool. To the extent that it continues to pursue neo-liberal politics, New Labour is likely to have to reckon with a resurgence of the left within its ranks by those who continue to accept the desirability of the political party as the best possible institution mediating between citizens and government. New Labour can also count on the continued opposition of those outside its ranks such as anarchists: anarchists in Britain and elsewhere are and of course always have been sceptical about the possibility of achieving genuinely democratic change via parties and states.

Anarchism is a movement with a long history and a legacy of contestation spanning the entire globe. Some argue that wherever people have practised self-government there has been anarchism, which means that it is an integral part of the history of humankind from its earliest manifestations right up to the present. From ancient nomadic communities to the Zapatista movement in Mexico and the antiglobalisation critics of capitalism everywhere in the world today, anarchist theory and practice challenge the assumption that humans are *naturally* selfish and aggressive creatures who need nuclear families, private property, police, jails and sovereign states in order to protect themselves from each other. Anarchists generally believe that institutions like the traditional family, property, the police and the state are in no way inevitable 'facts' of humans living together in society. These phenomena are evidence of the institutional repression that inevitably results when the forms of mediation between humanity and nature are flawed. Anarchist rejection of existing institutions, such as the state, is uncompromising, and its dismissal of existing forms of mediation, such as the law, is often total. This means that if anarchist critique has the virtue of remarkable coherence, it is not always easy for anarchists to know where to begin transforming critique into positive transformation. The party, however subversive and left-wing its claims may be, is bound up with an implicit defence of the state as an acceptable model of human relations. This becomes clear when studying party-led revolutions in, for example, Russia, China, Cambodia and Cuba. The trade union is also a compromised institution. But the trade union has firm links with the world of labour. Thus in terms of the history of the left, militants referred to as anarcho-syndicalists have often looked to radicalise unions against their reformist leadership in order to mobilise the working classes to liberate humanity not only from the liberal democratic state, but from the state in general. Yet there are also a great many anarchists who deny the idea that the union could ever be suited to the project of comprehensive social change.

It has been seen that in the Charter of Amiens (1906), French revolutionary syndicalists declared that the trade union could be transformed into the ideal institution for staging the overthrow of capitalism. At the Congress of Amsterdam the following year, several prominent anarchists such as Errico Malatesta (1853–1932) and Peter Kropotkin (1842–1921) contested syndicalist strategy.

Malatesta points out that organising workers on the basis of their various trades might encourage them to conflate the defence of interests of their particular branch of industry with the realisation of human emancipation. Within a capitalist framework railway workers could go on strike, but only at the expense of miners and other workers who needed to sell the products of their labour power via the railway network. The syndicalists generally counter by insisting on the unifying tendencies of the General Strike, to which Malatesta and others reply that since the workers are much poorer than the bosses, a truly revolutionary programme would have to be based on the combined efforts of workers in different industries above and beyond trade differences. The antisyndicalist sentiment in French anarchist circles had been brewing since the turn of the century. Writing in *L'Anarchie* in October 1905, André Lorulet expresses the anarchist position:

For us, there are no classes. We only recognise individuals. Amongst these individuals, some are disposed toward good relations with us. To them we respond with reciprocity, since they are anarchists, whilst the rest contribute to the functioning of the society that oppresses us. They support this society with adherence to its laws, by voting, by joining unions, and obeying its general principles: they are our enemies. Whether they are workers or bosses is of no consequence . . . We address our propaganda to both.[40]

Lorulet echoes recurrent themes in the work of Malatesta and the Russian anarchist Mikhail Bakunin (1814–76), arguing that regardless of their position in the division of labour, many workers regard the union as the best means to attain higher living standards, increased consumption, and power over other groups in society such as women, the unemployed, and even other workers in less prosperous industries. Bakunin insists that one of the chief defects of Marxism is its fetishising of skilled industrial workers—the very people who in his estimation are most apt to emulate bourgeois lifestyles as soon as they reach a certain level of wealth. He is convinced that the peasants and the urban poor are more likely to retain their spirit of revolt and become an important force for revolutionary change, and, indeed, he would probably have felt vindicated by the struggles of the landless peasants in contemporary Brazil. Bakunin argues that producer and consumer co-operatives and working-class credit societies are better suited to the task of organising a new economy than the large trade federations held in such high esteem by the syndicalists. The anarchist shoemaker Jean Grave makes a similar point in a different way. He observes that while they lead to the improvement of working-class living standards, unions tend to foster the creation of a labour aristocracy situated between the working class and capitalists. He reckons that in the long run, the trade union could only be counted on to defend this politically unreliable segment of the working population. Similarly, one of the founders of modern anarchism, Pierre-Joseph Proudhon (1809–65), prefers the idea of worker *autogestion* to union management of industry.[41]

Although famous for the quip 'property is theft', Proudhon is not against private property in principle. His theory of anarchist mutualism aims at establishing a framework for the just distribution of property based on the exchange of equivalents between bargaining units with equal power. In capitalism workers are forced to sell their labour power at exploitative rates, forcing them further and further into subservience and dependence while the capitalists increase their private fortunes. Rather than entrusting the organisation of production to the state, industrial union or factory council, Proudhon wants a radical redistribution of property such that each individual can exchange the equivalent of labour time for property with any other individual. Provided that everyone worked roughly the same number of hours, they would have more or less the same amount of property. Under these conditions the market would cease to be distorted by the fact that some buy labour power while others sell it; the market would now be balanced by different trading partners exchanging equivalent units in labour and property. No one partner could gain enough leverage to buy any other, so that a state of perfect equilibrium would be reached quickly and maintained. For Proudhon autonomy means nothing if not this freedom from having to sell one's labour power to someone who has every interest in keeping labour costs at a minimum while reducing quality to the lowest possible standard acceptable to the consumer.[42]

Proudhon realises that in most cases the individual independent worker co-operates with other workers in the manufacture of a good or service. He recommends workers combine in what he calls mutualist associations. These are a bit like Cole's guilds, though with the important overall difference that while Cole assigns consumer councils the task of aggregating consumer demand at the individual and collective levels, Proudhon has a more traditional vision of the consumer disposing of private income in the way they see fit. He envisages three main sectors of production. Individual proprietors manage the agricultural sector and skilled individual workers populate the artisanal sector, mutualist firms compete in the industrial sector. However, rather than allowing price to be swayed by competitive bids to monopolise individual markets, price is to be fixed by the labour hours necessary to produce a given product. Proudhon argues that one needs to set up a People's Bank authorised to issue notes to each producer corresponding to the number of hours they had spent working. Thus notes indicating the number of labour hours could be traded for the equivalent in goods and services. The People's Bank would provide credit without interest to help mutualist firms buy the necessary tools for their enterprise.

The goal is to establish an economy in which all income is derived exclusively through labour. In this economy workers have access to land and property, but do not have the option of earning money by renting land or machinery. In *On the Political Capacity of the Working Classes* Proudhon outlines the bases of his idea of anarchist incentive:

The superior worker who conceives and executes more rapidly, secures a greater yield and a better quality of product than another, who knows how to combine his technical talents with the genius of management, thus exceeding the average wage, will receive a greater salary. He will be able to earn the equivalent of one and a half, twice, or three days of work in a single day . . . If justice disregards no one, it does not disregard talent either.[43]

Some of Proudhon's opponents, such as the Bakuninist James Guillaume, regard Proudhon's theory of mutualism as an inconclusive break with capitalist notions of just reward, individual freedom and the limits of political community. Like Bakunin, Guillaume wants to go further towards the abolition of commerce than Proudhon is prepared to do. Guillaume envisages the creation of a Bank of Exchange in each local commune, which is to receive all the goods produced within its territory. The value of the goods is to be determined by local commune members and trade unionists on the basis of statistics concerning costs and considerations of relative scarcity rather than on the basis of labour hours. In return for depositing goods produced, individual workers are to receive vouchers entitling them to what they need, with the idea that as the different Banks of Exchange and communes co-ordinate their efforts to an increasing degree, exchange itself will give way to distribution on purely needs-based criteria. This may well be similar to what Marx and Engels have in mind when they speak of the administration of things to follow the withering away of the state. But whilst the founders of historical materialism seem to suggest that this degree of spontaneous co-operation is likely to be a by-product of the most advanced historical evolution in the dialectic between forces and relations of production, many anarchists see co-operation as a question of ethics, education and natural solidarity among humans. Kropotkin's ideas offer a good example of the anarchist position.

In *The Conquest of Bread* (1892), *Fields, Factories and Workshops* (1899) and *Mutual Aid* (1902), Kropotkin argues that neither representative government nor the wage system is compatible with a truly democratised economy and society. From his perspective the lesson of the Paris Commune is not merely that the working class cannot lay hold of the ready-made state machinery and wield it for its own purposes. *Autogestion* has to be enriched and extended beyond the workplace to education, the family and environmental protection as well.

Fields, Factories and Workshops outlines his proposal on the subjects on the basis of three main theses. First, anticipating the ideas of Jose Bove and many others in the contemporary struggle against global capitalism, he maintains that there are no objective technical reasons why industry and agriculture must necessarily be large-scale operations. Second, food—humanity's most vital resource—can be produced in plentiful quantities for local markets by using intensive farming techniques. Third, in a related vein, decentralised production for local consumption is by no means utopian. Kropotkin links these goals with the need to provide everyone with a strong educational and technical grounding in the practical sciences of agriculture and industry. *Mutual Aid* and *Fields, Factories and Workshops* stress that in the right society each person can choose the producer and civic associations in which they would like to be active. He reasons that if people are allowed to exercise their talents and follow their inclinations, they are far more likely spontaneously to co-operate than if they are forced to do dull and arduous work for the sole purpose of making a living. If work is allowed to become a mere means and drudgery, people are of course likely to work slowly and badly. For Kropotkin the aim of decentralising industry and agriculture is to give people the sense that they are meaningfully involved with their work and with other producers. He is convinced that this kind of involvement will lead to increased productivity rather than the stagnation and decline predicted by advocates of 'free' markets, mass production and mass consumption.[44]

In the essay 'Modern Science and Anarchism' (1913), Kropotkin articulates his opposition to Proudhon's labour-hour cheques and competitive incentives. His view is that since the aggregate wealth and skill in any region of the world is the result of the collective efforts of countless generations past and present, it is pointless to try to award people individual wages as if individual contributions could somehow be disentangled from the collective enterprise of housing, clothing, feeding and educating an entire society. To the objection that without individualist incentives no one would want to work, he responds that everyone wants to work at things that interest them and give them joy. The progressive intensification of the division of labour results in the pernicious situation that a tiny of minority of people do work they enjoy, and the great majority need to be bullied into doing work they do not want to do but have to do in order to survive. Under such conditions it is not surprising that the latter are reluctant workers, who need surveillance and discipline, and aggressive and apolitical citizens. From Kropotkin's perspective it is cynicism—not realism—to justify this system on the grounds that 'things have always been this way' or that talent will always rise no matter what the structural constraints may be. In opposition to Spencer's social Darwinism in his day and in anticipated opposition to Hayek's uncritical celebration of market forces, Kropotkin explains why the reproduction of human society depends on its ability to develop more complex forms of social co-operation corresponding to the growing complexity of human needs. The satisfaction of fundamental physical needs becomes possible thanks to people working together in sufficient numbers to guarantee the bases of survival. Thereafter, the question of the satisfaction of a wide range of emotional, intellectual and aesthetic needs can be properly addressed. By perpetuating scarcity, the wage system prevents most people from discovering their more complex and creative impulses. By confining people to repetitive and for the most part unchallenging tasks, the division of labour helps reinforce the stultifying effects of the wage system. The division of labour accustoms people to accept the separation between necessarily dull work during the week, compensated by necessarily fleeting relief in largely commodified forms of entertainment at the weekend. The words 'compensated' and 'relief' in this context serve as a reminder that the transition from simple need satisfaction to complex need satisfaction is prevented by a system that would prefer to see people multiply and fetishise their fundamental needs rather than progress to more complex forms of freedom, autonomy and creativity.[45]

Events such as the Spanish Civil War (1936–39), which saw the defenders of the Spanish Republic pitted against Gen. Francisco Franco's fascist militia, indicate that the anarchist co-operation and solidarity envisioned by Kropotkin and others have been real operative forces in history rather than the romantic dreams of isolated intellectuals. Like Proudhon in France, opponents of centralised political authority in Spain applauded the ideals of the French Revolution while disagreeing violently with the Jacobin attempt to monopolise the revolution and implement them 'from above'.

In 1871, the bitter rivalry between Marx and Bakunin produced a split within the First International. While the majority of European sections of the International followed Marx, who moved its centre to New York, the Spanish remained faithful to Bakunin in a conscious preference for anarchism over Marxist communism. The first anarchist groups in Spain were mainly printers, schoolteachers and students. They went from one rural village to the next, united in a general campaign to educate the peasantry. When trade unions were legalised in 1881, anarchism spread to the cities of Spain, and especially to Barcelona, where many Andalusian peasants migrated in search of employment. The Spanish labour movement was militant, but desperately under-resourced. When the unions united as the National Confederation of Labour (CNT) in 1911, there was no strike fund. This remained the case for years to come. But what the movement lacked in terms of money was offset by hatred of the forces of the state and capitalism. By 1927 the Spanish Anarchist Federation (FAI) welcomed all those (even criminals) who opposed the bourgeois order. The exploits of some of its more violent members, such as Buenaventura Durruti (1896–1936), have contributed to the proliferation of legends about anarchist feats of bravery and resistance to the Spanish state.[46]

Although the anarchists were the most powerful contingent in opposition to Franco's army at the outbreak of the civil war, they were often in conflict with the other factions of the republican cause. Dissent between anarchists, socialists and communists made it extremely difficult to establish local communes on a stable foundation. Despite this internecine conflict on the left, more than 1,000 anarchist collectives were formed during the civil war, ranging in size from one hundred to several thousand people. In the region of Aragon approximately three-quarters of the land was self-managed by co-operatives working in conjunction with local communes. The most important decisions were made by the collaboration of town commune and political committee, where the latter was usually comprised of CNT activists. For every ten or so workers a delegate was sent to the committee to relay information and receive guidance. As a result of the expropriation of large estates and the collectivisation of peasants' smallholdings, all arable land was placed in the hands of the community. Though wage labour as the sale of labour power to private buyers was abolished in much of Aragon, proprietors with individual landholdings could continue to work their land if they chose to do so. Historical documentation suggests that the relations between individual proprietors and collectivised enterprises varied from relatively peaceful co-existence to outright confrontation. In the event of a clash, individual landholdings were usually made communal.[47]

Though various methods of production and distribution were adopted, all the collective enterprises made significant steps towards the communitarian anarchist goal of distributing goods and services on the basis of spontaneous solidarity and need. In some cases, this was achieved in the manner proposed by Guillaume and Kropotkin: by placing produced goods in a central warehouse and allowing them to be available upon request. The realities of the civil war meant that such radical principles of distribution could only be applied to basic necessities. Nonetheless, figures for agricultural production during 1936–37 showed that self-managed enterprises boasted higher levels of production than their traditionally managed counterparts, thus providing evidence for the claim that the wage system and the division of labour decrease motivation and creativity. Workers asked: what incentive is there to increase output when such improvements benefit the despised figure of the landlord? Things are much different when workers work together to satisfy their needs and help others. Satisfying needs and helping others was more difficult in the cities than it was in the countryside, though of course the example of Barcelona in those years became a symbol of anarchist organisational achievement. Co-ordinating different branches of industry presented problems, familiar to syndicalists and council communists, that did not really affect semi-autonomous agricultural communities. While small agricultural communities could achieve high levels of autarchy by pooling their resources and bartering where necessary, large-scale industry did not have this option. Each branch of large industry had to rely on several others to maintain production, and it was often the case that different branches were located in different cities. For example, in order to repair buses metalworkers needed tools for which they could not offer food or anything else of immediate use, thus raising the difficult question of money and credit. For many anarchists in Spain and elsewhere, money is inseparable from the wage system and therefore an anathema. But compromises had to be made in the face of the hardships imposed by the conflict with Franco.[48]

At the outbreak of the war, a Central Labour Bank and an Economic Council were created to help plan production, provide credit on favourable terms and facilitate transactions between co-operativés. The fact that some workers had saved more money than others was compounded by the reality that workers with families had different needs than those without them. The Economic Council attempted to manage this situation by planning and co-ordinating production and redistribution, which in turn raised the question about the authority of the redistributing body. While libertarian socialists like Cole favour a constant dialogue between equally empowered producer and consumer councils mediated by the commune, anarchists in Barcelona and other urban centres found that the absence of something like an anarcho-communist state endangered the project of constructing a socioeconomic alternative to capitalism. Apart from the Spanish communists, who took their directives from Moscow and favoured centralisation, this was not a call for a central state. It was an acknowledgement of the problems of trying to co-ordinate production and aggregate needs without recourse to states and markets, combined with militant determination to fight for anarchism.[49]

That fight was eventually lost in the specific case of the Spanish Civil War, though not without bequeathing a wealth of revolutionary experience and evidence for future generations of libertarian militants. The left in Europe and elsewhere has continually looked back to these events in Spain as proof that people do not need repressive laws forcing them to work or paternalist states commanding them to respect each other: in other words, it is clear that spontaneous solidarity and co-operation are every bit as much a part of human history as competition and distrust. Whilst this chapter has looked at the collective dimension of solidarity and co-operation, the next two chapters indicate that individual spontaneity and creativity also have a long history on the left.

Suggestions for Further Reading

Gombin, Richard. *The Origins of Modern Leftism*, London, Penguin, 1975.

Jennings, Jeremy. *Syndicalism in France: A Study of Ideas*, London, Macmillan, 1990.

Joll, James. *The Anarchists*, London Methuen, 1979.

Kinna, Ruth. *Anarchism: A Beginners' Guide*, Oxford, Oneworld Books, 2005.

Marshall, Peter. *Demanding the Impossible: A History of Anarchism*, London, HarperCollins, 1992.

Mattick, Paul. *Anti-Bolshevik Communism*, London, Merlin, 1978.

May, Todd. *The Political Philosophy of Post-structuralist Anarchism*, University Park, Penn State University Press, 1994.

Portis, Larry. *Georges Sorel*, London, Pluto, 1980.

Schecter, Darrow. *Radical Theories: Paths Beyond Marxism and Social Democracy*, Manchester, MUP, 1994.

Smart (ed. and Introduction by), D.A. *Pannekoek and Gorter's Marxism*, London, Pluto, 1978.

Ward, Colin. *Anarchism: A Very Short Introduction*, Oxford, OUP, 2004.

Wyatt, Chris. 'G.D.H. Cole: Emancipatory Politics and Organisational Democracy', DPhil thesis, University of Sussex, 2004.

Notes

1 The project to build networks instead of pyramids alluded to in the title of this chapter is taken from Ward, *Anarchy in Action*, p. 22. For a concise guide to the most important ideas and major figures of the anarchist movement, see Ward, *Anarchism*. There are issues raised by the fact that only a relatively small group of artisans and agricultural labourers work *directly* upon nature, i.e. the relation between humanity and nature is in almost all cases mediated by law, history and society. This presents problems for Marx and a number of the movements considered in this chapter, which will receive more attention in Chapter 6.

2 This objection to Lenin and Bolshevism is made forcefully by, among others, the great socialist feminist radicals Emma Goldmann (1869–1940), Rosa Luxemburg (1870–1919), and Alexandra Kollontai (1872–1952). If Goldmann can be characterised as an anarchist, Luxemburg can be seen as an anti-Leninist Marxist. Along with A. G. Shlyapnikov, Kollontai was a member of the libertarian Workers' Opposition who argued for workplace democracy based on soviets rather than state dictatorship based on the party. Shlyapnikov was expelled from the CPSU in 1933, but Kollontai went on to become a Soviet diplomat in Norway and Sweden.

3 Recent years have witnessed the proliferation of co-ops in northern Spain and social centres (*centri sociali*) in Italy. Whilst the aims of the co-ops and social centres are not as far-reaching as the syndicalist union or the factory council during the period of their greatest popularity leading up to and immediately following the First World War, they represent a continuation of those older forms of libertarian militancy.

4 For the English case see Macdonald, *Syndicalism*. With reference to the more militant unionists in France, Macdonald writes, 'Syndicalism is a programme of trade union action aimed at the ending of the present capitalist system. Its organisation is exactly the same as that of our trade societies; it asks the workmen to combine in unions, to unite the local branches of those unions in trades councils, and to federate the national organisations in an all-comprehending central body, which in France is the famous Confédération du Travail, commonly known by its initials, the C. G. T. Syndicalism might have borrowed all this part of its system from the old-fashioned British unions. In fact, it is British trade unionism applied to revolutionary purposes' (p. 1). For a more recent look at English syndicalism, see the essays by the Tyneside syndicalist Tom Brown collected in *Tom Brown's Syndicalism*. Although Western and central Europe provide the focus of the current study, one should also mention the syndicalist Industrial Workers of the World, the IWW or Woblies, as they were called. They were led for many years by 'Big Bill' Haywood, and had considerable influence in the North American labour movement in the years 1880–1914.

5 Jennings, *Syndicalism in France*, pp. 19–21. Jennings's book provides a very thorough introduction to the history of French syndicalism and to the ideas of Pelloutier, Sorel and other syndicalist theorists.

6 Pelloutier, *Histoire des Bourses du Travail* [*History of the Bourses du Travail*], pp. 168–71.

7 These excerpts from the text of the Congress are reprinted in Jean Maitron, *Histoire du mouvement anarchiste en France, 1880–1914* [*History of the Anarchist Movement in France, 1880–1914*], p. 296. In this context 'complete emancipation' can be seen as the syndicalist equivalent of the young Marx's notion of human emancipation.

8 Sorel's views on Marxism and his conversion to revolutionary syndicalism are given full expression in three works published in 1908. See *La décomposition du marxisme* [*The Decomposition of Marxism*], *Les illusions du progrès* [*The Illusions of Progress*] and *Réflexions sur la violence* [*Reflections on Violence*]. In his *Reflections on Violence*, Sorel's best known work, he expounds his theory of the General Strike, revolution and the role of violence as a galvanising force for collective action. Exegetical space is limited here, but interested readers should consult Horowitz, *Radicalism and the Revolt against Reason*, Hughes, *Consciousness and Society* and Portis, *Georges Sorel*.

9 Sorel, 'Étude sur Vico' ['Study of Vico'].

10 Sorel, 'L'avenir socialiste des syndicats' ['The socialist future of the unions']; Portis, *Georges Sorel*, pp. 74–80. From a syndicalist standpoint the General Strike is always revealing of the spatial and temporal gulf between the revolutionary workers and reformist parliamentary leaders. Perhaps the most famous examples are the strikes of 1904 in Italy and 1926 in England. In general terms it is a strike in which the sectional and corporate interests of the different sectors of the working classes are overcome in a show of universal solidarity across trades. For a theoretical view incorporating elements of Western Marxism and revolutionary syndicalism, see Rosa Luxemburg, 'The mass strike, the party and the trade unions', in *The Mass Strike and Other Writings*.

11 Arturo Labriola is not to be confused with Antonio Labriola the Western Marxist briefly discussed in Chapter 2 in relation to Gramsci. While both were Neapolitans whose theoretical departure was Marx, Arturo Labriola was a syndicalist who was equally interested in Sorel, the southern question, and concrete questions of trade union control of industry.

12 Labriola, *Storia di dieci anni 1899–1909* [*The History of Ten Years: 1899–1909*], pp. 301–5.

13 Labriola, *Sindacalismo e riformismo* [*Syndicalism and Reformism*], pp. 15–16.

14 While syndicalism has to a large extent been a Mediterranean European phenomenon, council communism has tended to thrive in central Europe, including Hungary, and northern Europe. It is interesting to note that both syndicalist and council communist movements have flourished in Italy at various times. Gramsci had a major role in the organisation of the Italian factory council movement of 1919–20, which directly preceded the formation of the PCI in January 1921. It is also of interest that in the years immediately following the October Revolution in 1917 the Left Opposition was a constant and embarrassing reminder to the Bolshevik leadership that the Soviet state was meant to be a Union of *Soviet* Socialist Republics.

15 Luxemburg, 'The mass strike, the party and the trade unions', in *The Mass Strike and Other Writings*, pp. 64–65; Gombin, *The Origins of Modern Leftism*, pp. 80–81.

16 For an undeniably biased but in many ways convincing defence of Luxemburg's prognoses about social democratic reformism and Leninist vanguardism, see Mattick, *Anti-Bolshevik Communism*, Chapter 2.

17 Like the young Gramsci of the *New Order* years (1919–20) and Korsch and Lukács in the same era, Pannekoek intuits that in the period beginning with the Italian General Strike of 1904, the Marxist theories of history and revolution require drastic revision. This was necessary if Marxism was to remain a dialectical theory of reality rather than a quasi-religious 'materialist' dogma or the legitimating ideology of a party dictatorship of the kind the USSR was eventually to become. That is, revolutionary leftists with council communist sympathies in the years roughly spanning 1900–22 understand that a process of restructuring of the relations between labour, capital and the state in the countries of advanced capitalism was under way. Adopting the extremist position of the council communists for the moment, one might say that the process was likely to result in a libertarian revolution or some form of coerced integration of labour power within a highly authoritarian state. It will be seen in the next chapter that radical contestation of the capitalist prerogative to direct work dramatically resurges in France and Italy in 1968–69 and continues, especially in Italy, into the 1970s and 1980s.

18 Gerber, *Anton Pannekoek and the Socialism of Workers' Self-Emancipation, 1873–1960*, pp. 110–11, 118–20.

19 The case of the council republic in Munich in 1918–19 seems to support the council communist thesis that the period of capitalist expansion accompanied by imperialist aggression and world war is marked by radical contestation in the workplace and urban district on the one hand, and the high probability of political reaction against revolutionary movements on the other. The suppression of the short-lived republic was accompanied by the imprisonment of many of its leading members, such as Gustav Landauer (1870–1934), author of *Aufruf zum Sozialismus* [*Call to Socialism*], 1911, 1923). Landauer was released from prison in 1924, only to be murdered in a Nazi concentration camp ten years later.

20 Gerber, op. cit., pp. 132–33.

21 Programme of the KAPD, reprinted in Kool, *Die Linke gegen die Parteiherrschaft* [*The Left against the Domination of the Party*], p. 324.

22 As noted in Chapter 2, Korsch is normally regarded, with Lukács and Gramsci, as one of the founding theoreticians of Western Marxism. The period preceding his *Marx and Philosophy* (1923) is marked by the publication of *Was ist Sozialisierung?* [*What is Socialisation?*] in 1919. The book offers a militant defence of factory councils as an alternative to syndicalism and party-based versions of centralised command planning.

23 The role of factory and neighbourhood councils in the Hungarian Revolution of 1956 is celebrated by Hannah Arendt in *On Revolution,* in which she highlights one of the gigantic problems of council democracy from the Paris Commune to the events in 1956, to wit, that radically decentralised and participatory forms of democracy do not square with centralised economies. Arendt's suggestion that this may well be an insoluble problem holds true for

the more dogmatic versions of council communism. But it does not take into account libertarian socialist and anarchist perspectives, as will be seen later in this chapter.

24 Claude Lefort, 'L'insurrection hongroise', in *Socialism ou Barbarie?* [*Socialism or Barbarism?*]. The journal *Socialisme ou Barbarie?* played an important role as a rallying point for Western European Trotskyists and a variety of independent radicals in France and elsewhere in the 1950s and 1960s. It received contributions from figures such as Jean François Lyotard (1924–98) and Cornelius Castoriadis (1922–97), and had an impact on the situationists (see Chapter 5). The journal was a focal point for libertarian socialists and communists who were very critical of state socialism in Eastern Europe, though without ever relenting in their critique of capitalism.

25 For a libertarian socialist theory of *autogestion* developed within a wider framework provided by the dialectics of legality-legitimacy, see Schecter, *Beyond Hegemony*. The book argues that law is not legitimate unless it reconciles humanity with external as well as with internal or what one might call human nature, and that the reconciliation of external nature and humanity can be envisaged in practical terms as libertarian socialism. The relations between legality and legitimacy are examined as alternatives to liberal notions of democracy and justice in an attempt to theorise the bases of a society which is solidaristic at the collective level (reconciliation with external nature) while at the same time respecting the absolute particularity of each individual (reconciliation with individual nature).

26 Hobson, *National Guilds*, p. 132. The project of transforming the highly inadequate autonomy institutionalised in liberal regimes into much freer forms of action and association is common to all the movements looked at in this chapter, as well as the Italian Autonomists to be considered in Chapter 5.

27 For a detailed examination of the guild socialist movement and the ideas of its most important theorist, G. D. H. Cole, see Schecter, *Radical Theories*, Chapter 4.

28 Hobson, *National Guilds and the State*, London, G. Bell & Sons, 1920, pp. viii–ix. See also Penty, *Old Worlds for New*, pp. 58–59.

29 Penty, op. cit., pp. 50–51.

30 Cole, *The World of Labour*, p. 352, my emphases.

31 For all their conspicuous differences, liberal democracy and state socialism are forms of state that subordinate the living labour of discrete individuals to the homogenising ideologies of individual liberty and egalitarian democracy in the first case and collective liberty and collective welfare in the second. Cole indicates a way out of the oppression practised in both regimes without relying on a simplistic doctrine of worker control or naive conceptions of spontaneous co-operation. For a more detailed exposition, see Wyatt, 'G. D. H. Cole: Emancipatory politics and organisational democracy'.

32 Simmel, *The Philosophy of Money*, Part 2.

33 The idea that systemic differentiation and social complexity are incompatible with large-scale self-management is shared by systems theorists such as Niklas Luhmann (1927–98), and to a lesser extent by theorists of communicative action such as Habermas.

34 Sidney and Beatrice Webb headed the Fabian Society during Cole's years of political activism. At this time it was firmly committed to collectivist socialism based on central planning and a certain degree of pedagogic concern for working-class

education. The Webbs argued that industrial technology combined with the expert planning of socialist technicians would result in maximum productive efficiency and a just distribution of wealth. They sought a twentieth-century socialist version of the ideas of Claude Henri de St Simon (1760–1825) and Auguste Comte (1798–1857). These ideas found their most complete expression in their book *For a Socialist Commonwealth of Britain* (1920). Today the Fabian Society organises lectures and other cultural events related to socialist theory and other topics.

35 Cole, *Guild Socialism Re-stated*, p. 65.

36 Ibid., pp. 71–73; Carpenter, *G.D.H. Cole: An Intellectual Biography*, pp. 59–64.

37 Cole, op. cit., pp. 108–16. For a discussion of Cole's ideas on pluralism and democracy in relation to other theorists such as Rousseau and J. S. Mill, see Pateman, *Participation and Democratic Theory*, pp. 38–41.

38 Schumpeter (1883–1950) is best known as the author of *Capitalism, Socialism and Democracy* (1942) (London, Routledge, 1994), in which he argues that modern democracy is nothing more than a technical mechanism for facilitating orderly changes in government elites, i.e. nothing for which one can legitimately claim ethical or normative qualities. In *Political Theology* (1922) and *The Concept of the Political* (1933) (Cambridge, MIT Press, 1992), Schmitt (1888–1985) develops his argument that liberal democratic practices of legality are never fully resistant to the extra-legal claims of legitimacy articulated by the people and/or their political representatives. When and where necessary, and especially in times of crisis, liberal law will cede to democratic legitimacy. Needless to say, democratic legitimacy can assume highly authoritarian political forms such as the kind Schmitt himself endorsed during the 1930s.

39 Lorulet, quoted in Maitron, *Histoire du movement anarchiste en France, 1880–1914* [*History of the Anarchist Movement in France, 1880–1914*], p. 256.

40 Bakunin, *Marxism, Freedom, and the State*, pp. 47–49; Grave, *L'Anarchisme*, pp. 242–45. Readers interested in Bakunin should consult Carr, *Bakunin*, and Kelly, *Mikhail Bakunin*. Bakunin's break with Marx is a well-documented, if somewhat farcical, chapter of the history of the left which has been the subject of numerous anecdotes. In *God and the State* (written on the eve of the Paris Commune in March 1871 and published six years after Bakunin's death) Bakunin remarks that whilst the impulse to anarchism is really a pre-theoretical instinct to rebel, 'The government of science and men of science, even be they positivists, disciples of Auguste Comte, or again, disciples of the doctrinaire school of German Communism, cannot fail to be impotent, ridiculous, inhuman, cruel, oppressive, exploiting, maleficent.' (Bakunin, *God and the State*, p. 55). The Freedom Press edition contains an introduction by Paul Avrich, the anarchist historian of the Kronstadt events. Paul Thomas provides a very insightful analysis of the tensions between Marx and the anarchists in *Karl Marx and the Anarchists*.

41 Proudhon, *De la capacité politique des classes ouvrières* [*On the Political Capacity of the Working Classes*], pp. 75–84.

44 Ibid., pp. 95–96. Readers interested in Proudhon's ideas should refer to Crowder, *Classical Anarchism*; Joll, *The Anarchists*, Chapter 3; and Ritter, *The Political Thought of Pierre-Joseph Proudhon*.

45 Ward, Introduction, *Fields, Factories and Workshops*, pp. 9–14. Ward's (b. 1924) ideas are summarised, along with those of other important anarchist theorists and activists in the post–World War II period, including Paul Goodman

(1911–72) and Murray Bookchin (1921–2006), in Kinna, *Anarchism*, pp. 77–79, 90–91 and 142–47.

44 Kropotkin, 'Modern Science and Anarchism' in Woodcock, *The Anarchist Reader*, p. 173. Also see Kropotkin's 'Anarchist Communism' in Baldwin, *Kropotkin's Revolutionary Pamphlets*, pp. 64–70.

45 Thomas, *The Spanish Civil War*, pp. 508–10. Gerald Brenan offers a compelling picture of the events, personalities and ideas marking the Spanish Civil War in *The Spanish Labyrinth*. Readers interested in this period should also consult George Orwell's wonderful account in *Homage to Catalonia*.

46 Miller, *Anarchism*, pp. 161–62. See also Richards, *Lessons of the Spanish Revolution*, Chapter 9.

47 Brenan, *The Spanish Labyrinth*, Chapters 13 and 14.

48 Bookchin, *The Spanish Anarchists*, pp. 308–13; Borkenau, *The Spanish Cockpit*, pp. 166–70; Leval, *Collectives in the Spanish Revolution*, Chapter 8; Miller, *Anarchism*, pp. 166–68; Marshall, *Demanding the Impossible*, pp. 464–67; and Joll, *The Anarchists*, Chapter 9.

5

The Revolt against Conformism and the Critique of Everyday Life: From Surrealism and Situationism to 1968 and Beyond

At an international congress of writers in Paris in 1935, the surrealist poet and novelist André Breton declared, 'Marx said "change the world". Rimbaud said "change life". For us these two demands express the same imperative.'[1]

In addition to being considered by many the poet of the Paris Commune, Arthur Rimbaud (1854–91) is well known as the author of *A Season in Hell* (1873) and *Illuminations* (1875). A number of his poems offer a lyrical denunciation of the class inequalities caused by capitalism signalled by Marx. But they also contain a powerful critique of the stifling monotony of everyday life and the suppression of individual sensuality in industrial societies. This critique is also found in Nietzsche's writings, and is developed in different directions by Freud, the Frankfurt School and others. Soviet-style and social democratic states have been more and less faithful, for the most part in rather unimaginative ways, to the ideas of Marx, whilst neglecting the political implications of the artistic protest of people like Nietzsche and Rimbaud. The thinkers and movements of the left considered in this chapter attempt to move theory and practice beyond the dull choice between state socialist or social democratic pragmatism versus apolitical existentialism and aestheticism.

André Breton's remarks at the 1935 writers' congress indicate his determination to combine Marx's diagnosis of the relations between humanity and external nature based on the *collective* human effort to transform nature in the labour process, on the one hand, with Nietzsche's probing interrogation of the relations between humanity and human nature based on the elaboration of *individual* aesthetic values in music, painting, sculpture, poetry, dance and theatre, on the other. Stated slightly differently, this chapter examines various attempts in the twentieth century to formulate some kind of political symmetry between collective use values (Marx) and individual aesthetic values (Nietzsche). Breton thinks that both of these distinct but dialectically related aspects of reality come together, however fleetingly and poetically, in Rimbaud's work. He argues further that the political task of surrealism is to unite the critique of capitalism with a critique of the values implicit in bourgeois art and life in such a way that the very distinctions between reality and art, external nature and internal nature, as well as that between reason and desire, are overcome in a new reality or 'surreality'.[2] It will be shown that the attempt to overcome these dualisms is a common theme in the radical political contestation of surrealism and situationism. It will also become clear how this contestation comes to fruition in the events of 1968 in France and 1969 in Italy, and how it contributes in various ways to the emergence of new social subjects that today are known as new social movements (NSMs).

From Breton's perspective, the left's hope to overcome capitalism can be seen as an attempt to overturn liberal democratic property relations while at the same time transforming our daily experience of urban space, objects, architecture and linear time. Surrealism and other movements seek to heighten or intensify daily experience so that experience itself is capable of yielding richer and more imaginative forms of knowledge and freedom rather than merely more refined techniques for surviving and consuming. For Breton this means re-evaluating and defending the cognitive and political significance of desire and the unconscious in relation to Kantian and Hegelian conceptions of rational consciousness and linear notions of historical progress. The point about external and internal *nature* with regard to Marx, Nietzsche and Rimbaud, concerns the project to find new ways of *living*. This goes back to the point made in Chapter 1 that although humanity is part of natural life it is not reducible to nature, and that there is a difference between living and surviving. That difference between surviving and living can be encapsulated in the concept of transcendence of necessity, which in this context of this chapter is concerned with the poetics of everyday life and the combined imperative to transform economic as well as cultural institutions. Before proceeding further it might be helpful to summarise briefly how the issues taken up in the following discussion relate to ideas touched upon in previous chapters.[3]

It has been seen that the economy can provide humanity with a measure of freedom from brute necessity. But this freedom is to a significant extent thwarted if socioeconomic, political and cultural institutions oppress individual sensuality and creativity with merely instrumental forms of reason. To speak in terms of the Frankfurt School and some of the Western Marxists, capitalism produces external abundance in the form of multiple goods and services, while simultaneously reproducing internal, human scarcity in the form of one-dimensional and dehumanised individuals impoverished by bureaucratic control and industrial discipline. Hence, like Cole and some of the other libertarians considered in the previous chapter, critical theorists emphasise that the specific institutional forms (legal, social and political relations) humanity creates in the process of transforming external nature have an immense impact on the possibilities for overcoming external as well as internal scarcity. In an immediate sense they have direct implications for the environment. In a more mediated sense they influence whether individuals regard life as a series of tests they pass for rewards or fail with punishment, or if on the contrary they experience life as an open-ended adventure of continual discovery. People who regard life as a series of tests are likely to become neurotic and attribute a very different set of values to life than those for whom life is an unconstrained search to know what life is.

To speak in Gramsci's terms, capitalist hegemony is not simply a question of who owns the means of production or who has how much money. It is a question of what Gramsci, following Vico, refers to as common sense, as well as who counts as an intellectual and why, the role of culture and intellectuals in society, etc. Part of Gramsci's point is that capitalism is a way of life—it is much more than just a means for organising the economy—and that life can be changed. By extension, there is nothing inherently bourgeois or capitalist about art, travelling, going to university, or being an intellectual or poet. If for Vico all people are poets in a figurative sense, for Gramsci everyone is an intellectual. The project to build a new hegemony entails releasing the poet and intellectual in each person from bourgeois notions of test performance and success, so that they may discover their own means of expression and unique values. Hence, albeit in very different ways, there is continuity between a whole range of thinkers on the left, from Gramsci and Marcuse to Cole and Breton, who maintain that the collective revolution in property relations focusing on external nature and the economy has to be accompanied by a profoundly individual revolution in values, internal nature and culture. Seen in this light, Breton's statement above can be interpreted as a way of saying that in order to change life and facilitate the expression of authentically individual values, one also has to change the world and socio-economic institutions so that value becomes a measure of creative vitality and not just a measure of a more or less efficient response to the pressure to conform in order to survive. Stated in these terms the utopian quality of left politics comes clearly into focus. The expression of individual values without a collective dimension invariably gets caught up in the individualist implications of the existentialist or aesthetic revolt of the dandy (though Sartre thinks he may have an answer to this with his theory of existentialist Marxism). If unaccompanied by a revolution in individual values and modes of daily life, the collectivist economic revolution becomes mired in the bureaucratic structures of state socialist authoritarianism and social democratic reformism, i.e. in more and less oppressive forms of expert management and party rule. Hence there is a great deal at stake in the various projects considered in this chapter to transcend the poor compromise between philosophical and aesthetic individualism on the one hand, and bureaucratised collectivism on the other, which in different degrees permeates the daily life of citizens in liberal democratic, social democratic and state socialist societies. Part of what is at stake is the possibility of imagining alternatives to either wielding power or being subservient to it. If philosophical aestheticism and various forms of technocracy can be seen as unsatisfactory variations on the bourgeois liberal model they seek to oppose, the left can be seen to be searching for the bases of altogether new ways of institutionalising the relations between humanity and nature. Once again one sees continuity with previous attempts to institute radical change during the history of the left: this idea of subverting power without seizing it is a large part of the strategy of the anarchists in the Spanish Civil War and anarchist struggle in other contexts. As will be seen in the next chapter, this is a continuity that is also palpable today in some of the currents within the broad movement against global neo-liberalism.[4]

Subverting Power without Seizing it: Antecedents to 1968

Rimbaud's call to change life by fusing poetry and revolution can be seen as a response to some of Charles Baudelaire's (1821–67) ideas on the distinctness of modern urban experience. It can be argued that Baudelaire and Rimbaud are poets thinking about the specificity of modern urban existence, much in the way that Marx reflects on the rhythms of life in industrial cities and analyses the novelty of the forces propelling them. For Baudelaire the Industrial Revolution spells the irrevocable end of the days when the poet might quietly contemplate the beauty of nature in the serenity of private seclusion. The incipient technological revolution drives people together into urban spaces in such a way that experience becomes 'de-naturalised', and to a significant extent collective, indeed, oppressively collective for the author of *Les fleurs du mal* (*Flowers of Evil*) published in 1857, the same year as Marx's *Grundrisse*. Marx makes a closely related point when he traces the developments leading to the enclosure of common land and the mass exodus of peasants and craftsmen to the towns and cities in search for work. In the factories the labour process, like experience generally, becomes collectivised to the point of no return, such that Baudelaire, Marx and Rimbaud are all drawing out the full implications for notions of production, poetry and politics. Baudelaire's response to this state of affairs is somewhat guarded, fluctuating between denunciation, ironic sarcasm and exhilaration. He is ambivalent about the rapidly changing structure of the daily experience of the traditional epistemological subject of literature and philosophy, whose existence had previously been stabilised by the relatively fixed boundaries between private internal self and the public external world. The increasing fragmentation and urbanisation of experience results in dramatically attenuated attention spans. These phenomena tend to produce an almost inevitable rupture in the customary relations between the poet as autonomous creator and his or her audience as a receptive and educated public. But it also means that the boundaries between social classes are becoming more fluid, and that the canonised subjects of poetry such as God, nature, beauty, the sublime, etc. can be replaced by an infinitely wider and more ephemeral range of subjects and experiences, embracing seemingly insignificant objects as well as chance encounters in the street. As Baudelaire's American counterpart Edgar Allan Poe (1809–49) had shown, the grandeur of beauty now had its rivals in the smallest details of everyday life, including ugliness, the seemingly accidental, the bizarre and the macabre. It is important to note that this structural transformation of social and aesthetic experience has radical political potential. Instead of having to go to a museum or university to acquire recognised bourgeois qualifications, any alert individual walking down a boulevard and onto more isolated streets could now become an autodidact schooled in the social mediation of time and space reflected in changing architectural forms. Depending on the itinerary, a casual urban stroll could turn into a quasi-cinematographic experience of the most recent episodes of colonial history as well as the key issues of current politics. While Baudelaire remains committed to the notion of the poet as a privileged interpreter of signs with special powers, for Marx and Rimbaud the advent of industrialisation heralds the coming of a new, universal human being whose poetic powers will be liberated in the eventual transition from the oppressive collectivisation of advanced capitalism to the spontaneous community of the coming society. Hence in Marx and Rimbaud one can discern the early signs of what contemporary theorists such as Antonio Negri and Paolo Virno discuss in terms of the multitude and general intelligence (Chapter 6). It will be seen in this chapter that the surrealists and situationists attempt to translate Marx and Rimbaud's diagnosis of the structural transformation of social and aesthetic experience into a revolutionary form of politics beyond the stagnant rituals of established parties and states, i.e., beyond what Guy Debord refers to as 'the society of the spectacle'.[5]

Rimbaud applauds and radicalises the disordering of the senses registered at various moments in Baudelaire's poetry. While it can be argued that Baudelaire remains a Kantian or Hegelian to the extent that he believes that subjectivity is structured by rules that invest experience with objectivity, the poet of the Paris Commune strives to break those rules.[6] For Rimbaud, poetic inquiry is not so much a search for certainty as a search for the unknown and even the impossible, i.e. a poetic equivalent of the political project to subvert power without seizing it. The impossible implies a mad love of life that is so strong that it knows no fear of death, no strategy or calculation, and no limits to the imagination. Admittedly love in this sense is not immediately liveable—it is practically impossible. Yet for Rimbaud the search for the poetic impossible is an important battle in the struggle between the impossible (but real) and the probable (and oppressive). Hence in his boldest moments he strives to overcome the distance between poetry and life by writing a poetry of life as distinct from lyrical meditations on the consolations of poetry in the face of the desolation of life. Far from constituting an epistemological limit or an impediment to expression, the arbitrary relation between words and things gives Rimbaud the power to transform the world rather than simply to represent it. Instead of plodding dialectically toward a Hegelian synthesis of reality and art or reason and desire, poems like 'The Drunken Boat' seem to anticipate something more like Walter Benjamin's notion of a dialectic at a standstill. In other words, the conflict between antitheses is not resolved for the sake of the new, 'higher' synthesis. Syntheses of this kind usually legislate the subordination of art to reality and desire to reason. As a consequence, they are likely to lead to coerced reconciliation in aesthetics and hierarchy in politics. Instead of dialectically sublimating conflicting forces, in Rimbaud's poetry contradictory desiderata are simultaneously held together in ways that are otherwise almost impossible except in very complex musical compositions.[7] As the term 'simultaneously' itself implies, the poet is transformed at the subjective level while linear time is deconstructed at the objective level of experience. It is this transformative power of Rimbaud's poetry that Breton and the surrealists seek to enlist in the pursuit of explicitly political objectives. In the work of this young vagabond they discern the possibility of a kind of pluralist avant-garde of radical experience suggesting the possibility of new ways of living for the antinationalist nomads of the future. After a brief discussion of Breton and the surrealists it will become clear that it is this alternative conception of an avant-garde that fuels the imagination of the situationists as well as the protagonists of 1968.[8]

The practical aspirations of surrealism can be considered an attempt to harness the political potential of Dada by transforming Dada's satire of bourgeois-capitalist society into a sustained critique of capitalist social relations. In this way the surrealists think it might be possible to channel Dadaist energy beyond the nihilist tendencies of the Dada movement in practice. The Romanian Tristan Tzara (1896–1963) launched Dada in 1916 with Hugo Ball, Richard Huelsenbeck, Kurt Schwitters and Hans Arp. Tzara was in his element as the dynamic leader of this anarchic movement, contributing to the performance of incoherent multilingual poems at the Café Voltaire in Zurich, where he would provoke the audience into wild frenzy, which would then be followed by more Dadaist provocation and further counterattack by the audience. Tzsara insists that poetry is more than a written creation producing a succession of images and sounds—for him it is a way of life. In 1920 he moved to Paris, where he continued to organise highly controversial Dada evenings and joined Breton's companions working on the review *Littérature*. After a series of disputes about the relationships between art and politics, Dada and surrealism eventually went their separate ways. But the participants in both movements were agreed that after the senselessness of World War I, there could be no return to traditional forms of art or traditional relations between artists and society. From their perspective, to ignore the structural transformation of social aesthetic experience with such a return could only be reactionary in politics and outmoded in aesthetics. Art now had to revolutionise society and save humanity from the savagery of war that capitalism and imperialism had wrought upon it.[9] Despite the marked differences implied by the Dadaist faith in the power of spontaneous nonsense versus the surrealist insistence on the importance of the unconscious, both movements stress that revolutionising society means rousing it from complacency and inertia with satire, scandal and subversive art. Whilst Marxism would necessarily have its place in this attempt to translate the poetic derangement of the senses into revolutionary politics, it would also have to be a supple form of Marxism capable of combining political economy with ample space for libertarian aesthetics and experimental forms of urban geography. This requires a brief word of explanation.[10]

While it might be argued that Marx's base and superstructure model offers a somewhat mechanical theory of history and a passive model of subjectivity, Dadaism and surrealism re-evaluate the political role of the superstructure by affirming the revolutionary potential of artistic production. In the writings of his more dogmatic followers in the Second and Third Internationals, Marx's theory is often interpreted to mean that in the historical development of any industrial society, a moment is reached where the productive forces of the base (material) are constrained by the legal, political, artistic and religious institutions of the superstructure (ideal), such that the former tend to seek further expansion by shattering the limits set by the latter. An exemplary statement of this view is the thesis that the discourses of human rights deployed in the French Revolution respond to the bourgeoisie's need to liberate labour power from the shackles of feudal institutions rather than any genuine commitment to the political emancipation of humanity. According to this model the forces of production look like the protagonists of history, while revolutionary consciousness is a passive by-product of the inexorable tendency of productivity to increase. The communist revolution would seem to occur when a sufficient level of development of the productive forces has been attained, thus rendering possible an abolition of social classes and a withering away of the state. In Chapters 2 to 4 it is seen that the failure of this expansion of productive capacity 'automatically' to engender a revolutionary consciousness on a mass scale among industrial workers elicits different responses on the part of Western Marxists, critical theorists and the various strands of libertarian socialism. The Dadaists, surrealists and situationists continue this line of critical dialogue with historical materialism. Albeit in very different ways, they suggest that moving into the twentieth century one can palpably imagine, due to real, objective increases in industrial productivity, that the communist society anticipated in the work of Marx and Rimbaud will be characterised by abundance and classlessness. More important, the withering away of the state in a classless society will also signal the end of art as a separate, idealised sphere of production housed in churches and museums and cut off from everyday life.

For many of the artists associated with Dada and surrealism, one of the lessons of World War I and the arrival of the twentieth century is that the way to further the revolution is decidedly not by relying on further increases in capitalism's proven industrial productivity or on an elitist political vanguard. It is achieved by attempting to accelerate the already incipient tendency of the distinction between daily life and art to wither away, which will only come to full fruition with the revolution. The idea is to move beyond the straitjackets imposed by material/ideal, reform/revolution and pre-/post-revolution schemata. Dadaists attempt to do this by elevating ordinary objects into works of art through the use of photography, cinema, collage and other mechanical techniques. The surrealists, and later especially the situationists, call for a relaunching of the class struggle in a political sense, not in any narrowly productivist sense. In seeking to promote a society without classes or an artificially separate sphere of activity designated as art, the situationists seek to rearticulate the class struggle as a project to break down the division of labour and the corresponding distinction between active planners/experts and passive executors/workers. The aim of the situationist class struggle is to combine a libertarian socialist commitment to *autogestion* with an aesthetic commitment to unite planning and execution. Rather than directly pursuing control of the means of production and state power, i.e. by becoming a new 'socialist' ruling class led by the party and capable of maintaining industrial discipline in the name of the socialist *Vaterland,* as would subsequently happen in the USSR, the working class makes refusal of salaried work its first demand. Hence while the Dadaists and surrealists want to accelerate the already manifest tendency of the distinction between daily life and art to wither away, the situationists demand the transformation of quantity (factually unprecedented levels of real wealth, technological development and abundance) into quality (refusal of salaried work as a now superfluous form of discipline appropriate for an earlier, scarcity-ridden stage of production). These can be seen as two complementary ways of acting on the fact that the transcendence of material necessity has become a real possibility rather than a flight of wishful thinking, and that the possible end of wishful thinking signals the beginning of a new 'here and now' for the reality of the imagination.[11]

Following the example of Marx and Engels in 1848, both Dadaists and surrealists published manifestos declaring the aims and strategies of their movements. Breton wrote the first *Manifesto of Surrealism,* which was published in 1924. In the first couple of pages he writes that 'man, that incurable dreamer' increasingly finds himself in a situation where despite the relative wealth or poverty of the individual in question, he or she is surrounded by unidentifiable threats and a vague sense of malaise. He suggests that this is the result of the fact that people in advanced capitalist societies increasingly find themselves caught up in a whirlwind of events in which the individual has not really taken part, such that the events are experienced as 'missed events' ('événements manqués') in which the individual is a spectator rather than an active participant.[12] The sense of unidentifiable threat and general malaise is a recurrent theme in two twentieth-century painters who had a significant impact on the surrealist movement, Giorgio de Chirico (1888–1978) and René Magritte (1898–1967). Especially in Magritte one perceives an attempt to illustrate the *visual* dimension of thinking that is obscured in *linguistic* constructions of reality. Like Freud, Magritte perceives an immense world of repressed energies and (figuratively and really) forbidden associations lurking 'behind' the apparent monolithic unity of grammar, logic and reason.

Breton and other surrealists such as Paul Éluard (1895–1952) and most notably Louis Aragon (1897–1982) argue that due to the socioeconomic and political interests propping up the façade of that linguistic unity, we are at present allowed to know only a fraction of the possible knowledge that liberated experience might yield someday. Thus the revolution of everyday life advocated by the political adherents of surrealism envisages a bursting asunder of the limits on experience designated by Kant and Freud, the possibility for which they find in the work of Lautréaumont, Marx, Rimbaud, de Chirico, Magritte and others.[13] This attempt to read Marx and Freud together in order to supplement the critique of political economy with a critique of sensual repression is highly reminiscent of Marcuse and some of the other exponents of the Frankfurt School. But while the critical theorists generally seek to elaborate Hegelian conceptions of the dialectical and historical aspects of experience, and thereby stress the need to reconceptualise what is meant by reason, the surrealists are keen to develop what they consider the aesthetic dimensions of experience and the revolutionary potential of dreams and the unconscious, and thereby force us to reconsider what is meant by desire and the imagination. In terms of the history and future of the left, these can be regarded as complementary rather than contradictory projects.[14]

Breton argues that the dichotomies rational/irrational and waking world/world of dreams serve to blunt the imagination and severely curtail the human understanding of what is real in a possible world found beyond the dogmatic demarcation of those boundaries. In his estimation the rigidity implied by these dichotomies in thought is translated into repressive institutionalised realities with the categorical separation of the individual-private/public-political. If Marx and Rimbaud had already demonstrated the futility of trying to prop up these divisions, surrealism had to indicate the political-poetic path forward. Hence in *The Communicating Vases* (1932) he writes:

> Thus we arrive at a synthetic attitude capable of reconciling the need to transform the world radically with the need to interpret it to the fullest extent possible . . . It is simply not possible that in the new society private life, with its insignificant opportunities and disappointments, will be allowed to function as the grand distributor as well as the brake on energies. The only way to prevent this is to begin preparing a great epistemological breakthrough at the level of subjective consciousness which is devoid of weakness and shame.[15]

A picture of how lyrical life might be on the other side of the reigning dichotomies governing consciousness, society, and the division of labour is portrayed by Aragon in the *Paris Peasant* (1926), and by Breton in *Nadja* (1928) and *Mad Love* (1937). Breton's fictional work strives to achieve the effect of a kind of antiliterature corresponding to the desire to abolish the distinction between art and life. Instead of constructing an obviously fictional world recounted by an identifiable protagonist surrounded by psychologically developed characters, he attempts to combine aspects of documentary reporting and detective writing with techniques from photo-journalism and the typical diary. For example, *Nadja* begins with the question, 'Who am I?', and then goes on to describe a serious of chance encounters between Breton and a mysterious woman who is both imaginary and real at the same time. But these encounters are not really the result of chance, as such, and indeed, Breton suggests that there is a world of surreal associations and secret relations between things, events, and persons that is disclosed in random wanderings (*flânerie*) as well as in moments of individual revolt against the daily routine. A world of magic affinities is obscured by our common-sense understanding of the relations between cause and effect, means and ends. This world is unlocked and revealed when the 'I' of common sense is placed in abeyance so that a much wider and richer spectrum of experience becomes possible.

If Freud had been correct to show how the apparently monolithic individual subject is actually a field of contradictory impulses and site of rational and nonrational inclinations, he betrays the revolutionary implications of his own discoveries by developing techniques to normalise and stabilise the 'I' of subjective action, i.e. to make him or her mentally stable and economically productive. Rather than trying to make the person fit for what are widely considered 'normal' life experiences such as family, work, leisure, retirement and war, the surrealists want to dismantle and deconstruct subjectivity in the radical manner suggested by Rimbaud's poetry, and thereby to disrupt standard concepts of time, space and normality as well. In different ways they suggest that the very notion of a temporal present is a fictional construct that presupposes a stable, conscious ego. That is, it is a fictional construct with significant political implications concerning the way people think about the 'useful' employment of time and the 'useful' construction of urban and rural space.[16]

Both the *Paris Peasant* and *Nadja* attest to the marvellous and even miraculous aspects of 'everyday life' ('la vie quotidienne') in Paris and other modern urban settings. Aragon and Breton maintain that one need not travel far for adventure. One needs to see ordinary things with new eyes instead of desperately searching to see new lands and fashionably marketed exotic places with the same tired eyes. Indeed, de Chirico, Magritte and a host of modern painters had already indicated that the image on a canvas need not be exotic, and that a city square or a mirror can open up new dimensions of reality according to the principle that it is not what one represents, but how one represents it. In other words form (and by analogy, the superstructure), is more than simply the decoration framing essence. This principle leads to the surrealist conclusion that all of the experiences necessary for utopia are already *here*—friendship, sensual encounters, chance discoveries, poetry, great books, the imagination and the intoxication of all the senses. Hence the challenge is not to search for a new world, but to revolutionise the *now* of the one we currently inhabit.[17] In charting a line of poetic-political experience from Baudelaire and Rimbaud to Breton, however, one notes a gradual shift in tone and an increasingly urgent call for radical change. By the time of the surrealist intervention in revolutionary politics, Breton intimates that the sense of the marvellous and miraculous is not an innate faculty, or a timeless psychological disposition, or a natural right as such. It is a political achievement in the Marxist sense that needs to be vigilantly defended as the reigns of specifically capitalist forms of social integration tend to expel all noninstrumental forms of reason and experience from everyday life, and thereby reduce individual subjectivity to functional utility and competent conformism to capitalist criteria of usefulness. This defence became the central project of the Situationist International (SI), which was taken up to varying extents by the movements of contestation in France and Italy in 1968 and 1969.[18]

The SI emerged from the dissolution of the Lettrist International and COBRA movements, which were founded in the immediate aftermath of World War II. The post-war period in Western Europe was marked by the rise of these and many other movements determined to succeed in what the surrealists had begun, i.e. to accelerate the dissolution of art as a sphere separate from daily life, and to do this in a way that also subjects the economy and state to a consistent and unrelenting critique. There was no need to explain the reasons for the necessity of the task, given the collapse of the Popular Front in France, the triumph of Franco over the republican forces in Spain, and the onslaught of a second conflagration on a world scale. Moreover, the experience of the Resistance to fascism and the preponderant role played by communists in resistance movements in countries like France and Italy aroused great hopes about the possibility of converting the end of fascism and militarist occupation into radical social transformation.[19] The young militants associated with the Lettrist International and COBRA were deeply impressed by Breton and the surrealist project, but were also convinced that surrealism ultimately remained too committed to traditional divisions between daily life and artistic creativity and, as such, was doomed to wind up being a fairly academic and elitist affair, despite the intentions of its founders.[20]

The founder of Lettrism, Isidore Isou, was born in Romania in 1925 and moved to Paris after the Second World War. Here he wrote *An Introduction to a New Poetry and a New Music* in 1946, after which he made the controversial film *Treatise on Slaver and Eternity,* which he presented at the Cannes Film Festival a few years later. Isou can be understood as a Dadaist seeking to cut through the fine airs of the culture industry and art galleries in order to return to what he considers to be the childishness and gratuity of all true creation. If Baudelaire managed to considerably shorten poetry to poems in prose, and Mallarmé had succeeded in finding the poetic resonance of a single word, Isou claims to find intensity and reality in single letters. The link with Dada is evident when one compares Kurt Schwitters's attempt to do something similar in music in the 1920s with his notion of the *Ur* (original) sonata. In any case the tension between the aesthetic and political tendencies within lettrism led to a split in 1952.[21] The more political members formed the Lettrist International (LI) and announced the creation of the journal *Potlach,* which published 29 issues between June 1954 and July 1957. The journal provided a voice for some of the future participants in the SI, including its most prominent member, the filmmaker Guy Debord (1931–94). A similar schism led to the break-up of the COBRA group, a politicised association of avant-garde artists and dissident architects mainly from Copenhagen, Brussels and Amsterdam, including the Danish painter Asger Jorn

(1914–73). The SI united the most politically militant wings of the Lettrist International and COBRA on 27 July 1957, at a congress in the small Piemontese town of Coscio d'Arroscia in the province of Cuneo.[22]

From Situationism and the Occupation of the Sorbonne to New Social Movements and *Autonomia*

Debord's theory of what he would famously call 'the society of the spectacle' in a book with the same title published in 1967 emerged from his disparate readings of Marx, surrealism, the history of council communism, and the urban sociology of Henri Lefebvre (1901–99). Lefebvre is known as a theorist and critic of everyday life in advanced capitalist societies and author of over 60 books. Debord followed Lefebvre's courses at the Paris University of Nanterre which, with the Sorbonne in the Latin Quarter of Paris and the University of Strasbourg, was to become a nodal point of the 1968 events in France. Lefebvre's lasting contribution to twentieth-century social and political thought, the *Critique of Everyday Life,* was published in three separate volumes in 1947 (*Introduction*), 1960 (*Foundations of a Sociology of Daily Life*) and 1981 (*Critique of Modernity*).[23] Although he echoes Benjamin's criticism of the surrealist emphasis on dreams and the unconscious, which both thinkers reject as a flight from reality, Lefebvre takes up and elaborates Breton's notion that people in twentieth-century society increasingly find themselves caught up in a whirlwind of 'missed' or 'failed' events in which the individual is a passive spectator to an already rehearsed and predictable spectacle.[24]

If fascism represents the pathological high point of confusion and manipulation in the first half of the century, the post-war order in Europe and North America witnessed the introduction of a range of new, more subtle forms of ideology and techniques of domination accompanying the structural transformation of the base of the capitalist economy and the corresponding passive revolution of the liberal democratic superstructure. This transformation is sometimes referred to in terms of the transition from Fordism (various degrees of state planning of the economy, large trade unions, extensive use of assembly lines) to post-Fordism (reduced role for the state and unions, flexible working arrangements in place of assembly lines). While the evolution of the base is marked by the shift from tremendous industrial production to industrial decline and sustained growth in the tertiary sector, the superstructure registers the shift from class society to mass society, the emergence of consumer culture and youth culture, and the phenomena of commodified leisure time and leisure activities. Despite the continued use of Marxist terminology in practically all his writings, Lefebvre concedes that Marxism is in urgent need of updating in order to be able to explain such issues as mass society, consumerism, youth culture, and leisure time, not to mention the

bureaucratic deformation of the USSR and its satellite states. In his estimation Marxism had hardened into an academic ideology in the west
and an apology for state power in the east, with the consequence that it is
saddled with a persistent sociological deficit, i.e. it has no real theory of
social action apart from that based on the reductive notion of class interest, and it is philosophically stagnant as well. He argues that the antidote
to this problem is not to jettison Marxism, but rather to infuse it with a
sociologically informed theory of the modalities of daily life and an
analysis of mass society. A theory of social action adequate to the complexity of social life has to carefully consider that society is not neatly
divided into proletarians and capitalists or radicals and conservatives,
and that each person, regardless of their class origins, is likely to be conservative with respect to some issues and radical with respect to others.
While this no doubt poses problems for Marxism and Marxist ideas on
political organisation, it poses even bigger problems for capitalism and
liberal democracy. For if Marxism in practice (state socialism) admittedly
has proven to be awkward and authoritarian in its attempt to coordinate
people's daily lives with representative political institutions, liberal
democracy in practice severs the link almost completely. Hence for Lefebvre the choice is between boldly reforming Marxism and jettisoning the
idea of political transparency altogether in favour of the spectacle.[25]

One of the key features of post-war Western European society is that
the economy manages to defeat scarcity for the great majority of the
population, but it does this by intensifying rather than dismantling the
division of labour. It is true that the political system is designed to adjudicate conflicts mainly to do with money and its possible redistribution,
and that the malaise and sense of 'missed' or 'failed' events in people's
lives continues to be experienced as the appropriation of time and
energy in the workplace. But this passivity is also felt in a great variety of
other situations usually neglected by Marxists and others on the orthodox social democratic and communist left who are active in the standard
institutions of political representation. Appropriation of experience—as
distinct from political representation—is accomplished by experts in the
medical profession, the mass media, government-sponsored social and
economic research, universities, manufacturers of fashion articles etc.,
and is accentuated further by the professionalisation and commercialisa-
tion of activities such as sport and traditional forms of music and dance.
The picture is rounded out further when one considers the erosion of
regional culinary traditions (and related trades) with the rise and spread
of motorways and supermarkets. For Lefebvre this means that the concept of alienation first employed by Marx to analyse the relation
between humanity and external nature mediated by the labour process
needs to be broadened and applied to a much wider sphere of action
than production in the narrowly defined economic sense taken up by

the institutional left. This is a difficult task, because while on the one hand Lefebvre wants to extend the concept of alienation beyond work and the economy, on the other he concedes that almost all social relations are now mediated by money and the patterns of its circulation. Hence, as Simmel notes, money is more than a medium of exchange, and exchange is more than an economic category of social action. Money and exchange manage to take on a life of their own capable of becoming an imperious measure of reality relegating other modes of being and action to the status of the trivial and unreal. Thus in advanced capitalism people continue to be alienated from their fellow workers and the products of the labour process, as Marx suggests, but they are also alienated from other aspects of their lives that were not previously regulated by contract, commercial ties and calculations based on the model of profitable exchange and efficient use of time.[26]

In short, where people were once alienated from the labour process, they are now alienated from life in general. The two main implications for politics and political representation are clear. First, and in direct anticipation of 1968, one can say that whereas unions and communist parties could once plausibly claim to represent workers' protest against workplace alienation and economic exploitation, socioeconomic and political representation in this traditional sense has become useless, and, from a situationist perspective, even reactionary in the sense that it affirms rather than challenges the right of some people to buy the labour power of others, and to characterise this relation as free. Second, in anticipation of Hardt and Negri's notion of the multitude (see Chapter 6), Lefebvre complements his greatly extended definition of alienation with a correspondingly enlarged definition of the proletariat, which in his estimation now includes virtually everyone, with the exception perhaps of company directors and bankers. The situationists follow Lefebvre in deploying his inclusive idea of opponents to social relations mediated by capitalism. In this regard Lefebvre and the SI rearticulate the vision of human emancipation sketched in Marx's early writings.[27]

As the preceding discussion indicates, surrealism attempts to come to grips with this state of affairs. But Lefebvre argues that the surrealist moment of struggle has passed, so to try to rearticulate surrealist motifs unwittingly amounts to a futile defence of the privileges of the artist in a society where the integrity of art (like that of virtually all trades requiring an extensive period of concentrated preparation and training) is in a process of rapid decomposition and evolution toward what is now referred to as pop art (the analogy being 'flexible' employment in the place of trades). Yet there is no ready Marxist solution due to the protean dimensions of power and money in modern industrial societies and the generalised condition of proletarianisation experienced across previously prevailing class boundaries. Despite his scepticism concerning the continuing relevance of surrealism, Lefebvre summarises the situation in terms evoking surrealist as well as Marxist motifs. Surrealism can no longer hope to re-enchant reality, so to speak, since:

> We have become too sensible for these myths, which imply naivety; we no longer believe in mysteries, but pretend to believe in them; and there is nothing so tiresome as the false naivety, the false stupidity of certain poets who in other respects have all the tactics, the tricks of the trade, the technical subtleties of literature at their fingertips (Claudel, Pierre Emmanuel, etc.). But we are not sensible enough to get beyond abstract, formal, metaphysical reason in our lives and in our consciousness. Thus we are caught in a state of uncertain transition between old and new reason; and our consciousness is still only a 'private consciousness' (individual, isolated, becoming universal only in abstract form, deprived of genuine contact with the real and of any consciousness of its practical and everyday character). We perceive of everyday life only in its trivial, inauthentic guises. How can we avoid to turn our backs on it? . . . *The Proletarian qua proletarian can become a new man.* If he does so, it is not through the intervention of some unspecified freedom which would permit him to liberate himself from his condition. Such metaphysical freedom is nothing more than a vestige from the former universal human nature supposedly common to all people. It is *through knowledge* that the proletarian liberates himself and begins *actively* to supersede his condition[28] [his emphases].

Lefebvre suggests that in the place of now outmoded practices of political representation in which the political party mediates between state and society, and in some cases eventually becomes synonymous with the state if it is 'revolutionary' enough (i.e. as in Leninism), the revolution of everyday life is precipitated by a new form of revolt he calls *contestation*. Contestation is not politics in the party political sense at all; it aims at the reinvention of daily life and the redefinition of pleasure, poetry, happiness, art, imagination, love and the praxis of revolution itself. Part of what this entails is a decisive break with the political fetishisation of the working class by career politicians and professional academics, and a major emphasis on the importance of epistemology referred to in the quotation above. In Volume II of his *Critique* (1961), he argues that in the overwhelming majority of cases, the fact is that work has become a routine parcelled up into a series of fragmented tasks rather than anything that anyone can legitimately confuse with a trade based on an apprenticeship yielding quantitative and qualitative knowledge. From this moment on it becomes absurd to argue that workers should seize control of the means of production.[29]

But it is equally absurd to urge them to reform capitalism and liberal democracy by voting for social democratic and communist proposals for redistribution. The problem is that while money is indispensable for survival, the things one can buy with money generally reinforce the division of labour and existing social hierarchies by institutionalising passivity and reducing people to the role of permanent spectatorship. Having more money in a capitalist society does not change this—it subtly enforces the refinement of strategies for survival rather than facilitating the step from the transcendence of what one is towards what one might become outside one's designated role in a rigidly defined social order. In the final chapter of Volume II, entitled 'A theory of moments', Lefebvre points out that in a civilisation centred on private life, professional occupation and status, people become consumed in the melodrama of their individual lives and personal successes and failures. The 'I' and (wherever possible) the family tend to become bulwarks against the unpredictability of life and the perceived hostility of the external world. Experiences are accumulated on the model of units of linear time and money, and are then classified as worthwhile or as a waste. The political and epistemological challenge raised by the possibility of contestation is to break out of the melodramatic cycle of predictable achievement–boredom–new achievement, and to embrace the tragedy of the impossible in Rimbaud's sense. Lefebvre calls for the transformation of daily life into a tragic as opposed to a dramatic fête in which the search for the impossible is permitted to change our very understanding of the sense of life, time and what might be possible. He reasons that whilst the existing socioeconomic and political system can neutralise practically all traditional political demands through moderate redistribution of money and the mediation of career party politicians, it cannot absorb a movement determined to transform daily life into a fête. Since the abundance created by capitalism and the manifest redundancy of the distinction between life and art makes this transformation possible for the first time in history, according to Debord and the other members of the SI there is no reason to settle for less than the realisation of life as tragedy, affirmation and celebration.[30]

It has been noted that like Lefebvre, the situationists are sympathetic to the young Marx's vision of human emancipation. It will be recalled from Chapter 1 that in his critique of Hegel the young Marx draws on Feuerbach's notion that the critique of alienation begins with the critique of religion, and that the critique of religion quickly becomes a critique of the state. Marx goes further than Feuerbach by transforming the critique of religion and the state into a critique of political economy. In the final stages of human emancipation Marx envisages that the state, as an instance of alienated political power, will 'wither away'. But whereas thinkers in the Marxist tradition such as Marx, Gramsci, Trotsky and others suggest that traditional forms of artistic creativity will flourish on an unprecedented scale when the state withers away, the situationists follow Rimbaud and Breton in striving for the immediate withering away of art as something separate from life. For the latter the answer to the riddle of theory and practice is generalised *autogestion* and creativity in actual situations, and emphatically not the continued exposition of works of art in museums, galleries and churches. State legislation promulgating free entrance to such institutions does not go anywhere near the root of the problem. Debord insists that there is a big difference between the state socialist attempt to put creation at the service of the revolution (usually resulting in pathetic examples of socialist realism worse than the art commodities created at the service of the capitalist market), and the situationist desire to put revolution at the service of creation (liberating individual subjectivity from all social relations mired in the institutionalisation of power and money). For the theorists of the SI it is mistaken to popularise or democratise art and education in order to make them accessible to the masses, as if the latter are dumb but likeable children who in the process of growing up deserve their share of 'the good things in life' in return for a productive working life quietly spent inside the machinery of the national economy. The point is to abolish the museum and university as instances of alienated creativity in the same stroke that abolishes work as wage labour. Hence the situationists follow in a revolutionary trajectory, from Marx, through Dada and surrealism to Lefebvre, which sees no possible compromise between human emancipation and the desire to abolish *all* forms of alienation.[31]

The SI's emphasis on the spontaneous construction of situations has precedents in surrealist *flânerie* around the Place de l'Opéra and the Buttes de Chaumont park in the nineteenth arrondissement of Paris in the 1920s and 1930s, and in the nocturnal pranks of some of the members of the LI in some of the poorer suburbs of Paris. The occupation of the church Notre-Dame in 1950 is perhaps the most famous of the LI stunts with an impact on the situationists.[32] The first issue of the SI journal *internationale situationiste* of 1 June 1958 provides a list of key terms and definitions, including situationism (situationisme), psychogeography (psychogéographie), drift (dérive), diversion (détournement), unitary urbanism (urbanisme unitaire) and the constructed situation (situation construite). All of these are related aspects in the situationist project to relaunch the theory and practice of revolution as an emancipatory revolution of daily life rather than as a seizure of power or as a design to engineer social justice within the narrow limits permitted by the ruling imperative to maintain steady levels of economic growth. Terms like pyschogeography, drift, and diversion are not easy to translate exactly. In addition to their linguistic meanings they have culturally specific connotations, which the situationists want to load further still with political significations. But the general idea is to politicise the ideas of contestation, creativity and fête, and to articulate them in a nondogmatic way to more recognisably political terms such as *autogestion* and revolution. The members of the SI maintain that in an era in which politics and art are no longer separate from daily life and the proletariat has come to include all alienated people, there is a wealth of political content in discussions of urban geography, films and projects for the realisation of nonfunctional architecture. The converse holds: to fetishise political parties, constitutions, solemn legislative ceremonies in parliament, national holidays with military parades—the state in the usual sense—is to fall prey to the increasingly *spectacular* quality of modern society, or what Debord sees as the spread of the spectacle to all areas of life, and to capitulate to the passive role of the spectator within it.[33]

Hence the point of situationist contestation is not fairer access to jobs and universities or free access to museums and libraries; indeed, one of the slogans of the SI widely taken up in the revolts of 1968 is 'grant our concessions and we'll ask for more!'. The challenge is to mobilise the proletariat in the extended sense to refuse wage labour, unmask the spectacle, and take control of its life in all areas. Extending the definition of the proletariat beyond the factory gates meant, among other things, embracing two relatively new social actors recently attaining prominence in post-war industrial societies in the 1960s: youth and immigrants from former colonies. The situationists were receptive to Lefebvre's idea that even if one is a Marxist, one must look at social action in sociological terms rather than in terms of historical laws, preconceived ideas about class, or what the party line on a given issue happens to be. This entails recognising that the same person can be conservative in some ways and radical in others, as well as the fact that, whether privileged or poor, youth can be volatile and radical. The ambiguous sociological and political status of youth in this sense finds its complement in the ambiguous status of the university. Although it can be considered a key institution in the reproduction of the class structure and hierarchy, in moments of crisis the university can be transformed into the most vulnerable link in the chain of social command. This is because it is continually capable of generating a radical critique of the idea of a university itself and its role in society in general. Students are privileged in the sense that they have access to the world of books and ideas, but unlike other groups their existence is uncertain because they have not yet been allotted a place in the social order. It must be borne in mind that during the period in question tremendous changes in social structure were causing palpable effects in Western Europe and North America. In Europe, the transition to mass political democracy and social integration, which at the official institutional level was nearing completion when women voted for the first time (in 1948 in Italy, for example), was now being extended further with the advent of mass university education. In April 1968, one month before the university occupations and the strikes in factories in France, very little attention was paid by the press and academics to potentially radical forms of contestation beyond the reformist demands of the CGT and the PCF. In fact, however, the situation had been explosive from the early 1960s onwards. At the level of student struggles, the events of 1968 in France were preceded by what became known as the 'scandal of Strasbourg' in 1966 (and students at Berkeley and other American universities had been demanding university reform since 1964). At the more global level they were preceded by the general climate of upheaval caused by the exacerbation of Cold War tensions resulting from the Sino-Soviet split, the Cuban revolution, and struggles for postcolonial independence in places like Algeria and Vietnam, to name but two of many. In the early and mid-1960s, the idea of a loose coalition between students, immigrants and workers across continents gradually began to emerge and lend credibility to the idea of an international proletariat in struggle with the society of the spectacle. The events leading to 1968 came quickly thereafter.[34]

At a conference in the town of Dijon in 1963, the resolution of the National Union of French Students (UNEF) contained a critical analysis of the role of the university in French society, and called for unity with the world of work. Students at the University of Strasbourg issued a statement in the same year, declaring that while university reform was an urgent priority, the reform of the university passed by way of a thorough reform of society as a whole, and in fact, Strasbourg was the first town in which students went to the streets in droves to protest against their assigned roles in society. The catalyst was a short brochure by the situationist Mustapha Kyahati on the problems of the university system. In November 1966 the local branch of UNEF declared itself in solidarity with the SI and promised financial support for the publication of Khayati's 32-page *De la misère en milieu étudiant (On the Poverty of Student Life)*. This act of solidarity with what was considered by the establishment an extremist group on the fringe of French society incensed the university administration, which was subsequently in a state of shock when it turned out that the text was read and enthusiastically approved by large numbers of what were casually assumed to be happy students. In *On the Poverty of Student Life* Khayati pillories student passivity and the paternalist authoritarianism of the French university system, and ridicules the conservatism of the political class incarnated at that time by President Charles de Gaulle. The scandal of Strasbourg ensued when the executive committee of the UNEF, a post which was considered to be a springboard to 'a good career', declared that its main purpose was to dissolve itself, and that it would put a motion with that aim to the General Assembly of students. The University of Strasbourg accused several members of the executive of illegal use of funds and took them to court. Meanwhile, Khayati's tract was translated into ten other languages and republished the following year in France with a print run of 10,000 copies. It is remarkable for its stinging wit and brilliant analysis of the links between the predictability of student life and the monotony of working life, and concludes with the exhortation that was to become one of the most popular graffiti slogans of the following year, 'live without dead time and enjoy without hindrances' ('vivre sans temps mort et jouir sans entraves').[35]

The events of 1968 and its prolonged aftermath with the 'hot autumn' in Italy the following year, as well as the rise of NSMs, began with a very local-level protest in January on the part of a small number of *enragés* (the 'furious') at the University of Nanterre against the conspicuous police presence on campus. But it soon became clear that René Riesel and the *enragés* of Nanterre were not speaking for a tiny minority, and that there was in fact mass student disaffection with the teaching of seminars, the scheduling of lectures, the format of exams and the content of courses. There was also the problem that students were treated like children—student residences were strictly separated on the basis of gender and were policed by uniformed guards. The protest against police presence widened into a contestation of the general principles regulating French university life. This contestation came to a head with the movement of 22 March, which raised questions about the US military actions in Vietnam and the complicity of the French government with American imperialism.

In the eyes of the public the movement was lead by Daniel Cohn-Bendit; but Cohn-Bendit denied this role and denied that the movement had leaders at all or even a goal, and that it was the media that was looking to focus on people's faces and personalities rather than on an analysis of the situation. In any case on 22 March, after the arrest of several members of the National Vietnam Committee, 150 students at the University of Nanterre invaded the chamber of professors demanding the right to organise political meetings in their seminars and individual subject faculties. Special police units came to the scene to restore order, but most of the students occupied the halls of the university and fought back, leading to arrests, injuries and accusations in all directions. In a matter of hours the Nanterre contingent of the movement of 1968 was organised.[36]

Throughout the month of April sit-ins and occupations were held in an attempt to draw up plans for the reorganisation of the French university system and French society in general. A wave of new pamphlets, manifestos, journals, newspapers and organisations sprang into existence, expressing solidarity with student movements in other countries as well as support for anticolonialist struggles abroad and workers' struggles at home. A recurrent theme was the issue of knowledge and the question of objectivity. In many quarters it was argued that knowledge cannot be objective or scientific in a society where the conditions for such systematic inquiry are undermined by hierarchical institutions and rampant inequalities. That is to say, the university cannot function as an island of tranquil research in the midst of a society torn by conflict and bureaucratic usurpation of citizens' rights. These impressive instances of contestation would not have been nearly enough to challenge de Gaulle and the power of the spectacle had it not been for the simultaneous eruption of wildcat strikes and the establishment of factory councils taking charge of shop-floor decisions in the Renault plant at Billancourt (Paris) and other factories. Where the PCF tried to present itself as a respectable party of order that could deliver better wages and competent industrial management, the student assemblies and factory committees demanded the end of hierarchy and alienation in education and work. In terms reminiscent of some of the ideas discussed in the preceding chapter, the French historian Richard Gombin summarises the situation and notes that:

> Only the future will tell if the unions will be supplanted by new structures such as factory committees, or a French equivalent of the British shop stewards . . . It has been noticeable that the traditional framework has tended to disappear: the radical contestation of all aspects of power within the factory, the attempts at self-organisation, even self-management, criticisms of the very role of the unions, and the unleashing of conflicts in whole sectors of the economy mark the distinctive signs of a mode of action which may well be described as libertarian.[37]

In the hope of restoring order, the trade union confederation CGT attempted to keep workers and students apart to the greatest possible extent; the PCF went so far as to denounce the students as *agents provocateurs*. But things accelerated instead. The street fighting between police and revolutionary groups that continued into the early hours of 11 May in the Latin Quarter has gone down in history as the 'night of the barricades'. On 13 May the Sorbonne was occupied by a coalition of *enragés*, situationists and a score of other far-left organisations that had formed since 1963. These events gave rise to the formation of a multiplicity of committees demanding the continuation of the occupations, which met together in the halls and seminar rooms of the Sorbonne on 17 May. It is reported that although meetings went on throughout the night and the subsequent days, no group or organisation attempted to dominate the May movement or mobilise it for its own objectives. Hence it can be argued that with the factory committees in the workplace and the student committees in the universities an embryonic network of generalised *autogestion* was in the process of formation. Some observers even began to speak of a dual power situation reminiscent of Russia in 1917, in which the spontaneous authority of the councils and committees rivalled the power of the party system and the state. The major difference of course is that while the councils played a major role in both cases, there was no equivalent to the Bolsheviks in 1968 capable of transforming the revolutionary movement into a seizure of power. In this specific respect 1968 might be more comparable to the Paris Commune.[38]

One of the lasting legacies of 1968 is precisely this refusal to renounce the freedom of the movement for privileges of party and state power, and it is this spirit that has animated a large number of the NSMs (feminist, ecologist, gay, peace, etc.) that have sprung up since then. It is moreover clear that the difficulty of sustaining movements (suggesting fluidity, spontaneity, and absence of hierarchy) against the bureaucratic and authoritarian tendencies of parties and states continues to present the left with enormous challenges. This raises questions, posed at the outset of this chapter, which are relevant beyond the context of May 1968: how might it be possible to destabilise power without seizing it or drifting into ineffectual marginality thereafter?[39] Can there be a viable politics of desire and spontaneous creation in the manner defended by the situationists, or does the quest for the impossible in this sense always stop short at its poetic invocation, i.e., as in the case of surrealism?[40]

It is common in historical commentaries on April–May 1968 to note that while there was large-scale agitation in Japan, several European countries and especially in the United States prior to the occupations of universities and factories in France, in January 1968 nobody really anticipated the wave of protest that was about to unfurl on de Gaulle and the French establishment. Like Breton and the surrealists before them, Lefebvre and the SI had identified a palpable sense of malaise and yearning for change which was nonetheless impossible to define with the existing social science terminology. What began as the protest of a handful of *enragés* against police presence on the campus of the University of Nanterre in Paris developed into a movement of contestation calling into question the basic institutions of French society including university, work, the police, gender roles and the state itself. It is also common in analyses and documentary studies of those brief months to emphasise just how quickly those established institutions, which had seemed almost invulnerable to critique, appeared to be on the verge of collapse practically overnight. Observers on the far left are particularly keen to point out that the conservatism of the PCF, CGT and de Gaulle stood out in marked contrast to the boldness of the students and the striking workers. There is more than just irony in placing the PCF and de Gaulle on the same side of the barricades. Years after 1968, the crisis of political representation spotted in the offing by Lefebvre has become visible on a world scale with the rise of international movements like ATTAC and the world and European social forums (Chapter 6). That is, the crisis goes well beyond French borders. The example of Italy in this period offers a very good case in point, which foreshadows some of the strategies of global contestation today.

A virtual collapse of political representation and an explosion of worker and student unrest in the years 1967–78 threatened to plunge Italy into a civil war. In his account in *Street Fighting Years,* the British revolutionary Tariq Ali describes the situation across Europe thus: 'Politics in Britain at the time, and even more so in Europe, were very exciting. It was now clear beyond any doubt that there was a massive process of radicalisation under way, which in France and Italy transcended the campuses and entered the factories.'[41] What happened in Italy had roots going back to the late and in many ways botched unification of 1861, the seemingly permanent fear put into the Italian bourgeoisie by the occupation of the factories in 1919–20, fascism and the turbulent years of resistance to Mussolini's regime, as well as the highly problematic (that is to say merely partial) dismantling of the fascist elements of Italian state and society after 1945, and the rise of right-wing terrorism.

In the elections of 1948 women voted for the first time at the national parliamentary level in Italy. The monarchy was abolished in a simultaneously held referendum, and Italy became a republic. The Christian Democratic Party (DC), which formed during the war under the leadership of Alcide De Gaspèri and which played a very minor role in the resistance forces dominated by socialists (PSI) and communists (PCI), won a resounding electoral victory with the open financial and ideological support of the USA. The Cold War conflict between the USA and the former USSR was beginning to invade all aspects of politics. This tendency was especially pronounced in Italy due to its recent fascist past and the remnants of fascist government structures, the prestige of the left accrued during the Resistance, the Italian border with former communist Yugoslavia, and the tradition of critical Marxist thought and action that had been established by Labriola and especially Gramsci. Gramsci's successor at the head of the PCI, Palmiro Togliatti, returned from Russian exile with Gramsci's *Prison Notebooks,* which were published and widely translated in the immediate post-war period. Togliatti insisted that the PCI was a Gramscian party committed to the construction of an alternative hegemony in Italy and the transformation of common sense and daily life. The reality, however, is that despite its massive support amongst the working classes and trade unionists, and despite a very firm footing in civil society and an active role in the organisation of local cells and popular festivals in almost all towns and cities, by the 1960s the PCI had become a responsible political party and a force for stability. The more pertinent issue, however, is that the general crisis of political representation that devastated the PCF in France after 1968 also presented the PCI in Italy with insurmountable problems.[42]

While Italy had experienced a post-war economic boom on a scale comparable to those in Germany and Japan, Italian educational and political structures remained in many respects antiquated and elitist. As a result of the boom it was not uncommon for the average household to have a car, a refrigerator, a radio, a television and a wide range of other very recently manufactured appliances, and yet to be characterised by high levels of illiteracy and poor health care, especially in the South. Mafia links with the DC assured the party's presence in national politics. Moreover, a complex association of former fascists, secret service officials, army officers, bankers, journalists and Masonic lodges coalesced in a clandestine network of antirepublican organisations with the express intent of overthrowing Italian democracy and restoring some kind of fascist order. The openly fascist MSI (Movimento Sociale Italiano, the Italian Social Movement) was flanked by a number of more secret extra-parliamentary groups to its right, which had contacts with the anti-democratic networks working toward the organisation of a restoration coup. The collaboration of these forces contrived to produce a menacing atmosphere of imminent and violent conflict captured by the term 'the strategy of tension'. The project of the extra-parliamentary right was to unleash a wave of terrorism indicating that the Italian state was too weak to guarantee order, which in its turn would provoke a popular demand for the resurrection of an authoritarian state.

The strategy of tension exploded into bloody violence at 4.30 on the afternoon of 12 December 1969. The detonation of a bomb in Piazza Fontana in Milan resulted in the death of 16 people. While state complicity was difficult to ascertain with absolute certainty, state incompetence was proved beyond the shadow of a doubt when two anarchists who had nothing to do with the bombing (subsequently shown to be the work of right-wing terrorists) were arrested and accused of the crime.[43]

With the PCI looking increasingly integrated and ineffective, the Italian left was compelled to reorganise itself on the basis of extra-parliamentary revolutionary groups active in factories, universities and neighbourhoods. The effectiveness of these groups had already been established in the course of the autumn of that same year, when a massive wave of strikes, occupations and protests had engulfed the country in what became known as the 'hot autumn' ('autunno caldo'). In some respects the autumn of 1969 was starkly reminiscent of the events of April and May 1968 in France. But in contrast to France, where stability was quickly re-established when de Gaulle's Prime Minister Georges Pompidou succeeded the General as President of the Republic in 1969, the 'hot autumn' turned out to be a prelude to one of the most violent chapters in modern Italian history. It was followed by the 'years of lead' ('anni di piombo'), as they were called, in reference to all the shooting and to the abduction and murder of Aldo Moro by the Red Brigades (BR) in the spring of 1978. There was nothing inevitable about the violent turn of radical contestation in Italy in these years. A combination of factors, including the inability or unwillingness of the state to put an end to right-wing terrorism, played a significant role. There is little doubt that the PCI's decision to adopt a cooperative role and try out a 'historic compromise' with the DC in 1975 in order to further demonstrate its professional competence convinced some people that the Italian political system could no longer be reformed: it had to be overthrown by force. It will be useful to provide a couple of words of explanation about the rise of an extra-parliamentary left in Italy and the violence that is unfortunately sometimes associated with it before concluding this chapter.[44]

Since the rise and spread of factory councils in 1919–20 there has always been widespread support for an autonomous revolutionary movement in Italy, rooted in the workplace but independent of even the ostensibly most left-wing political parties. Gramsci's early writings on workplace democracy in *L'Ordine Nuovo* (*New Order*) were regarded by many Italian militants as just as important if not more important than the far more famous *Prison Notebooks*. This conviction gained ground after World War II, as Togliatti and his successor Enrico Berlinguer seemed increasingly determined to transform the PCI into a parliamentary party capable of enforcing the same kind of factory discipline as any other political party, and to do this in Gramsci's name. In his mature writings and pronouncements on fascism Gramsci advocates political alliances with moderate antifascist forces for the purpose of undermining Mussolini's dictatorship. In some of these works it is possible to read Gramsci as an advocate of reformist compromise and national unity. But by the early 1950s, a wide range of thinkers and activist to the left of the PCI began to object that with the onslaught of the Cold War and the post-war 'economic miracle' ('miracolo economico'), the period of 'classical' fascism was clearly now over. The first wave of fascism corresponded to the capitalist imperative to introduce a considerable degree of planning into the economy while maintaining the prerogatives of capital to determine the rhythms and products of production. With the help of its international allies, the Italian bourgeoisie had managed to do this, and no longer needed thugs like Mussolini to continue its domination of Italian society.

To the left of the PCI it was increasingly argued that Gramsci's continuing relevance consisted in his factory council writings and in the specific prison notebook entitled *Americanism and Fordism*, in which he evaluates the transition from craft and industrial production to Fordist and post-Fordist assembly lines and new forms of flexibility in the workplace. To many activists it became clear that with the consolidation of DC power the time had come to abandon the Gramsci of national unity and antifascist humanism dear to Togliatti and Berlinguer, in order to reaffirm the Gramsci of council communism and worker autonomy.[45]

The theoretical origins of the radical contestation of 1968–77 can be found in the positions taken up in the journals *Quaderni Rossi* (*Red Notebooks*), edited by Raniero Panzieri (1921–64) and *Classe Operaia* (*Working Class*), edited by Mario Tronti (born in Rome in 1931). Although they dissolved in 1967–68, these journals outlined the main tenets of a movement known in Italy known as workerism (*operaismo*) culminating in the formation of groups demanding full working-class autonomy from capital and political parties like the PCI. From an *operaista* perspective, the problem with social democratic parties and communist parties operating within parliamentary democracy is that in one fundamental respect they do not differ from liberal democratic parties or even from right-wing populist parties. Within this system they must adopt a populist logic, which is always capable of being absorbed and distorted by the institutions of mainstream representative democracy. This is a logic that posits a representative identity between the people and the state. In left populism this identity is distilled in the working class and represented in the party, and then symbolised in the media by the party leader. On the one hand this is a mode of representation that is trapped in the society of the spectacle. On the other it implicitly accepts a crude model of power according to which the state is a kind of repository of power units, which are unequally distributed throughout society. Inequality calls for more (communist) or less drastic (social democratic) redistributive measures, and the party is assumed to be the best vehicle for administering this redistribution. If it is the great merit of Foucault to have broken with this model of power at the theoretical level, as will be seen in the next chapter, it is the great merit of a number of Italian extra-parliamentary groups to have challenged it in practice. The aim of Workers' Autonomy (Autonomia Operaia) and other groups in the late 1960s and early 1970s became a refusal of wage labour at the point of production, as well as refusal of political representation in a parliament that recognises 'the people' only in terms of the spurious universality conferred by equality of citizenship for everyone regardless of the reality of their position in the production process. Hence the point for *operaismo* is not to formulate a left-wing humanist version of the people, whose best essence is supposedly embodied by the saintly figures of poor workers in need of redistributive aid. On the contrary, one must insist on the specificity and centrality of class in a political system that systematically effaces the differences between classes with all-inclusive and generic modes of representation.[46]

Autonomia formed in 1973 with the intention of galvanising the forces of contestation that came to fruition during the 'hot autumn' and its aftermath. Along with Antonio Negri, formerly of the extra-parliamentary Workers' Power (Potere Operaio), a number of other university professors in Padua and Trent began to articulate a vision of autonomous workers' organisations locked in struggle with the state precisely at that site where they thought that the capitalist state finds its *raison d'être*—the point of production. The movement, which tended to hover a bit between network and extra-parliamentary party, enjoyed considerable support in Italian factories, universities and city neighbourhoods. In marked contrast to the defensive and redistributive demands of traditional parties and unions, Autonomia pursued an offensive strategy animated by the conviction that the working class is the driving force of capitalism and decidedly not the passive agent of capital: workers make the commodities and offer the services that everybody is more or less forced to buy, and it is workers who have the power to refuse work. Like Debord and the situationists, Negri and the militants of Autonomia suggest that what Gramsci refers to as Fordism has transformed industrial workers with well-defined trades into a generalised social worker (*operaio sociale*) of post-Fordism. For the most part this is an elaboration of the inclusive redefinition of the proletariat initiated by Lefebvre in the *Critique of Daily Life*. But rather than following the council communist platform of Gramsci in 1919–20 or Lefebvre in demanding the spread of *autogestion,* Autonomia made refusal of work one of its top priorities. In retrospect it seems clear that there are obvious limits to what the strategy of refusal can offer until there is a concrete alternative to capitalism and wage labour of the kind outlined by thinkers like G. D. H. Cole. Further problems arose as Autonomia reiterated the need to pass from the defensive to the offensive without specifying how this could be done without direct recourse to force. There is little doubt about the corruption of the Italian political class in those years and its complicity with the Mafia and secret lodges with links to fascist organisations. But it is also very doubtful that the solution of meeting force with force could have produced anything but bloodshed and further repression, as the example of the BR illustrates. In fact, a kind of stalemate was reached between the intransigence of groups like Autonomia and the resolution of the repressive elements of the Italian state and its international supporters to restore order on terms favourable to the further development of capitalism. Negri was accused of inciting violence and forced into exile in France for many years after spending time in prison in Italy at the end of the 1970s. He has subsequently emerged from clandestinity and rose to considerable international fame with the publication of *Empire,* written with Michael Hardt in 2000, which will be considered in the final chapter of this book.[47]

Rather than signalling a permanent impasse, the stalemate alluded to above is indicative of some of the far-reaching changes in the theory and practice of the left heralded by the evolution of contestation from surrealism and situationism to the events of 1968–77 and Autonomia. The crisis of traditional forms of representation, such as the union and party, is coterminous with the rise of the widest imaginable array of NSMs. Some, like the disparate descendants of Autonomia, remain committed to the centrality of class struggle, while many others have opted for new terrains of struggle to do with gender, identity and other issues concerned with the politics of daily life and possible developments in the implementation of human rights. If the organisational form of the party has been challenged by the reality of movements and networks, the notion of the left intellectual has also undergone considerable change with important implications for future practice. Figures such as Sartre and Breton have been succeeded by less traditional radical thinkers who do not occupy the role of the 'intellectual' as such, much in the way that the craft worker has been replaced by the general social worker as part of the transformations that have contributed to the rise of student and youth movements. In contrast to predictions about the coming of a totally administered mass society sometimes conjured up by critical theory in its more pessimistic moments, it appears that contemporary social reality is characterised by the complex and contradictory simultaneity of contestation, consensus and conflict. This contradictory situation is at the centre of the reflections of the theorists and movements considered in Chapter 6.

Suggestions for Further Reading

Ali, Tariq. *Street Fighting Years,* New York, Citadel, 1980.

Lefebvre, Henri. *Critique of Everyday Life,* Vol. I, London, Verso, 1991.

Lumley, Robert. *States of Emergency: Cultures of Revolt in Italy from 1968–1978,* London, Verso, 1990.

Marcus, Greil. *Lipstick Traces: A Secret History of the Twentieth Century,* Cambridge, Harvard University Press, 1989.

Nadeau, Maurice. *The History of Surrealism,* Cambridge, Harvard University Press, 1989.

Nicholls, Peter. *Modernisms: A Literary Guide,* Berkeley, University of California Press, 1995.

Plant, Sadie. *The Most Dangerous Gesture: The Situationist International in a Postmodern World,* London, Routledge, 1992.

Roberts, John. *Philosophising the Everyday: Revolutionary Praxis and the Fate of Cultural Theory,* London, Pluto, 2006.

Ross, Kristin. *The Emergence of Social Space: Rimbaud and the Paris Commune,* Minneapolis, University of Minnesota Press, 1988.

Wright, Steve. *Storming Heaven: Class Composition and Struggle in Italian Autonomous Marxism,* London, Pluto, 2002.

Notes

1 Breton, speech at the Congress of Writers, reprinted in *La position politique du surréalisme* [*The Political Position of Surrealism*], p. 68. Breton joined the French

Communist Party (PCF) in 1927. Relations with the PCF were always strained by his libertarian conception of communism, and by the time of the 1935 writers' congress he was no longer a member. This did not prevent him being a life-long supporter of unorthodox revolutionary politics.

2 Breton, *Manifeste du surréalisme* [*Manifesto of Surrealism*], p. 24. Two additional surrealist manifestos written by Breton were published in 1930 and 1942. It is often said that the first surrealist work is Breton and Philippe Soupault's (1897–1990) *Les champs magnétiques* [*The Magnetic Fields*]. For a comprehensive overview of the origins and development of surrealism, see Nicholls, *Modernisms*, Chapter 12.

3 Synthesising Hegel, Lacan, Deleuze and film theory, Slavoj Zizek has developed the political significance of desire and the unconscious in innovative and original ways. For an analysis and assessment of his contribution to a new theory of political radicalism, see Feldner and Vighi, *Beyond Foucault*.

4 Since the leader of the Zapatista Army for National Liberation (EZLN) declared in January 1994 that revolution in Mexico was imminent, there has been much debate about whether Marcos and the Zapatistas represent another episode in the long history of attempts to destabilise power without seizing it. For a wide-ranging analysis that relates the movement in Mexico to the history of the country as well as the ideas of Guy Debord and Antonio Negri, see Mentinis, *Zapatistas*.

5 For an analysis of Baudelaire's ambivalence about the end of integral experience in the context of modern industrial sociopolitical reality, see Peter Collier, 'Nineteenth–century Paris: vision and nightmare', in Timms and Kelley, *Unreal City*, pp. 33–37, and Nicholls, *Modernisms*, pp. 16–21. For Baudelaire's praise of Poe's originality, see the chapter on Poe in Baudelaire, *L'art romantique* [*Romantic Art*], Chapter 16.

6 Any good collection of Rimbaud's poetry will include those poems directly inspired by the events of 1871. These include 'Parisian War Song', 'The Parisian Orgy', 'Paris is Re-populating' and 'The Hands of Jeanne-Marie'. For a brilliant analysis of the poetics of Rimbaud's political ideas, see Ross, *The Emergence of Social Space*, especially Chapter 4. The English version published by Macmillan in the same year contains a useful introduction by the Marxist literary critic Terry Eagleton. Readers of French should consult Gascar, *Rimbaud et la Commune*, and the painter André D'Hotel's *Rimbaud et la révolte moderne*.

7 This is the achievement of another poet with considerable influence on the surrealists, Stéphane Mallarmé (1842–98).

8 Nicholls, *Modernisms*, pp. 29–30. The possibility of a cultural avant-garde with radical political implications can be discerned in the work of Comte de Lautréaumont (Isidore Ducasse, 1846–70) and the figure of Guillaume Apollinaire (1880–1918), inventor of the term 'surrealism'. In anticipation of Gramsci's notion that everyone is an intellectual, in his *Poésies* Lautréaumont maintains that real poetry must be made by everyone. Apollinaire defined his poetry as the search for the unity of art and life in a new lyrical humanism.

9 It is worth noting that there are differences in approach between 'northern' Dadaists working primarily in Germany and 'southern' Dadaists working primarily in France. While the former, including artists such as George Grosz (1893–1959), Wieland Herzfelde (1896–1988), Raoul Hausmann (1886–1971), John Heartfield (1891–1968), Erwin Piscator (1893–1966) and others, had close

ties with anarchist and communist movements, the later were more inclined to confine their energies to artistic creativity.

10 In this endeavour there is little doubt about the influence on both movements of Alfred Jarry's (1873–1907) grotesque theatrical comedy about *King Ubu*, which manages to combine the more dramatic elements of Shakespeare with the burlesque traditions of popular marionette theatre in order to satirise a brutal *coup d'état*. The play anticipates Dada and surrealism in that, rather than attempting faithfully to reproduce real life, Jarry's language evokes a kind of extra-intensified reality removed from the normal spatial and temporal boundaries that define the real. He also depicts action in its own terms without relying on traditional notions of individual character development or psychological motivation, and thus prefigures some of the themes in the work of Beckett, Adamov, Albee and Genet. Legend has it that Breton learned about Jarry by way of Jacques Vaché (1895–1919), an injured soldier and poet he met in a medical hospital in Nantes at the beginning of World War I. On his return from the front in 1916, Vaché sent Breton his *War Letters,* in which he expresses his indifference to all of the political and cultural inanities, including art, which in his estimation had a hand in causing the great debâcle. It remains uncertain whether his death at the age of 24 of an opium overdose was suicide or the just result of his majestic indifference. In any case Breton credits him, along with Jarry, as being one of the key figures in the transition from the symbolism of poets like Mallarmé to Dada and surrealism. See the brief homage by Breton in *Les pas perdus* [*The Lost Steps*].

11 In anticipation of the discussion of 1968 to follow, one can regard the events of May that year as a very good example of how elements within the superstructure can emerge as catalysts of militant protest. Schematic versions of historical materialism tend to identify the economy (base) as the 'motor' of social change, and then go on to identify the legislature and the executive as the key state institutions most immediately affected by that motor at the level of the superstructure. Yet the events of 1968 suggest that an apparently remote part of the superstructure, such as the education system, can actually be much more effective than economic crisis as a laboratory for new social and political values. Though Deleuze and Guattari take this thesis beyond the parameters of historical materialism, they nonetheless consider their work to be a development within their particular brand of Nietzschean Marxism (Chapter 6).

12 Breton, *Manifestes du surréalisme* [*Manifesto of Surrealism*], p. 12. One could also translate the word 'manqué' with the English 'failed'.

13 One of these other sources is no doubt the prodigious influence of the life and work of Picasso (1881–1973), painter of the antiwar canvas *Guernica,* and consistent (if independent) political supporter of the PCF.

14 It should be noted that while the attempt to recuperate the Hegelian dimension of Marxism is common to many of the exponents of Western Marxism and critical theory, there is also dissent within and between both groups about how best to go about doing this. Moreover, thinkers such as Adorno can be seen to be developing a non-Hegelian kind of dialectics, or what Adorno refers to as negative dialectics.

15 Breton, *Les vases communicants* [*The Communicating Vases*] (1932), pp. 149 and 153. Part III of the book contains Breton's vision of a surrealist Marx-Freud synthesis which offers a kind of a political-poetic version of the Frankfurt School

critique of instrumental reason. One cannot be certain, but it is a fair guess that Breton's scathing critique of private life and its petty ambitions and disappointments is directly inspired by Balzac's (1799–1850) portrayal of the increasing power of money over all things and people in nineteenth-century French society in the *Comédie humaine*. The novels by Aragon and Breton cited are available in English.

16 Breton, *Nadja*, p. 9. For an analysis of the stylistic innovations and political implications of *Nadja* and the *Paris Peasant*, see Nicholls, *Modernisms*, Chapter 12, and Ian Walker, *City Gorged with Dreams*, Chapters 3, 4 and 6.

17 The French journalist Pierre Assouline describes the photographer Henri Cartier-Bresson as the 'eye of the [twentieth] century', and explains Cartier-Bresson's commitment to surrealism as a belief in spontaneity and revolt against all forms of routine and against liberal democratic and state socialist dogma. On this account surrealism in art and politics suggests news ways of conceiving of the revolution of daily life without bureaucratic structures and leadership. See Ansouline, *Cartier-Bresson*, pp. 62–67, and Walker, *City Gorged with Dreams*, Chapter 8. It will be seen below how the idea of transforming the here and now into open-ended situations is taken up by the situationists.

18 While Baudelaire quips that he abhors the idea of being 'useful', Rimbaud, speaking for his comrades in the Paris Commune and elsewhere, says that no, 'we are not going to work'. Both poets manifest a kind of aristocratic disdain for wage labour which is taken up by surrealists and especially situationists who pose the question why, and for whose benefit, exactly, are we working? The link between the flourishing of modern creativity and the critique of wage labour crystallises in the situationist argument that individual genius and joy will only come to full fruition with collective rejection of the current mode of production. They suggest that when this happens the humanism and creativity that flourished in the Renaissance will be possible for all of society. But while for the SI the Renaissance fetishises the 'work of art' and traditional relations between artist and public, the task of the revolution in the twentieth century is to transcend the production of 'art objects' with living situations. In a manner akin to Marx's claim about the need to abolish philosophy with revolution, situationism demands that humanism abolish itself by realising its claims in practice.

19 There is not enough space here to recount the history of the Popular Front in France and the Resistance in France, Italy and Germany. These episodes are nonetheless two important chapters in the history of the left in Europe. It should be mentioned in passing, however, that in the spring of 1936 the Popular Front government under the leadership of the socialist Léon Blum managed to unite socialists, radicals and communists in order to pass a series of wide-reaching reforms positively affecting the working hours, wages, holiday entitlements and retirement plans of French workers. His government only managed to stay in power for a year. Despite a certain amount of historical controversy concerning the reasons for the demise of the Popular Front in April 1937, there is a broad consensus that it was to a significant extent undermined by a financial speculators precipitating a run on the franc. Blum briefly returned to power in 1938, but he was unable to hold the coalition forces together. His government was replaced by a much more moderate centrist government which eventually signed the accord with Hitler at Munich in 1938.

20 For a very informed discussion of the difficulties of the movement to maintain a credible political profile, see the historian of surrealism Maurice Nadeau's account in *The History of Surrealism*.

21 For an entertaining and extremely well-researched account of the affinities between Dada, surrealism, lettrism, situationism, the events of 1968 and the punk scene of the 1970s and 1980s in Great Britain and the United States, see Marcus, *Lipstick Traces*. Marcus's book contains a good deal of information about Isou and Henri Lefebvre, two key figures in this period who are not at all well known outside France.

22 The artists, architects and urban planners of the COBRA movement (1948–51), many of whom joined the Association of Free Artists (1948–57) attempted to develop a distinctly antifunctional vision of urban space in direct opposition to architects such as Le Corbusier (Charles-Édouard Jeaneret, 1887–1965). Jorn, the Dutchman Constant Anton Nieuwenhuys, better known as Constant (1920–2005), the Italian Giuseppe Pinot Gallizio (1902–64) and others were founding members of the movement and its projects for a new urbanism, which they referred to as the Imaginary Bauhaus, before joining the SI in 1957.

23 The 1957 edition of the first critique contains a lengthy and elucidating introduction in both French and English. The English version of Volume I with the 1957 introduction is translated by John Moore and published in London by Verso (1991; paperback edition 1992).

24 See Walter Benjamin, 'Surrealism: the last snapshot of the European intelligentsia' (1929), now in his *Reflections*. Despite the critical standpoint on surrealism adopted in that essay, Benjamin does applaud the surrealists for attempting to 'harness the forces of intoxication for the revolution'. Due to lack of space it will not be possible to look at the views of two other figures closely associated with the surrealist project to revolutionise daily life, Georges Bataille (1897–1962), author of *The Accursed Share* (1949) and Antonin Artaud (1896–1948), author of *The Theatre and its Double* (1938). On Bataille see Marcus, *Lipstick Traces*, pp. 394–96; for Artaud see Nicholls, *Modernisms*, pp. 293–98.

25 Henri Lefebvre, *Critique de la vie quotidienne* [*Critique of Everyday Life*], Vol. I, pp. 61–66, and Vol. III, pp. 113–14.

26 Simmel, *Die Philosophie des Geldes* [*The Philosophy of Money*], pp. 209–10, 428, 449–51, 491, 721.

27 For a look at the links between Lefebvre's ideas and situationist demands, see the last chapter (entitled 'Lipstick Traces') of Marcus, *Lipstick Traces,* and Plant, *The Most Radical Gesture,* Chapter 3. Relations between Lefebvre and the SI eventually became strained. To the latter, which cultivated an air of secrecy and total refusal, Lefebvre looked like an establishment figure with a permanent university post. On a slightly less personal note, they disagree about the fundamental category of labour itself, in that whilst Lefebvre advocates the humanisation of work, the SI categorically rejects work in all of its forms.

28 Lefebvre, op. cit., Vol. I, pp. 132–33 and 144 (his emphases). For an analysis of the relation between the social relations characteristic of advanced industrial capitalism and the evolution of artistic production towards pop art and punk, see Chapter 1 of Frith and Horne, *Art into Pop*.

29 The theory of contestation is also developed in relation to 1968 in Lefebvre's *L'irruption de nanterre au sommet* [*The Irruption of Nanterre at the Summit*], pp. 73–82.

It becomes clear that the aesthetic and philosophical difficulty of representing an object with a word, explored by Magritte and others, finds its political complement in the impossibility of representation without positing some kind of spurious identity between the representative leaders and the represented people. This suggests that the demand for the greatest possible *autogestion* aims at institutionalising a kind of harmony between philosophical-aesthetic reality and uncoerced political community. In the introduction to a book published in the same year as Lefebvre's *L'irruption*, Gilles Deleuze suggests that modern thinking is born out of the philosophical and political failure of the idea of representation, which can be seen as parallel to Adorno's ideas on nonidentity. See his *Différence et répétition* [*Difference and Repetition*], pp. 1–2.

30 Levebvre, *Critique de la vie quotidienne* [*Critique of Everyday Life*], Vol. *II*, pp. 344–57. Against this background one begins to see the particular way in which figures like Rimbaud and Vaché offer the example of a non-Leninist avant-garde that puts a much higher value on life than on survival. It is in this sense that the notion of impossibility itself takes on new meaning. For if disavowal of survival makes life impossible, it also opens up the possibility of a new life which is lived, however briefly, instead of sporadically peeped at from the perspective of ever-diminishing units of time. Claude Lefort, a longstanding contributor to *Socialisme ou Barbarie?*, describes the goal as that of developing a sense for the possible without losing one's sense of the real. See Lefort, 'Le nouveau désordre', in Morin et al., *Mai 68*, p. 62. The articles by Morin and especially Coudray provide a very insightful theoretical analysis of May 1968 and its implications for the future of the radical left.

31 Debord, *La société du spectacle* [*The Society of the Spectacle*] (1967), first published by Buchet-Chastel, pp. 147–48 (thesis 191 of 221).

32 See Marcus, *Lipstick Traces*, pp. 279–322, and Sadler, *The Situationist City*.

33 'Définitions', in Patrick Mosconi (ed.), *Internationale situationiste* (hereafter *SI*), pp. 13–14. Mosconi has collected all twelve issues of the *SI* published in the years 1958 to 1969. This is a very valuable volume that gives a good indication of the range of people involved in this at times secretive, almost clandestine group of libertarian militants. While the works of Debord and Raoul Vaneigem (born in Belgium in 1934) are available, translated into English and other languages, in paperback editions, Mosconi's *SI* contains the articles of a number of more marginal but highly original situationist thinkers, such as Jorn, Constant, Michèle Bernstein, Mustapha Khayati and Attila Kotanyi.

34 Thus what today is referred to as the multitude has its origins in situationism and the contestations of 1968, which in their turn have origins in the writings of Marx, Rimbaud and surrealism. It has been necessary to show why in some detail, which is also why it has not been possible to analyse the relation between postcolonial struggle and the left. The space required to do this, like the space required to look at the NSMs in the required detail and depth, exceeds what is possible in this study. It would be impossible to look at the currents of the left covered here as well as postcolonial movements and NSMs without trivialising the importance of the latter by attempting to simplify post-colonial and new social movement thought and action in a few summary pages. It is hoped that readers will excuse these gaps and bear in mind that it has already been necessary to omit major episodes such as the Russian Revolution and the

history of social democracy in order to lend coherence to the analysis of the theoretical perspectives offered in this book.

35 The text succinctly unites all the major situationist themes, and counts as the first of the three major theoretical contributions to the left made by members of SI (along with Debord's *La société du spectacle* [*The Society of the Spectacle*] and Vaneigem's *Traité de savoir-vivre à l'usage des jeunes générations* [*The Revolution of Everyday Life*]. Khayati's text is analysed in relation to the 'scandal of Strasbourg' and discussed by an unnamed member of the SI in *SI*, n. 11 (1967), pp. 519–27.

36 Zegel, *Les idées de mai*, pp. 24–25.

37 Gombin, 'The Ideology and Practice of Contestation seen through Recent Events in France Today', p. 32. This article provides information on the links between student and worker struggles as well as details about the structure of the factory committees that spontaneously arose in 1967–68. For a more general analysis of libertarian currents on the left, as well as a libertarian interpretation of 1968, see Gombin's *The Origins of Modern Leftism*, Chapter 4.

38 René Vienet, *Enragés et situationnistes dans le mouvement des occupations* [*Enragés and Situationists in the Movement of the Occupations*], pp. 24–34 and 135–38. Although this account is frankly pro-situationist, it is nonetheless regarded as a very reliable source of information about May 1968 and its aftermath. It contains a large number of fantastic photographs as well as an appendix of relevant documents, including Khayati's *On the Poverty of Student Life*. It is worth noting here that Sartre vigorously defended the occupations and lent his intellectual prestige to the cause of revolution in May 1968.

39 This relevance becomes clear when one considers the trajectory of movements such as Solidarity in Poland, the African National Congress (ANC) in South Africa, the Zapatistas in Mexico, etc.

40 Instead of trying to become respectable or an institutionalised force in French politics, the SI dissolved in 1972. Debord explains why in some detail in a text written with the Italian Gianfranco Sanguinetti in 1972, entitled *La véritable scission dans l'internationale: circulaire publique de l'internationale situationiste* [*The Real Split in the SI*].

41 Ali, *Street Fighting Years*, p. 237. For the British context see Chun, *The British New Left*.

42 Although it had never been nearly as Stalinist as the PCF and had no responsibility for what had happened in the name of communism in the former USSR and its satellites, the PCI leadership took the fall of the Berlin Wall in 1989 as a cue to exit the historical stage. In 1991 it became the Democratic Party of the Left (PDS), which eventually became Democrats of the Left (DS). The DS is now a centrist party and the central coalition partner of Italy's current government under the leadership of Romano Prodi. During the Cold War the PCF and PCI were major electoral forces in Western European politics; at the height of their popularity they could count on anywhere between 25 percent (PCF) and 33 percent (PCI) of the vote in parliamentary elections. They are now nonexistent (PCI) or marginal (PCF). The theoretical and practical reasons for that demise are implicit in the analysis in this chapter and Chapter 6 of this study.

43 The arrest of Giuseppe Pinelli and Pietro Valpreda remains a source of embarrassment for the Italian justice system. In the course of his interrogation, Pinelli jumped out of the window of a police station and died in what was offi-

cially declared to be a suicide. There is little doubt, however, that Pinelli was provoked into leaping to his death. The Milanese playwright Dario Fo (born in 1926) staged the incident in a drama entitled *Accidental Death of an Anarchist*. Through their innovative production of alternative theatre in workers' clubs, bowling alleys and other unusual urban spaces, Fo and his wife Franca Rame occupy a unique place in the history of the left in the twentieth century. (Rame has suffered for her political convictions, being kidnapped, tortured and raped at the hands of neo-fascists in 1973.) For an excellent analysis of their importance set within the turbulent years considered here, see Lumley, *States of Emergency*, pp. 120–34. Lumley's book provides a wealth of information about all aspects of the Italian situation in this period and is a must read for anyone interested in revolutionary politics since 1968. Readers interested in Fo and Rame should also consult Behan, *Dario Fo*.

44 For an historical account of the 'hot autumn' and the violent turn in political contestation in these years, see Lumley, *States of Emergency*, Parts III and IV. Almost all historical accounts indicate that the BR was just one of the groups of the extra-parliamentary left in the 1970s. Unsurprisingly, spectacular exploits such as the Moro abduction resulted in huge media coverage, which contributed to the view that extra-parliamentary contestation and violence were synonymous. While in no way excusing BR violence, it must be borne in mind that they began with kidnappings and farcical mock trials in which no one was hurt. As ring-wing terror persisted and police repression against the BR and other extra-parliamentary groups calling for more democracy was increased, a core of BR activists took matters into their own hands, and things took a horrible turn for the worse. There are some parallels with the German case and the rise of the Red Army Faction (RAF). An important figure in the German context is the student leader and activist Rudi Dutschke (1940–79), who was the victim of an assassination attempt in 1968 that eventually lead to his death 11 years later.

45 Some felt that Gramsci had to be abandoned altogether along with the entire tradition of humanist Marxism which had been dismissed by Althusser in *For Marx* (Chapter 2). For this view see Asor-Rosa, *Scrittori e popolo* [*Writers and the People*].

46 For a look at the factors contributing to the appearance of *Operaismo* out of *Quaderni Rossi* and *Classe Operaia*, as well as the rise of Autonomia Operaia thereafter, see Wright, *Storming Heaven* Both Lumley's (*States of Emergency*) and Wright's studies offer a good idea of the vast number of revolutionary organisations and networks that came into existence in Italy at this time. In addition to Autonomia some of the more famous ones are Potere Operaio (Workers' Power), Lotta Continua (Continuing Struggle), GAP (Gruppi Armati Partigiani, Armed Partisan Groups), Avanguardia Operaia (Workers' Vanguard) and Manifesto. In total, however, Wright estimates that there were dozens (p. 126). Beyond this staggering manifestation of intellectual and practical militancy, it is safe to say that the number of newspapers, bulletins and pamphlets that proliferated greatly exceeds the number of organised groups.

47 On the question of refusal of work, see Tronti, 'The Strategy of Refusal' in Lottinger and Marazzi, *Italy, Autonomia*, pp. 28–35. This collection includes contributions by Fo, Bifo (Franco Berardi), Debord, Negri, Deleuze, and many former members of Potere Operaia and Autonomia, such as Renato Curcio, Oreste

Scalzone and Sergio Bologna. See too the essays collected in Virno and Hardt *Radical Thought in Italy.* Needless to say, the break-up of Autonomia and the BR does not mark the definitive end of radical contestation in Italy. A network of pirate radio stations organised by students and nonstudent youth, as well as an extensive movement of squatters associated with what is called the 'Movement of 77' continues to have a marked presence in Italian cities. Some of the work of the social centres (*centri sociali*) in contemporary Italy is directly inspired by the Movement of 77 and other NSMs, which took over where Autonomia left off. See Lumley, *States of Emergency,* Part IV, Chapter 20 and Conclusion.

6

Towards a New Form of Internationalism?
From the Critique of Everyday Life to
Global Anti-Capitalism

Previous chapters have examined the reciprocal influence of decisive moments in the history of political contestation and the elaboration of theoretical frameworks capable of illuminating key aspects of the historical process. In a variety of ways the left has attempted to understand history, and on the basis of that knowledge tried to contribute to changing the structure of society as an integral part of the struggle for human freedom. Thus for many years left-wing movements have attempted to grasp reality, intervene to transform it, and then explain new realities with comprehensive theories about freedom and power. This is clear if one keeps in mind the close relationship between the French Revolution and the Hegelian theory of the state criticised by Marx in his writings of 1843, the Paris Commune and Marx's *The Civil War in France,* fascism and the *Prison Notebooks,* the events of 1968–77 and the unorthodox ideas developed in the *Critique of Everyday Life* and the *Society of the Spectacle,* etc. In the period spanning the *Communist Manifesto* in 1848 to the occupation of the Sorbonne in 1968, the representatives of the left looked at in Chapters 1 to 5 are generally confident that the right combination of critical analysis and political activism will eventually create a society in which the free development of each becomes the condition for the free development of all. In the contemporary world there are numerous examples of continued belief in the left project to transform society, most notably on the part of the theorists and activists associated with movements of global resistance to neo-liberal capitalism. In their book *Empire* (2000) Michael Hardt and Antonio Negri attempt to give articulate theoretical expression to the aspirations of thousands of demonstrators who participated in the protests against the World Trade Organisation (WTO) in Seattle in November–December 1999. Many observers regard the Seattle events as the start of a new movement that has subsequently gained dynamism with the protests against the meeting of the representatives of the most developed economies of the world (G8) in Genoa in 2001, and the founding of the World Social Forum (WSF) in Porto Alegre in Brazil in the same year.

Yet amidst this optimism, one also registers the presence of doubt from such diverse quarters as the critical theorist and philosopher T. W. Adorno as well as the Italian poet and film director Pier Paolo Pasolini (1922–75). These doubts can be regarded as symptomatic of a loss of belief in the inevitably progressive direction of history, and as indicative of a profound scepticism about humanism and humanity's capacity successfully to articulate the relation between theory and practice in ways that generate the knowledge necessary to make human emancipation possible. This is in some ways unsurprising given the devastation wrought by fascism, two world wars and the disappointing return to the very institutions that helped precipitate the fascist era in inter-war Europe in the first place—capitalism and parliamentary democracy. In the years following World War II, Adorno, Pasolini, Michel Foucault and others began to question the foundations and future of humanism itself.[1] The final chapter of this book examines the shift from the confident, macro-theoretical political humanism of the left to the more cautious, micro-theoretical analysis of thinkers and movements in the era of global capitalism and generalised technology, such as Michel Foucault.

As Hardt and Negri's praise of what they refer to in *Empire* as 'the multitude' suggests, it is not as if there is no more talk of revolution. But with the large-scale integration of the working classes of North America and Europe into the political mainstream, and the uncertain transformatory capacity of the NSMs, there has been a discernible evolution in the content and tone of analysis. Just as the working class has been effectively integrated, countries that in 1968 had inspired so much hope as alternative models, such as China and Vietnam, have become integrated into the world economy, and by and large have adopted state capitalist rather than libertarian socialist institutions. Hence the articulation and practice of left politics has been tremendously complicated by the widely shared assessment that, with the possible exceptions of Cuba or North Korea, there is no longer a social class or a state which is really outside the global system dominated by capital. This undoubtedly means that resistance has to be international. But it also implies that it has to be *auto-resistance* or a self-overcoming kind of resistance, so to speak, since there is no easily identifiable subject external to the system, and all people are to a greater or lesser extent involved in it at some level. This raises the question of whether there might be a possible synthesis of the Marxist emphasis on *autogestion* with the Nietzschean conception of self-overcoming that could work in practice.

It will be seen that the proliferation of a wide variety of social subjects in place of the (in theory) unified proletariat marks the possible emergence of a new form of internationalism with considerable promise—and risks too. It is possible to regard the Marxist proletariat as the historical successor to the revolutionary people who stormed the Bastille. In other words, one can detect a discernible movement from *republican humanism,* with its roots in the political ideas of Machiavelli, to the *Marxist humanism* of thinkers like Gramsci, Sartre and Lefebvre, who attempt to translate a number of Machiavelli's ideas on politics into a Marxist idiom. In the analysis of Autonomia at the end of the previous chapter it was suggested that the republican notion of the people as well as the social democratic and communist attempts to radicalise that notion remain locked within a populist logic that has had disastrous consequences for parties of the institutional left such as the PCF and PCI. It is also seen that this is a logic underpinned by a highly questionable model of power as well as authoritarian practices of representation. Hence the post-1968 crisis of humanism, which begins with the critique of daily life formulated by surrealists and situationists also entails a crisis of political representation and legitimacy. The discussion of *Empire* in the second part of this chapter takes up some of these important issues in the light of Foucault's theory of biopower analysed in the first part. A central question in that discussion can be formulated as follows: does the arrival of what Hardt and Negri call the multitude signal the paradoxical possibility of a post-humanist humanism that effectively breaks with the implicit populism of leftist humanism, or have we entered the era of cyber-subjects and quasi-animalistic nomadic tribes evoked by Donna Haraway and Gilles Deleuze?[2]

The Crisis of Humanism and its Aftermath

For thinkers such as Marx, Luxemburg, Gramsci, Lukács, Marcuse, Lefebvre and many others, humanity has a clearly defined epistemological and political task. That is to overcome the separations implied by the dichotomies subject-object, form-essence, theory-practice, ethics-politics, mental labour–manual labour, civil society–state and labour-capital. Marx initially formulates this task as the project of overcoming fetishism and most importantly, following Hegel, of overcoming alienation. For Marx the end of alienation is synonymous with the founding of a fully humanised world without religion and other forms of ideology in which the organised power of classes, states, parties and bureaucracies is abolished in favour of a community of free and creative individuals. Classes and states are obstacles to the realisation of the emancipated human being who, while only really active as an historical protagonist in a world on the other side of the division of labour, can nonetheless be glimpsed in the present in his and her alienated form as an exploited worker. In a parallel vein, alienated form is a shadow of the realised essence to come. It is destined to appear on the historical scene for the first time with the collapse of the dichotomies in a higher form of unity. Thus in his early writings Marx predicts that the revolution to succeed the French Revolution will unite state and civil society in a qualitatively higher form of pluralist and libertarian community.

But as seen in Chapter 1, this idea of *unity* is already called into question by Kant's discovery that humanity is part of nature but not reducible to nature because of consciousness. In the twentieth century the intractable problem of the *difference* between humanity and nature discerned by Kant has been reformulated in a variety of ways, each of which renders the humanist unity of form and essence problematic. This is not simply an abstract epistemological issue. When translated into political terms, one can regard the humanist unity of form and essence as the unity of the nation state and the people of its sacred territory. For Freud, the difference between humanity and nature is at the root of the conflict between the pre-socialised nature of each person and the institutions of collective socialised humanity, i.e. society.[3] Heidegger gives the problem a different twist by locating human *Dasein* in an ambiguous intermediary position somewhere between nature and objects on the one hand, and being, on the other. He thus posits an ontological difference between things in their quality as things and the *being* of those things. While humanity is a thing that participates in an ontic dimension of reality bound up with 'thingness', it is also the shepherd of being that can open itself to the ontological dimension of the world bound up with being. To open oneself up in this way is fundamentally not akin to reappropriating an alienated human essence. On the contrary, in Heidegger's writings it is to acknowledge the limits of the human and the insurmountable difference between the ontic and the ontological.[4]

Hence in humanist terms, which implicitly also question the status of humanism, difference can be formulated as that between nature and humanity (Kant), between society and humanity (Freud), or as between being and humanity (Heidegger), to cite only three of the most well-known ways of approaching this issue.[5] While Kant and Freud reckon with the permanent difference between humanity and nature, and Heidegger is adamant about the ontological difference between being and all other entities, it is seen in Chapter 3 that Adorno's philosophy holds out the possibility of an uncoerced reconciliation between humanity and nature. But for Adorno reconciliation is not a romantic unity between humanity and nature. It is mainly glimpsed in art and other unusual and fleeting instances of noninstrumental reason. For thinkers like Adorno and Foucault, left politics is not about liberating humanity from the obstacles to its essence or self-realisation. For Foucault, in particular, it is more centrally concerned with liberating life from subjective manipulation undertaken in the name of social science and other clumsy humanist interventions in the Dionysian flux of existence. Although a history of the left would be incomplete without a substantial discussion of Foucault, he is not part of an identifiable left-wing tradition or movement in the same way as the thinkers considered in previous chapters. This is a fitting way to introduce this final chapter, which attempts to analyse the most recent period as a phase in which the dominant protagonists of the past, most notably the industrial working class and its allies, are no longer central, and the individual project of self-overcoming has come to complement the collective concern with the self-realisation of humanity in its variously formulated liberal, republican and Marxist versions. With regard to this prospect of a Marx-Nietzsche synthesis, Foucault is an eloquent exponent of the Nietzschean position. Like Breton, who was radicalised by his experiences working with patients in mental hospitals during World War I, Foucault examines the issue of madness and related questions concerning sexuality, deviance, standards of medical health and pathology, as well as questions of population control. The link with Breton and surrealism is solidified in a couple of other ways as well.

First, Foucault is a brilliant literary critic and a highly original theorist of what Maurice Blanchot and Derrida refer to as the 'space' of writing. Foucault's essays about writing and literature are emphatically not attempts to rearticulate or salvage the relationship between the artist and society in the light of the crisis of tradition and the related demise of integral experience. Instead, he asks questions about the relationships between language as a system of signs, society as a system of boundaries and prohibitions, authorship as a painful act of potential self-transformation, and the power relations in society, which make writing something substantially different than the literary expression of some humanist essence issuing from the protected interiority of a beautiful mind or soul. In his work on the surrealist novelist and playwright Raymond Roussel (1877–1933), Foucault suggests that the state is omnipresent in social relations. It is not a sovereign unity standing above society and presiding over it in detached contemplation and concentrated authority. Hence it is in many ways more accurate to speak of *power* than to speak of the *state* as such. This idea will be developed in detail below because of its tremendous impact on social theory and political practice since 1968. What is important in this context is that Foucault observes parallels between the open-ended and protean forms of power and the indeterminate co-ordinates of literary production. Hence literature can shed light on politics and power, and the study of politics can illuminate the conditions of literature. Just as the issues concerned with education and student life looked at in the previous chapter pose a challenge to schematic versions of Marxism and the organisational strategies of Leninism, it is mistaken to consider writing and literature as marginal aspects of the superstructure subordinate to an economic base that determines all other aspects of a hypothetical sociopolitical totality. Indeed, it is difficult to consider the Western Marxist idea of totality without ascribing some sort of organising centre to it.[6]

The challenge of seemingly peripheral issues, such as education and art, for theory and practice is that they are neither causally determined by the economy nor completely unrelated to the economic structure of society. Roussel's seemingly eccentric literary oeuvre directs Foucault's attention to the possibility that language, like society, is a system without a unified centre or a unifying subject. In the same way that it may be more promising to focus on the modalities of power than it is to focus on the state as a power centre, it may be more precise to focus on the structures of language and the science of signs than it is to retain the notion of the author as autonomous creator. This opens up a series of parallels between the possible deconstruction of the models of subjectivity and individual freedom linked to the ideal of the supposedly autonomous writer, on the one hand, and the possible deconstruction of the bases of the monolithic state and the supposed political unity of the sovereign people, on the other.[7]

Like Rimbaud, Foucault is interested in the open relation between things and the words that represent them. Roussel's writing is of particular interest in the endeavour to discover the physiognomy of this openness, since it does not try to reconstitute the pristine origin of a pure means of expression in which there is a harmonious correspondence between formal language and real essence. It is rather a language that has its basis in the reality of language itself. Language is thus not the form behind which the literary essence embodied in the author shines forth. That is, Roussel's plays, poems and novels do not spring from a stationary, original source. His literature is more like an inventory of language in movement that is already under way and in the process of repeating and perpetuating its conditions of existence without recourse to a foundation or origin. For Foucault the implication is that it is misleading to posit humanity as alive, dynamic and creative, whilst positing words and things as dead, static and created. It is equally misleading to regard knowledge as the conceptually mediated reappropriation of thought and its alienated forms, as Hegel might, or to regard knowledge as the reappropriation of alienated labour, as Marx might. Roussel indicates that humanity is not the measure of all of nature or the measure of the reality of things, any more than authors are the measure of the reality of language.[8]

Second, Foucault develops a political critique of Freud while elaborating the epistemological significance of the work of a number of key surrealist artists who fall outside the scope of this study, such as Artaud and Bataille. Like Breton, Foucault acknowledges the importance of Freud's discoveries concerning the fluid boundaries between the self and the external world, the material reality of dreams, and the body as an unstable point of convergence between society, history and nature. He also concurs with Breton's assessment that despite his undeniable importance as a social theorist, Freud renounces the path-breaking implications of his own ideas.

This is because Freud ultimately regards the conflict between corporeal-psychic impulses of the individual and the demands of social order to be ancient and unsolvable. Foucault rejects Freud's diagnosis that the pain and repression caused by this conflict can be illuminated by therapy, but can never be overcome through new forms of creative social action and self-transformation. But there is also another matter of divergence related to Foucault's analysis of language and power alluded to above.

In the *Interpretation of Dreams* (1900) Freud indicates that desire is the reality of the unconscious and dreams are its language. This means that the unconscious expresses itself in images rather than words. For Freud there is a pre-linguistic stratum of wishes, fantasies and mania that only artists manage to mould into aesthetic values, whether they use language as a means of expression or not. Foucault agrees with this whilst challenging Freud's suggestion that the rest of humanity is destined to suffer under the weight of these emotions, which escape verbal or written expression and which are stored in the unconscious. According to this formulation, life is for the most part about enduring pain inflicted by nature and society that escapes articulation. Lack of articulation in its turn produces inevitable explosions of pent-up frustration. The implication is that progress in anything other than a technical sense is illusory, and that humanity will always have to reckon with feelings of guilt, inadequacy and aggression. Indeed, as technical progress continues apace while unconscious desires continue to be repressed, the threats of mutual destruction multiply. On this basis Freud is convinced that he has uncovered the origins of individual turbulence and collective conflict. From Foucault's perspective, however, Freud argues somewhat like Marx and Hegel, though with the notable difference that for Freud humanity is not able to reappropriate its alienated essence. Unlike the subjects of *Geist* and social labour, the Freudian subject cannot reappropriate its desires because it is permanently divided into the unconscious id, the ego, and the morally chastising superego, and because the discipline required to maintain social order will simply not permit it. Psychoanalysis develops techniques to provide the analyst with knowledge of the individual subject that may help them in their efforts to reach some sort of functional compromise between individual desire and social constraint. Thus in the transition from the confident modernist humanism of Hegel and Marx to the highly troubled modernism of Freud, the subject's relationship with the outside world becomes problematic. Nonetheless, the point of reference and unifying centre of action in all three cases is either individual (Freud) or collective (Marx) subjectivity. It is his reading of Nietzsche that enables Foucault to break with Hegel, Marx and Freud in order to embark upon the formulation of a critical genealogy of knowledge and power that questions the very notion and practice of humanist subjectivity itself.[9]

In Foucault's estimation there is an obvious connection between the psychoanalytic use of various correctional techniques to help people and the role of the analyst in the endeavour to rehabilitate them. The supposed objectivity of Freudian and other versions of psychoanalysis is based on the deployment of science and medicine; that is, the authority of medicine is enlisted in the project of healing mental illness. What is most problematic for Foucault is defining what constitutes mental illness and determining who is mentally ill. Freud asserts that the conflict between unconscious desire and social order affects everyone, which means that all people are repressed and neurotic to some extent. It also means that the boundaries between neurotic and psychotic, on the one hand, and efficient and highly motivated, on the other, are very difficult to determine with precision. Foucault is adept at asking questions such as: what does it really mean to 'help', 'rehabilitate', and 'heal' people in this context, and what criteria establish what counts as 'precision'? He is impressed with Nietzsche's ability to ask these questions with regard to the value positions which are expressed in terms of good and evil. Like Nietzsche, who discovers that the terms 'good' and 'evil' mean different things according to who says them and how they are said in different historical periods, Foucault discovers that the terms healthy/ill and normal/deviant mean different things according to the specific demands of specific regimes. The concept of regime is important, for it captures Foucault's notion that governments do more than attempt to establish their authority and protect the rights of their citizens.[10]

Governments are regimes in the sense that they make people work in ways that reward certain values and energies at the expense of others. Hence there is a deep misunderstanding about the nature of liberal democratic government, which is often said to be based on the consent of the governed and the protection of a form of individual liberty that is compatible with every other person's liberty, i.e. liberty as noninfringement, or what is sometimes referred to as negative liberty. Instead of being founded on practices of noninfringement, liberal democratic regimes make people work, play, rest, read, write and reproduce in ways that have the apparent neutrality of negative liberty and the apparent objectivity of science and medicine. This means that there are diverse practices of governance rather than central government as such. In terms reminiscent of Gramsci, Foucault suggests that liberal democratic hegemony is extremely difficult to challenge without seeming arbitrary and authoritarian. Whilst Gramsci already intuits the de-centred dimensions of power with his ideas on passive revolution and civil society, Foucault focuses on the de-centred dimensions of language, the relation between knowledge and power, and the changing definitions of mental illness in the period of liberal democratic ascendancy.[11] This inquiry does not lead him to a single source or origin from which it is possible to derive definitions of mental health and economic efficiency. Nor does it provide him with a foundation on which to give a clear account of what reason is or what is quintessentially human. It leads him to a systematic analysis of power that calls into question accepted notions of freedom, justice and democracy and at the same time renders problematic any straightforward continuum from the political right (bad, unjust, less human) to the political left (good, just, more human).[12]

Foucault's studies of literature, linguistics, madness, criminology and medicine support his thesis that if rights, progress, justice, democracy, mental health, reason and other phenomena are tools in a complex field of struggles to gain control of definitions and preside over institutions, power is a constant throughout history. But he adds that power is never exercised in the same way for too long. In theory, only the all-powerful are powerful enough to liberate humanity from power relations. But even if this were possible in practice, in Nietzschean terms this elite would only really have succeeded in imposing its own theory and practice of powerlessness as power. Moreover, to seek to emancipate humanity as a whole from power relations in this way is to misconstrue power in negative terms as a chain on the forces of production or a shadow of darkness obscuring the light of reason. Power is a positive force in the precise sense that it produces subjects, knowledge, codes of behaviour and standards of truth. Truth is not a matter of a priori objectivity or impartial logical consistency. There is no truth until the judge, scientist, doctor, military expert, etc. has spoken, and this power is not a simple function of class position or central state authority. He believes that in every society the law is a composite network of illegalities, propositions, prohibitions, rewards and incentives. That is, the law silently presupposes the pre-legal, non-legal and extra-legal dimensions of legality. If the pre-legal and extra-legal constitute the conditions of legality itself in ways that structure the mode of justice, there are extra-scientific factors that condition the mode of scientific research, extra-medicinal factors that condition standards of health and normalcy, as well as extra-economic criteria that influence what counts as efficient and productive. On this basis Foucault argues that the relation between knowledge and power is different in every society, which in turn means that the mode of truth production, or what he refers to as a *truth regime,* is also always unique in terms of its modalities and effects.[13]

In the historical period marked by the Industrial Revolution and the ascendancy and consolidation of bourgeois hegemony, liberal democratic truth regimes tend to extend their power over the minds and bodies of subjects in ways that undermine typical liberal distinctions between private/public and negative/positive liberty. In *Discipline and Punish* (1975) and his lectures at the Collège de France in Paris in the late 1970s, Foucault analyses this modality of power as a qualitatively new form of *bio-*

power which can be resisted through *bio-politics*. The exercise of bio-power in advanced capitalist societies endeavours to increase the scope of power beyond control of the labour process to include all aspects of life, including mental health and bodily welfare. Hence power no longer stops at the place of production and is not restricted to the exploitative mechanisms of wage labour, but rather seeks to induce docility and conformism in individuals in various areas of daily life that were previously relatively free from juridical regulation and police surveillance. This means that the difference between openly punitive institutions such as the prison and other institutions such as the army, hospital, workplace and university is one of degree rather than kind. Foucault analyses this subtle but palpable spread of power in terms of the rise of disciplinary and carceral modalities of control as opposed to the many forms of blatantly authoritarian brands of rule that preceded modern society. Bio-politics is the ethical and aesthetic revolt against this form of coerced conformism. One of the many questions raised by the theories of bio-power and bio-politics concerns the extent to which bio-politics can be conceived as a collective project. Might it be the case that it is always a question of the specific instances of subversion of one or a limited number of individuals against the bio-political manipulation that directly affects them, or might these diverse struggles achieve some kind of noncoerced unity in a qualitatively new form of protest movement? This question will be returned to below in relation to the idea of the multitude.[14]

The reworking of extra-legal propositions into legitimate legal form, like the manufacture of seemingly coherent logical propositions and truthful conclusions out of non-truths, is an art linked to governance that Foucault analyses in terms of the construction of *discourse*. Discourses constitute the bases of scientific disciplines such as psychiatry, jurisprudence, population studies, psychology, statistics, economics, criminology, medicine, geography, paediatrics, etc., and the foundations of the 'sciences of man' (also known as the human sciences) that emerge in concomitance with the rise of bio-power. The knowledge furnished by these sciences helps produce individual subjects and at the same time the same subjects may strive in various ways to resist the institutions and processes that produce them. For Foucault, however, there is nothing automatic or inevitable about this revolt. He suggests that in modern societies power is exercised as knowledge embedded in discourses. As language, discourse is a system with no unified subject or integral centre; it is a system of rules that entice, compel, encourage and invite diverse individuals to speak in certain ways and to be visible in a certain ways. Foucault maintains that power does not speak directly—it produces speech acts on the part of individual subjects. Similarly, power produces different fields of visibility—it is not the invisible core behind the visible exterior of a power edifice. His notion of language and discourse opposes a traditional view of the order of things, which usually posits a two-tier system of complementarity between citizen-law–individual consciousness–theory, on the first level, and nation-legitimacy–collective consciousness–practice on the second level. Foucault designates this system as the sovereignty model of power, which likes to imagine power as a homogeneous substance concentrated in the most visible state institutions and incarnated in key figures such as the president or prime minister.[15]

But power is not homogeneous, concentrated or continuous; it is heterogeneous, dispersed and discontinuous. Power as knowledge is articulated in discontinuous form in the unstable interaction between the *nonvisible enunciations* of discourse (énoncés) on the one hand, and the *nondiscursive, visible* institutions of society on the other. For example, if one takes the discursive formulations of penal law together with the visible institution of the prison, one has what Foucault in some contexts refers to as an archive. Against Hegel and Marx, Foucault refuses to regard the constellation of the discursive and visible nondiscursive elements of archives as one of cause and effect, thesis and antithesis, or base and superstructure. It is a relation constituted by networks, practices, procedures and strategies. This is illustrated by the penal law/prison example. Although in principle the prison is subordinate to the decisions of the legal system, it also has the necessary means to organise and administer its internal affairs. The autonomy of the prison from penal law and the economic system is neither relative, nor absolute, nor what Engels designates as 'autonomy in the last instance'. Foucault characterises the flow of power as multidirectional and capillary rather than from top to bottom or from centre to periphery. Hence the relation between penal law, prison reform and changes in surveillance techniques is not analogous to the base directly causing superstructural changes. Against Freud, Foucault refuses to isolate individual cases of mental illness from the overlapping fields of power and knowledge in which pathology is discursively constituted and institutionally practised. Therapy, which proceeds in abstraction from the realities of bio-power and the possibilities of bio-politics serves to reconcile people to the conservative idea that the relation between individual and society can never be anything more than cautious damage limitation.[16]

Foucault tends to analyse conflict in transversal and horizontal terms focusing on reward, surveillance, discipline and punishment in which the lines between oppressor/oppressed or knowledgeable/ignorant are blurred rather than vertical. Indeed, the problem with structuralism is that it retains the model of vertical causality and insofar only partially breaks with the humanist existentialism of thinkers like Sartre. For example, he reckons that if one adopts a genealogical approach to the study of a maritime military hospital, it becomes clear that there are criss-crossing circuits between penal law, medical expertise, military tradition and ideologies of national interest. The focus of genealogical inquiry is not directed towards distinguishing between the exploiters who buy labour power and the exploited who sell labour power or between the small number at the top of the power pyramid and the large number at the bottom. To do so is to fall back on the idea that the state is a unified distributor of identical power units, which it happens to distribute unequally according to class, gender, race and other factors, and it is to remain locked within a continuum of thinking that moves from the 'less' human right to the 'more' human left. It is symptomatic of reified thinking to rely on power units or quantifiable differences in this way. The problem with reified thinking is not only that it is insufficiently rigorous—it also sustains domination and mastery. Hence Foucault's analysis of power and his deconstruction of humanism indicate that there are powerful critiques of reified thought that do not necessarily point towards traditional left solutions such as those first suggested by Marx. Instead, he examines how knowledge and power interact in a fluid relation between legal and scientific discourse on the one hand, and prisons, hospitals, schools, banks, military academies, business schools and other institutions, on the other. He is particularly sensitive to transitions from one truth regime and its prevailing norms of knowledge and power to another, and what this transition entails in terms of new practices of discipline, new criteria of truth, as well as new techniques for making bodies and minds docile when necessary as well as vigilant and watchful when and where necessary.[17]

The transition from the sovereignty regime, based on heavy-handed policing and the territorial integrity of the nation state, to the disciplinary regime, based on subtle forms of surveillance and the establishment of institutions of international co-ordination, offers a primary example. The sovereignty model emerges with the rise of modern nation states and the gradual but steady erosion of intermediate institutions such as guilds, corporations, and other independent, nonstate bodies with their own legal status. Although the sovereignty model in Europe was initially used by the absolute monarchies against the aristocracies, Foucault explains that the bourgeoisie eventually assumes control of the sovereign state and attempts to exploit the forms of knowledge inherent in it. Over time one observes the traces of a rupture between the notion of universal knowledge and macro-power concentrated in the state and codified in rational law (of which the Hegelian state is the most confident theoretical expression), and a carceral model with the accompanying phenomena of micro-power dispersed in scientific disciplines and theoretical-practical archives. The juridical power of the law to coerce cedes place to the disciplinary power of knowledge to encourage the internalisation of norms of sexual propriety, medical health, scientific efficiency and economic productivity. That is, in the movement from the generalised state to the generalised prison, norms are internalised to a much greater extent than in the past. To put the matter crudely for a moment, in the past it was possible to produce relatively powerful bodies with juridical-oriented minds. Foucault reckons that if one makes an archaeological study of diverse archives such as prison records, hospital records, and statistics on population movements and longevity, one finds a discernible mutation. In the period roughly spanning the years 1770 to 1830 it becomes possible to produce more docile bodies with minds that are more independent of the law and the immediately identifiable political institutions of state, but which are more integrated in social institutions—most notably wage labour and other phenomena bound up with modernisation and urbanisation.[18]

Foucault is thus able to identify the early signs of what is today recognised as the crisis of the authority of the nation state and the political parties working within its territory. Since the fall of the Berlin Wall and the collapse of the former USSR, this crisis has been given fresh impetus by the World Trade Organisation (WTO), World Bank, International Monetary Fund (IMF) and various international de-regulation projects accompanying neo-liberal globalisation. The neo-liberal offensive is currently being challenged by the wave of activism following Seattle, Genoa, and the European and world social forums, and thinkers such as Negri and Paolo Virno have celebrated the appearance of the multitude as a new revolutionary collective subject. Yet there remain real questions about the possibilities of revolution in the twenty-first century, especially if by revolution one understands something like the events of February–October 1917 in Russia. As Negri, Virno, and others generally admit, the most important of these questions were already raised by Foucault in the 1960s and 1970s. They include: how is the struggle for human emancipation to be rethought in light of the reality that humanity, reason, law, and the state have all become problematic concepts? Do globalisation and postmodernism signify the end of what was once the left? If the distinctions between left and right have become increasingly obsolete in view of the increasing technocratic management of politics and its evolution towards a media-driven spectacle, is it time to think more in terms of global *resistance* to all forms of power rather than continuing to speak in terms of the left, human emancipation, alienation, etc?[19]

Foucault has stimulated a much-needed critique of the sovereignty model of power, which in many ways was uncritically accepted by state socialist societies in Eastern Europe and elsewhere. His work has also served to initiate a process of critical reflection on what reason and thinking might be without relying on standard definitions of humanism and subjectivity, of which there are remarkably similar left- and right-wing varieties. The discussion in this chapter so far suggests that it is mistaken to remain committed to the broad spectrum of traditional humanism, since one is confronted with a series of epistemological and

political problems that are not adequately resolved by adopting positions at its centre or left. It is surely necessary to rethink these issues, but
it is also necessary to question received notions concerning what thinking is. For Foucault thinking is not simply an innate capacity included in
the definition of what it means to be human, nor is it the autonomous
act of an isolated subject that grasps the world of external objects and
social relations from the safe recesses of an internal citadel. His studies of
Roussel and his research on the rise of the human sciences incline him
to regard thinking in a critical sense implying resistance as an event that
'happens', or can happen, when individuals overcome the subjectivities
assigned to them by discourses and institutions. Thus the space of
thought is not the individual human mind in any straightforward sense;
it is the unstable field of possibilities offered by the interstices between
discursive *énoncés* and visible social institutions. The history of state
socialism indicates that the left humanist attempt to *collectivise* the isolated liberal subject is an insufficient response to the problem of understanding thinking and knowledge and the related project of co-ordinating
theory and practice. The history of NSMs to date raises the hypothesis
that it may also be problematic to *broaden* the isolated liberal subject in
terms of gender, race, and other ostensibly alternative identities. Collectivisation and pluralisation of an already flawed model tends to exacer-
bate the problems inherent in the original. It also tends to perpetuate
reified and conformist thinking, which entrenches concrete domination
in institutional practice.[20]

Conformist thought sees power as a homogeneous substance issuing
from a centre that can be manipulated for different state-organised projects to 'help' people. This increasing concern with helping people and
protecting victims against possible dangers or insults results in what Foucault understands in ideal typical terms as a possible shift from carceral to
pastoral society, i.e. a society without margins in which almost everyone
is 'successfully' integrated. He demonstrates that in reality each individual subject is also an object constituted by discourses and institutions.
The subject can resist the processes of subjectification by proposing its
own values realised in distinct models of subjectivity, epistemology and
action. Resistance occurs when individual people refuse the generic
mantle of human nature as it is defined by reigning forms of power-
knowledge, in order to be more than human in an uncompromisingly
individual manner. In ways that are perhaps frustrating for activists eager
to propose a concrete programme of social change, Foucault defends the
view that people do not transgress the limits of the human as they are
constituted at any particular time by humanising language. It is language
that must be liberated from human fears, fetishes and needs. In that
process people may be able to transform themselves on their own terms
rather than re-establishing a traditional identity within a predictable

spectrum of alternatives which are more or less acceptable to the demands of bio-power on minds and bodies.[21]

For Foucault life has a much higher value than truth and, indeed, he argues that it has been the project of power throughout history to domesticate and if necessary imprison life, and to make life governable in the name of truth and knowledge. In his lifetime this epistemological stance did not lead to a de-politicised academic retreat from social struggle. Foucault was an enthusiastic supporter of the contestations of 1968 and active in defending the rights of prisoners and immigrants. His activism was informed by his research and the conviction that the attempt by power to domesticate and govern life in the name of truth has a very specific history in modern western societies, where minds and bodies are subjected to scrutiny, surveillance, control, and, above all, become objects of knowledge. Human needs in their great multiplicity are not satisfied. Instead, they become the focal point of a series of inquiries and statistical studies, the aim of which is to study how these needs can be categorised and rendered predictable in terms of regular patterns and recurring symptoms. Foucault's claim that modern society is not designed to promote human freedom or happiness as much as it is a qualitatively new project to discipline life in humanity in the name of human dignity and human rights is sustained by extensive independent research and innovative thinking. It is not tailor-made for a party programme or the needs of a social movement that he or somebody else might then attempt to lead. He regards representational and humanist epistemologies as strategies to make us see ourselves (and not beyond) when we see, and in the process to see someone else's vision of us as if it were freely chosen by us. Foucault's project of overcoming traditional subjectivity, knowledge and power is an attempt to enable people to see in their own ways, i.e. in ways that are discretely but firmly subversive of existing classifications, hierarchies and techniques of surveillance and discipline. His is not the end of history, but rather the aspired end of humanity as an object of knowledge and the self-appointed prison guard of life. Foucault offers an example of radical thinking rather than what is usually understood as left-wing thinking as such. It is not radical in Marx's Latin sense of going to an original root. It is an attempt to think subjectivity without recourse to foundations and origins, and insofar it has certain features in common with Heidegger's attempt to deconstruct and destroy the premises and consequences of Western metaphysics and humanism. Just as there are still many open questions concerning Heidegger's politics, the same applies to Foucault.[22]

It could be argued that despite his radical methodology, Foucault is a very unorthodox humanist and a relativist. This is illustrated in a very obvious way by his interest in Kant and Enlightenment at the end of his career. But it is also plausible on other grounds. By arguing that the individual subject can resist the processes of subjectification by proposing its own values realised in distinct models of subjectivity, epistemology and action, it would seem that he comes close to endorsing a liberal model of agonistic pluralism with which thinkers like Simmel and Arendt would have had a great deal of sympathy. The Nietzschean idea that one might become more than human in an uncompromisingly individual way sounds more like the last outpost of liberal humanism than a decisive break with humanist epistemology and politics. Moreover, if it is true that there is no truth until the judge, scientist, doctor, military expert, etc., has spoken, is this the case for every polity, such that all are equally distant from un-coerced reconciliation? In other words, if Habermas's theories of communicative action and the public sphere ultimately rely on a Kantian concept of reason and truth despite the fact that it is a Kantianism with an admixture of universal pragmatics, does Foucault not go to the other extreme by relativising truth and reason as ruses in the struggle between the forces of power and the forces of life? Although it is not a simple case of choosing Habermas and dogma or Foucault and relativism, and although there is no doubt about Foucault's insight and originality, there are many questions about Foucault's relevance to the left.

However, one can also restate the matter in a completely different way. If there is no way to integrate Foucault's critique of power, reified thinking and humanism (despite its contradictions) into a recognisably left-wing political programme, maybe the time has come to say that the left has ceased to be relevant to the experience of most people in advanced capitalist societies, where truth regimes and bio-power do indeed structure experience and influence the possibilities for individual and collective resistance. Is it simply the case that the left belongs to a constellation of ideas and forces that originated with the French Revolution, and which have come into their twilight with the crisis of Enlightenment, reason, humanism and the steady weakening of the territorial integrity of the nation state? As will be seen in the next section of this chapter, a number of these questions are taken up by Deleuze and Negri.[23]

The Struggle against Bio-power in Theory and Practice

Foucault's insight and originality make him impossible to ignore, and, indeed, even if it is clear that his ideas are not easily adaptable to the aims of parties and NSMs, a number of contemporary movements for radical change have nonetheless taken up diverse aspects of his project to resist power and subvert existing forms of subjectivity. At the theoretical level, there has been particular interest in his notion that power is something positive that enjoins, and not just a series of prohibitions and constraints that forbid. Gilles Deleuze (1925–95) is one of the most probing readers of Foucault's ideas on life, power, knowledge and the politics of self-transformation. In addition to a number of very original contributions to social theory written with Félix Guattari, Deleuze is an able commentator on the writings of philosophers such as Spinoza, Hume, Kant, Nietzsche and Bergson. While his interpretations of Spinoza are an important source of inspiration for Hardt and Negri as well as for Virno's concept of the multitude, his writings on Bergson and cinema have provoked various attempts to think about time in terms of parallels and transversals that resist the reified logic of temporal units and strictly linear chronology. Hence it is fair to say that even if the concept of the left has become problematic in light of some of the challenges posed by the theoretical boldness of Foucault and the failure of a concrete alternative to capitalism to materialise in the years between 1968 and the end of Autonomia, the search for a coherent articulation of the relation between experience, knowledge and the possibility of radical contestation that began with Marx continues today.

Deleuze's contribution to this search is a many-sided project embracing epistemology, aesthetics and politics. Perhaps the most politically relevant aspect of his oeuvre is his attempt to map out the lines of a plausible theory of immanence, i.e. a theory of this-worldly as opposed to transcendent reality. Foucault suggests that truth and reason are means in the struggle between the forces of life and organised power. To this extent one can regard him as a critical Enlightenment thinker who can be compared to Adorno. Rather than discussing Enlightenment, truth or reason in any detail, Deleuze takes up Foucault's concern with life and attempts to show that the immanent reality of life is natural, animal, human, industrial-mechanical, cyber-mechanical and cinematographic at the same time. Humanity is not the privileged measure of reality, since *productivity* and intelligence (life) are everywhere. By contrast, *wage labour* (power) is confined to an artificially restricted sphere of economic toil with predictable rhythms and crises, and official politics (another instance of power) is artificially confined to specialist committees governed by rules and arbitrary standards of elitist 'expertise' in Debord's sense of the term. To say artificially restricted in this context is another way of saying politically restricted. This leads to mass political disaffection and, indeed, for Deleuze the multitude is de-politicised. But this is really its strength. In a literally more vital sense it is productive in ways that are currently politically controlled by what Negri and Hardt refer to as the empire, and it is reined in and made banal by national identities in processes that Deleuze designates with the term *territorialisation*. Hence bio-politics in Foucault, Deleuze, Negri and beyond is a struggle for de-territorialisation and is centrally concerned with the articulation of new forms of knowledge and possibilities for living across existing boundaries between nations, genders, academic disciplines and other rigid distinctions and dualisms.[24]

With regard to the question of knowledge, it was seen in Chapter 3 that Adorno ultimately rejects Husserl and Bergson's solutions to the problems of epistemology posed by the idealism/materialism impasse and the Marxist argument that the time has come to realise philosophy in praxis. Adorno regards the philosophies of Husserl and Bergson as unsuccessful attempts to bridge the fracture between consciousness and the images of the world humans construct on the basis of consciousness: that is, they fail to give epistemological inquiry a firmer foundation than idealism or materialism. In this context firmer means closer to human experience of reality. While Kant attempts to project inquiry beyond the metaphysics of pure reason in rationalism and empiricism by introducing a dialectical element stressing the mediated dimension of all things real, much of radical philosophy after Marx seems to return to rather unmediated distinctions between the 'fictions' of internal consciousness and the 'facts' of the external world. For Husserl, the passage from consciousness to the world need not be constructed, as such, since consciousness is always consciousness of something. His phenomenology investigates the thesis that there is no consciousness in abstraction from the relations that consciousness entertains with the objects of consciousness (what in the phenomenological tradition is referred to as intentionality). But for Adorno and Deleuze, the phenomenological overcoming of the dualism between consciousness and world in Husserl is achieved with an implausible reconstruction of a form of transcendental subjectivity that remains locked within the antinomical structure of Kantian idealism and the dichotomies between subject-object, consciousness-world, rational-sensual experience, etc. As such, in phenomenology the passage is more like a return to the original source of consciousness than an actual contact with the world. Adorno submits that one must return to the Kantian question about the conditions of possible knowledge and experience, including the socioeconomic, political and cultural conditions, and comes to the negative dialectical conclusion that those conditions are only palpable in terms of their manifest absence. While Husserl fails to theorise the objective pole of subject-object dialectics, in Adorno's estimation Bergson makes the equally unsatisfactory and ultimately irrational move of dissolving the subject in the flux of time.[25]

But Deleuze regards Bergson's philosophy as a far more promising solution to the problems of the idealism/materialism dualism than Adorno and the Frankfurt School are willing to admit. For Deleuze, Bergson's philosophy hints at a possible unity between the human, the natural and the mechanical which challenges dualisms and dichotomies of traditional philosophy. Bergson anticipates the cinema as a form of mechanico-human experience corresponding to the immanent reality of movement in which light is transformed into mechanical images. That transformation does not change the fact that all of reality is *linked*—and emphatically not dialectically *mediated* by Hegelian *Geist*—in a series of discontinuous, montage-like cuts, edits and new beginnings that, like Roussel's conception of language, are always already in motion and that circulate without origins, centre or terminus. The task of thinking is to trace the intersecting lines, resounding vibrations and underground currents that constitute the links, in order to make them visible in concepts, texts, films, events, communities and other points of fleeting yet palpable contact. It is not simply that consciousness is always consciousness of something. Consciousness *is* something, and everything is light and movement. Bergson does not direct subjectivity inwards toward the conscious subject that controls perception, and, indeed, according to Deleuze Bergson implies there is more living force in perception than any individual or collective subject could possibly control.[26]

In Deleuze's estimation Bergson breaks from a phenomenological tradition that runs roughly from Kant and Husserl to Heidegger, Sartre and Merleau-Ponty, for all of whom in different ways perception is somehow something 'natural'. The parallel move in phenomenology is to equate experience with subjective experience, when in fact there is nothing absolutely natural or purely subjective about experience. If the 'normal' experience of time produces an illusory continuum out of minutes, hours, days, months and years, cinematographic experience does the same out of edits and re-arrangements. The link between philosophy, cinema and politics becomes manifest when one considers that in denaturalising the relation between subjectivity and perception it becomes possible to think about thinking in ways that had previously been excluded by the rigid distinctions between subject-object, machine-nature, consciousness-world. For centuries most philosophies have simply accepted the dichotomies between humanity-animals, man-woman, whites-blacks, etc. as natural. For centuries philosophy has vacillated between meditations about the essence of humanity and considerations about the essence of a transcendent reality of truth embodied in God, nature, reason or some combination of all three. Deleuze, following Foucault, attempts to renew the Nietzschean project of reconstituting philosophy as an open-ended search for new ways of looking at the link *between* humanity and the world that does not founder on the ruins of the attempt to locate a fixed point of absolute epistemological certainty which translates into liberal democratic, communist or other forms of authoritarian political dogma.[27]

If it is borne in mind that time is a construction both in and outside the cinema, it becomes possible to deconstruct so-called natural time, seemingly natural social relations and what counts as natural thinking, i.e. common sense. If Deleuze is correct, the political importance of this enterprise lies in the fact that what is ideologically constructed as natural actually serves to channel life energies and potentially boundless productive forces into predictable channels and circuits that attempt to control de-territorialising desires, and that help to justify the 'natural' right to property, the apparent inevitability of the sexual and industrial division of labour, the supposed efficiency of the mental and sensual division of labour, as well as the 'unfortunate necessity' of the international chain of imperialist command between nations (according to the logic that somebody has to be in charge, do they not, or, some hierarchical balance of powers is necessary to produce stability, is it not?). The project to de-territorialise desire is linked with Deleuze and Guattari's aspiration to re-evaluate schizophrenia in positive terms, and to indicate how it might be possible for citizens to become nomadic machines instead of the delicate souls cared for by the modern state and its therapists (doctors, lawyers, accountants, psychoanalysts, social workers and others). This project is the subject of their *Capitalism and Schizophrenia I: Anti-Oedipus* of 1973.

Just as there is nothing natural about time or perception, there is nothing natural or even individual about desire: it is a social phenomenon rather than a natural phenomenon which in Freudian terms runs up against social oppression. For Freud it is clear that apart from therapy there is little to be done about the conflict between natural desire and social stability. Deleuze and Guattari propose social desire and schizo-analysis as an alternative to individual natural desire and psychoanalysis. *Anti-Oedipus* builds on Deleuze's earlier work on Spinoza, in which the Dutch philosopher of the Baroque period is portrayed as the philosopher of the multitude and as a thinker who offers ways of thinking about immanence in non-Hegelian terms. Deleuze's Spinoza is a theologian for whom everything expresses its nature through God, and God is a substance composed of an infinity of attributes. On this reading Spinoza is a philosopher of affirmation who suggests that epistemology is not centrally concerned with the objects of knowledge as much as it is concerned with becoming aware of our different capacities to know. When we know something about an object or a relation we gain an insight into its capacity to realise its own potential in varying degrees. On Deleuze's reading, for Spinoza knowledge is not acquired as a result of the forward assault towards a stable core situated behind an illusory shell. In a related vein, for Spinoza ethics is less about refraining from doing unjust deeds as it is about finding out what we are capable of, and activating the forces within us required to realise that theoretical capacity in actual practice. In seeking this realisation all efforts are positive forces, such that desire and reason are complementary rather than contradictory impulses. Hence for Deleuze it is important to note that as the multitude we are separated from our powers and not alienated from them in such a way that we might reappropriate alienated essence. Oppression consists less in being subjected to the power of another subject than in being separated from one's own powers. This may seem like a trivial distinction, but for

Deleuze it indicates that the struggle for knowledge and freedom is not an idealist zero sum game in which one reacquires what one originally had at a 'higher' level of consciousness. The alienation/reappropriation model is based on the idea of a sovereign subject that successfully asserts itself in its quest for the recognition of other sovereign subjects. It proceeds on a path of conquest until it becomes the universal sovereign subject. In historical terms theorised by Hegel, in the modern world that subject is synonymous with the people of a nation organised in the state, which in Marxist terms becomes a universal class whose unified revolutionary consciousness makes the state superfluous. Spinoza's model is different in that it does not posit the return to a supposed primal state of unity, however enriched after successive stages of mediated disunity.[28]

Philosophers such as Kant and Husserl suggest that there are moments in daily life when experience becomes reacquainted with the conditions of experience itself. This happens in political terms when a people collectively reaffirms its unity and values in a series of decisions that confer political legitimacy on the state, and in a series of wars, if necessary, that reassert the territorial integrity of the state's borders. By contrast, Spinoza's multitude seeks to continually expand its productive capacity and to enlarge its potential for creation and many-sidedness rather than affirm its elastic but ultimately monolithic unity. Within the alienation/reappropriation framework desire is directed towards something which, when attained, becomes the spur for a new desire which continually eludes complete satisfaction, and which is experienced as a lack. Deleuze's multitude constantly changes its conditions of existence instead of rediscovering them, and it creates qualitatively new desires rather than satisfying new versions of existing ones. Hence the multitude is a movement in continual motion. It is expansive movement in many micro directions rather than a dialectical spiral heading toward a macro summit. The plenitude of the multitude is not to be confused with the (continually frustrated) satisfaction of the universal people or class. While the nation and class are suspicious of foreign elements, the multitude exists in a relation of curiosity and exploration vis-à-vis what is external to it. Power, as opposed to vital productive capacity, is constantly engaged in attempts to rein in the vital desires of the multitude in institutions like the family, the commodity economy and the nation state. The authors of *Anti-Oedipus* explain that Freud accomplishes something of great importance by raising the issue of sensual repression. But whereas the Freudian family *frustrates* the desires of the child, the anti-oedipal family *contains* them. While this may again seem like a mere quibble, for Deleuze and Guattari it means that according to the left-Freudianism associated with critical theorists like Fromm and Marcuse, desires might not be frustrated in the right kind of family. The point is to move beyond the family as a so-called natural unit of reproduction, just as it is imperative to move beyond the nation state as a supposedly natural political organism fuelled by an economy that must be defended from foreign competition and internal sabotage. Otherwise one might be tempted to think that the right state, like the right family, might one day be able to reconcile people to the Hegelian reason at work in their daily lives that usually eludes their comprehension. It is not difficult to see the appeal of this kind of theorising for the more militant activists in the world social forums and for other contemporary proponents of global solidarity. This point will be elaborated in a little more detail towards the end of this chapter.[29]

Instead of speaking in terms of modes of production, for Deleuze and Guattari there are three main truth regimes, each of which is a machine that operates according to different techniques designed to regulate the production of goods, affective impulses and needs of its citizens. After the primitive territorial and despotic machines comes the capitalist machine, which in contrast to its predecessors accelerates the dynamic motion of unrestrained accumulation. Commenting on *Anti-Oedipus* Steven Best and Douglas Kellner remark:

> Capitalism subverts all traditional codes, values, and structures that fetter production, exchange and desire. But it simultaneously 'recodes' everything within the abstract logic of equivalences (exchange value), 'territorialising' them within the state, family, law, commodity logic, banking systems, consumerism, psychoanalysis and other normalising institutions. Capitalism substitutes for qualitative codes an 'extremely rigorous axiomatics' that quantitatively regulate and control all decoded codes. Capitalism re-channels desire and needs into inhibiting psychic and social spaces that control them far more effectively than savage and despotic societies.[30]

But in the second half of the twentieth century, capitalist recodification and reterritorialisation is confronted with its own limits, according to Deleuze and Guattari. They suggest that capitalism helps produce the bases of its own demise, but not by producing a unified proletariat that seizes control of the means of production. The system has set a dynamic of de-territorialisation in motion that will eventually elude its normatising control—it will be unable to produce the subjects it needs to sustain capital-labour whilst reigning in and commodifying the desires of the multitude. A case in point is the schizophrenic.[31]

For the authors of *Anti-Oedipus*, schizophrenia is not a pathological deviation from mental health any more than the nuclear family is a naturally healthy reproductive unit or than capitalism corresponds to some innate disposition to compete and accumulate. Modern schizophrenia is the result, among other things, of the frenetic decoding and de-centring processes that accompany the steady dissolution of tradition, state control of national boundaries and other factors that once bridled national economies, and contrived to produce more and less stable class, gender, racial, regional and national identities. The same applies to traditional notions of mental health and arbitrary standards of physical handicap.[32] Hence for Deleuze and Guattari it is now possible for people to experience ambivalence and contradiction as dimensions of plenitude rather than as demobilising problems. They submit that the schizophrenic nomad—that is, a person who refuses to be interpellated according to a territorial boundary or a traditional identity—is now the most destabilising figure on the contemporary social landscape. Following Artaud, Deleuze and Guattari regard the schizophrenic nomad as a desiring machine-body freed from the disciplined subject whose productive energies are tied to the destiny of the capitalist machine and its heteronomous laws of operation. The fact that many people can be taught to desire their own repression in the service of the capitalist machine should not distract attention away from the fact that many machine models are possible. While the rigid 'molar lines' of territorial political representation underpinning the modern state sometimes appear invulnerable, the authors of *Anti-Oedipus* counter that there are also soft 'molecular lines', which elude representation and Fordist and post-Fordist criteria of efficiency. It is their thesis that molar discipline will not be able to contain molecular joy indefinitely. Indeed, in the period of neo-liberal globalisation it appears that the state is being forced to relinquish its control over subjects constituted as healthy individual contributors to the national collective effort to maximise private profits. This idea is developed further in *A Thousand Plateaux* (1980), the companion volume to *Anti-Oedipus*.[33]

Where *Anti-Oedipus* presents the image of molecular lines of desire permeating the nomadic, schizophrenic desiring machine that is each person, *A Thousand Plateaux* introduces the idea of the *rhizome*. *A Thousand Plateaux* abandons what there is of narrative structure in the earlier work of 1973 in order to present the reader with a kaleidoscopic array of different time frames, conceptual flourishes and textual detours, which offer a series of plateaux instead of chapters as such. The concept of the rhizome suggests an epistemology that departs from the arboreal conception of knowledge based on a stable configuration of trunks, roots and branches. Arboreal systems have dominated western thinking, which relies to a great extent on binary distinctions and other kinds of dualisms. Instead of erecting unified systems of knowledge and organising them around central principles, rhizomatics endeavours to disseminate polyvalent knowledge based on schizophrenic and cinematographic experience charting the multiplicities of time and the fragmentation of space. The rhizome is more like a winding subterranean offshoot than a trunk with visible branches and invisible roots. Rhizomatic knowledge is the knowledge of desire that resists authoritarian channels and planned cultivation; it is often random, though not arbitrary, and spontaneous, though not purely accidental. At the beginning of *A Thousand Plateaux* Deleuze and Guattari explain their methodology and their conception of writing as follows:

> In a book, like in anything else, there are lines of articulation or segmentation, strata, and territories. There are also lines of escape, movements of de-territorialisation, and of de-stratification. The comparative velocities of circulation of these lines result in relative delays, in viscosity, or, on the contrary, in precipitation and rupture. All of this, the lines and the measurable velocities, constitute an *agencement*. A book is such an *agencement,* and as such, without determinate authorship. It is a multiplicity, though one does not know what the multiple implies when it ceases to be attributable to a given author, that is to say, when it is raised to the state of the substantive. A mechanical *agencement* is directed toward the strata which together constitute a kind of organism, or, if one prefers, a signifying totality, or a characteristic of a subject, but it is also directed toward *a body without organs* which never ceases to undermine that organism, and never ceases to propel and circulate particles without signification, i.e., pure intensities, and to appropriate for itself subjects which it does not designate so much with names but rather as the trace of an intensity.[34]

Against the view espoused by some rather pessimistic postmodernists that bio-political truth regimes are now closed totalitarian systems with no margins of resistance, Deleuze and Guattari maintain that no system can successfully repress desire, and that it is the great merit of Spinoza to have shown why. If one reads Spinoza and Marx in light of the potentially revolutionary implications of cinematic experience, they suggest, it becomes apparent that productive desire continually seeks supple segmentary lines and lines of escape from the ordering processes encoded in the rigid segmentary lines that categorise people as boss/worker, male/female, human/animal, black/white, human/machine and combinations thereof. It is not that minorities in the post-1968 world seek majority recognition, even if this is asserted by a great deal of contemporary social theory. On the contrary, the protagonists of rhizomatic action aim at *becoming a minority* rather than fleeing minority reality. The implication is that minority action joyfully embraces becoming a queer and a criminal in Judith Butler and Jean Genet's sense. Plural and protean minorities are the real antithesis to the lifeless mass electorates of bourgeois democracy, and, what is more, there is a virtually unlimited number of minorities. Some wish to become a rat, as in the film *Willard,* others want to become one of Pasolini's boys of life, and others desire self-transformation in order to become giant insects with human minds like Gregor Samsa in Kafka's *Metamorphosis*. Their hope is that minority intensities liberate desire from acceptable forms of state-sponsored majority satisfaction, and open up new possibilities for collective action in constantly changing combinations. All of these minority nomads are a threat to existing forms of accepted knowledge, biological classifications, territorial boundaries and fixed identities necessary for the smooth functioning of educational, tax, health, economic and military systems. They are a threat, in short, to the power of what Hardt and Negri refer to as the empire, as will be seen below.[35]

It is clear that with Foucault and, more dramatically, with the work of Deleuze and Guattari, one is at a considerable distance from anything that Marx, Western Marxists, critical theorists and most of the libertarians looked at in Chapter 4 might recognise as left politics. The critique of daily life and the critique of the society of the spectacle examined in Chapter 5 thus represent a watershed in the historical and theoretical account offered in this book. What emerges at this point is the thesis that the left now finds itself in a very tricky dilemma. If it does not drastically reform, it runs the risk of being written off as obsolete by the plurality of new social subjects that have emerged in the wake of the contestations of 1968–77 in France, Italy and innumerable other places, and which has been theorised by Deleuze and Guattari. If it tries to adapt itself to this diversity it runs the risk of losing what has been distinctive about the left since Marx. While the revolutionary left has been extremely impressive in terms of its capacity to think and re-think the relationship between humanity and external nature, the emergence of the bio-political paradigm has presented it with an array of challenges that it has been struggling to come to grips with for some time now. The thinkers and movements looked at in Chapters 1–4 are adept in showing why human emancipation depends on the creation of an economy that liberates humanity from scarcity in external nature at the same time that it liberates humanity from socially perpetuated scarcity in the guise of inequality and exclusion. The authoritarian turn of the Russian Revolution and the emergence of new social subjects have cast considerable doubt on the ability of the working class and its allies to lead a revolution that liberates people from scarcity without producing an oppressive political bureaucracy and a grotesque leadership cult in the process. The problem goes deeper, however. If one follows the trajectory that moves from Nietzsche, Rimbaud and Breton to Lefebvre, Foucault and Deleuze, one notes that human emancipation is a problematic concept. Moreover, it is far from obvious that the solution to the problem of scarcity with regard to external nature is also the solution to the problem of conformism and oppressive integration with regard to individual human nature. Hence the left is now confronted with the task of theorising the bases of a possible *collective nonconformism,* which for many is a contradiction in terms. The critique of daily life displaces the focus of the analysis of the power mechanisms in modern society from a central axis such as the economy or the base. In so doing it displaces the centrality of class and party, and acknowledges that the paths to change are multiple, intersecting and diverging. Whilst Deleuze and Guattari regard themselves as radical modernists, Hardt and Negri believe that we are now in postmodernity, and that postmodern times require new forms of social action. Their optimistic reading of the contemporary situation is based on the thesis that those new forms of social action are provided by a new historical subject that has little in common with 'the people' of the nation state in traditional political theory, and which has equally little in common with the principal subject of contestation corresponding to the people within this traditional framework of analysis, i.e. the unified working class that figures so prominently in the ideas of the theorists examined in Chapters 1–4 of this book.

Though the authors of *Empire* share the widespread scepticism about the future potential of the working class, in the multitude they see a new nomadic proletariat that embodies the revolutionary subjectivity of the international communist movement in its heyday as well as the immanent desire of Spinoza's God. As noted at the beginning of this chapter, at the time of its publication *Empire* seemed to capture the spirit of a new internationalist militancy and hope signalled by counter summits such as those in Seattle in 1999 and Genoa in 2001. The World Social Forum in Porte Alegre 2001 and the European Social Forums of Florence and Paris thereafter have lent a certain degree of plausibility to Hardt and Negri's thesis that contestation in the contemporary world is increasingly global, or de-territorialised, in Deleuze and Guattari's sense, but also subversively local, in the latter's sense of rhizomatic minorities. Hardt and Negri see *Empire* as part of a tradition of revolutionary political pamphlets in times of social transition, which includes Machiavelli's *The Prince* (1513) and Marx and Engels's *Communist Manifesto* (1848).

They remind readers that these works are so close to actual historical movements that they are more like guides to practical action than philosophical treatises. In Machiavelli's case the text communicates the urgency of the prince's mission to establish a stable order out of the ruins of the collapsing late medieval world. Among other things this means establishing new criteria of political virtue that steer the community away from the twin perils of fatalism and adventurism. For Marx and Engels it is a question of signalling the twilight of republican humanism and explaining why the Industrial Revolution creates the objective possibility of a qualitatively new form of democracy in which the formal equality of bourgeois citizenship is replaced by the real equality binding the libertarian community of communist producers. For Negri and Hardt it means rearticulating the reasons why communism is still the answer to the riddle of history. In fact, they suggest that despite the collapse of the state socialist model and the integration of the working class within the political institutions of industrial and postindustrial democracies, the world has never been closer to revolution.[36]

We are now closer to revolution than ever because the imperialist nation state has given way to an international form of global governance which has finally reached the objective outer limit of its expansion in the history of the struggle between oppressive political power and the productive desire of the multitude. Hardt and Negri thus reinterpret the bio-political theories of Foucault and Deleuze and Guattari, and find a confirmation rather than a refutation of Marx's thesis that capitalist social relations are the last possible form of antagonistic social relations. In their view, Marx is correct to argue that capitalism is the indispensable condition for a free society that will eventually emerge from the inevitable collapse of capitalism, but he was understandably unable to perceive that it would first require two world wars and the Cold War before the nation state would finally implode. That implosion takes the bourgeois populist conception of 'the people' with it, thus opening things up for the multitude. The authors of *Empire* argue that the modern territorial nation state that emerged in the wake of the French Revolution and the Industrial Revolution in Europe and North America constitutes the last stage in a process of territorialisation that has literally run out of territory to govern. In Hardt and Negri's usage the disappearance of the working class is bound up with the appearance of an international proletariat in the post-Autonomia world of global capitalism. If Autonomia was the most articulate expression of the dual rejection of wage labour and the political spectacle within the context of the nation state, the multitude is the visible reality of the dual rejection of wage labour and bio-political domination in the context of the emergence of the empire.[37]

It is important to emphasise that Hardt and Negri's empire is not synonymous with imperialism or nationalism, or even with the current hegemony of the United States of America. Imperialism and colonialism correspond to the period of competing nation states and the struggles of the working classes within them in the period roughly spanning the years from the French Revolution to the end of World War II. The years following 1945 are marked by rapid industrial reconstruction and remarkable capital accumulation, as well as the transition from the Fordist assembly line to post-Fordist forms of flexible organisation of the labour process.

During the Fordist period in Europe and North America, large labour unions and social democratic, socialist and communist parties defend the working class in a corporate bargaining structure dominated by the representatives of labour, capital and the state. Fordism is thus the typical mode of production in a nation state that in varying degrees is in a constant social struggle with capital and labour within the boundaries of its own territory, and at the same time is enmeshed in a political struggle for commercial and military hegemony with other nation states on the international level. Within Fordism, international relations are characterised by strategic alliances between states in the search for geopolitical supremacy, accompanied by colonial conquests as part of the project to secure cheap labour power and direct access to raw materials and natural resources. Within this context colonialism represents an important economic factor for the smooth functioning and steady growth of the national production machine. It is also a significant prestige factor for a bourgeoisie hungry for contact with and mastery of exotic cultures and races. Colonial conquest thus brings 'colourful' specimens of Third World quaintness to the metropolises of the capitalist mother country. The relative success of the British and French bourgeoisie in this endeavour to dominate the globe is often cited as a major cause of the military conflicts with their German counterpart in 1914–18 and 1939–45.[38]

The constellation of the imperialist and Fordist period of industrial production is marked by the territorial integrity of the nation state, the unproblematic political representation of the native people within it, the assumed racial purity and superiority of the native people of the mother country vis-à-vis its colonial 'imports' at home, and war with rival nation states abroad. Hardt and Negri maintain that all of this changes at the theoretical level with Foucault and at the practical level with the advent of the bio-political post-Fordist empire. They acknowledge that while it would be tempting to regard the United States as the centre of the empire, it is in fact a crucially important feature of the empire that, like language for Roussel, the empire has no directing centre analogous to the nation state of Fordist imperialism. The empire, like the bio-political regulation of internal human nature, is global, economic, cultural, scientific, sociopolitical and linguistic. As a consequence, it engenders forms of resistance which are global, multi-class, racially and culturally heterogeneous, nomadic and contaminated. Here contamination implies a reality that eludes binary purity in all of its guises, such as black-white, native-foreigner, animal-human, high culture-popular culture, machine-human, straight-homosexual, male-female, art-politics, etc. If the pre-industrial, pre-Fordist period is characterised by the struggle between the legitimacy of the church and that of the state, the Fordist period is marked by the conflict between the power of capital and the authority of the modern state. In this latter moment in the battle between production and power, the bourgeoisie is a historically progressive force that prepares the ground for the arrival of the post-Fordist multitude. It is in this sense that Hardt and Negri follow Marx and Engels in celebrating capitalism as a force capable of unleashing productive energies which it subsequently will not be able indefinitely to territorialise and bio-politicise. Within the Fordist context capital has the contradictory task of exploiting the working class without exterminating it, i.e. it has to get the most out of the workers while providing them with a stable material existence. The state, operating on the basis of the sovereignty model, has to guarantee the rights of formal equality for all citizens while endeavouring to maintain political stability in the face of the flagrant discrepancy between formal equality and real social inequality. According to Hardt and Negri, the disciplinary society analysed by Foucault does not fully emerge until the transition from Fordism to post-Fordism is completed. Hence in theoretical terms the authors of *Empire* weave together Marx and Foucault on political economy and power with Deleuze and Guattari on the multitude and desire.[39]

Fordism represents the unstable compromise between the forces of the state and capital, constructed on the basis of the exploitation of domestic surplus value and the accumulation of colonial wealth in cheap labour power and natural resources. In the short run the compromise results in tremendous levels of growth associated with the post-war boom years and the beginning of the complete internationalisation of the economy, referred to today as globalisation. As Marx predicted, the victor in the battle between capital and the state is capital. But in the long run the nation state and capital lose the disciplinary capacity to mutually regulate one another, with the result that the bases of Fordism collapse. The collapse of Fordism ushers in the crisis of social democracy and the welfare state as well as the definitive crisis of the territorial integrity of the nation state. As evidence, Hardt and Negri point out that states are now openly admitting their inability to regulate the flows of money, capital and information steered by multinational corporations and organisations such as the World Bank, WTO and IMF, and citizens are increasingly unconcerned with national elections. De-politicisation in this sense is marked by repoliticisation in another. That is, the demise of the state accompanies the demise of humanist politics in the strong sense of Schmitt, Arendt, Benjamin Barber and others. The end of politics and the state also signifies the end of the 'people' in its typical usage, and signals the appearance of the multitude.[40]

Hardt and Negri observe that in the political philosophies of thinkers such as Hobbes, Rousseau and Kant, one notes a clear distinction between the state of nature and civil society (synonymous with the state until Hegel), to which corresponds a clear distinction between an internal political space in which law replaces force, on the one hand, and an external international space in which conflicts continue to be resolved by the strength of the fittest reigning in the state of nature. Although the dynamics between state of nature/civil society and internal/external territory vary depending on the thinker in question, there is overall agreement on the integrity of territorial boundaries and the legitimacy of the sovereign state. In the transition from Fordism to post-Fordism the last remaining boundaries between internal and external are eroded. As a consequence, the distinctions between politics and production, public and private, and, significantly, between reason and desire become untenable. At the theoretical level, Hardt and Negri suggest that in the era of empire, the nationalist immanence of reason typified by the Hegelian state is gradually undermined by the international immanence of production (Marx) and de-territorialised desire (Spinoza). Marx's cogent critique of Hegel thus marks the end of any plausible theory or practice of legitimate liberal democracy. His critique is accompanied in sociocultural terms by Baudelaire's vague but fertile intuitions concerning the emergence of global experience and consciousness, and Benjamin's analysis of the demise of aura. Thus Marx, Baudelaire and Benjamin all testify to the early signs of the decay of the hegemony of the bourgeoisie as well as the crisis of its state. Hardt and Negri maintain that the collapse of this particular state form is particularly long and agonising since it entails two world wars, de-colonisation and national independence in what was once called the Third World, and the Cold War. However, these catastrophes are all preparatory stages in the formation of the newly emerging collective subjectivity and global consciousness on a mass scale made possible by the transition from nationalist imperialism to international empire. At the practical and historical level, Hardt and Negri submit that it is now possible to regard de-colonisation and the Cold War as part of a related process in which the de-territorialisation of state power is confronted with the de-territorialisation of productive desire beyond the illusory boundaries of the nation state and juridical sovereignty.[41]

On this reading, the American victory in the Cold War is no more a victory of Enlightenment and democracy against barbarism and totalitarianism than the end of colonialism in Africa and Asia. De-colonisation, the end of the Cold War, the dismantling of the welfare state and the remaining restrictions on international trade are all moments in the collapse of any viable distinction between the empire and what might be external to it. For Hardt and Negri this does not amount to the final victory of empire, however. On the contrary, the empire is confronted with its own inability to apply Fordist and post-Fordist strategies of regulation and governance. Whether dropping bombs on civilian populations, or hunting 'terrorists', or de-regulating markets, everything that the empire does is performed in the name of democracy and peace. Today, conflicts between states such as World Wars I and II, and attacks on colonial populations such as those perpetrated against Algeria and Vietnam, are vestiges of increasingly obsolete modes of power. This is a liberating message for the multitude, who are slowly becoming aware of the fact that they are in a war against bio-political control in which they have no enemies in supposedly foreign lands populated by 'other' nations or races. Those boundaries have been destroyed by the empire itself—and now it must exit from the historical stage as well. Drawing on the subtle distinction made by Deleuze with reference to Spinoza, Hardt and Negri insist that the multitude is separated rather than alienated from its productive capacities. It has to transform itself into a governing force rather than re-appropriate its alienated essence as the general will of the sovereign peo-ple or the general interest of the universally exploited industrial class. If it can invent the right nomadic forms of life and unfettered productivity, it may be able to replace the empire as the new protagonist of history.[42]

Despite Hardt and Negri's optimism about the political potential of the multitude, the question remains: will it really replace empire? It may be plausible to argue that the great advantage of the concept of the mul-titude vis-à-vis the concept of social class is its tremendous elasticity. Deleuze and Guattari argue that political theory must now become ontology, and, indeed, Hardt and Negri's multitude seems to be every-where and nowhere in particular in the manner of Heidegger's *Sein* (being). Is this a genuine theoretical gain, or has something been lost or perhaps neglected in the haste to translate Foucault's epistemological innovations and his ideas on governance and bio-power into social and political theory? The Conclusion of this book attempts to address this difficult issue.[43]

Empire suggests that as the limits of post-Fordist governance become clear, labour becomes increasingly immaterial and intelligence becomes increasingly generalised. The argument is that it is no longer possible plausibly to confine productivity to the wage labour form. Hardt and Negri thus reiterate the socialist feminist argument that unpaid work in the home and other contexts is productive in ways that are not reflected in the capitalist economy and its skewed modalities of remuneration. In a parallel vein, it is also no longer plausible to confine desire to the hetero-sexual couple or patriarchal family any more than it is possible to confine politics to the liberal democratic state form or the bourgeois public sphere. In his *Grammar of the Multitude,* Paolo Virno states the matter in the following terms:

> The contemporary multitude is not comprised of citizens or work-ers; it occupies a middle position between the individual and the collective. For this reason the distinction between public and pri-vate is no longer valid. It is in fact a consequence of the dissolution of these time-honoured couplets that one cannot speak in terms of the implicit unity of the people that becomes real and explicit in the state . . . The unity of the multitude is comprised of common places of the mind [luoghi comuni della mente], of linguistic-cognitive fac-ulties common to the human species, and of the general intellect. It is a matter of unity and a universality which is visibly different from state unity. That is, the unity of the multitude is not the unity of the people. The multitude does not need to converge in the general will because it already disposes of a general intellect.[44]

Virno maintains that the conflict lacerating capitalist society is not simply the Marxist contradiction between social, collective production and private, individual appropriation. It is the discrepancy between productive energy and the wage-labour form of production, on the one hand, as well as the discrepancy between the multitude's political aspiration to create new forms of collective life and the parliamentary appropriation of generalised intelligence and political aspiration, on the other. Whereas Gramsci holds that the working class must generate a set of organic intellectuals from within its ranks to challenge the traditional intellectuals of bourgeois hegemony, Virno argues that modern societies are characterised by a diffused general intellect that defies the conventional class analysis of Marxist and non-Marxist sociology. Much in the manner of Deleuze and Guattari, he implies that intelligence, productive capacity and political imagination are like waves of water breaking the socioeconomic and political dams that seek to channel them in exploitable directions. Hence the multitude is trying to construct new public spheres that defy the tendency of the bourgeois public sphere to mediate between the private sphere and the state in a manner that stabilises private interests while checking the abuses of state power. The bourgeois public sphere was complicit in the capitalist project to steer horizontal communicative and co-operative processes in a vertical direction, so that private social power and public political authority could achieve equilibrium at the expense of a potential expansion of communication and co-operation in a variety of directions. The rise of the multitude and the cybernetic diffusion of information and knowledge through the Internet and alternative public spheres have discredited the idea that there might be a single general will or some form of monolithic state authority. According to Virno the October revolution of 1917 was, among other things, a mistaken attempt to construct a socialist general will at the expense of an anarchic and solidaristic general intelligence of the kind that achieved visibility in Italy in the years 1969–77. For him the contemporary multitude embodies the continuation of the pluralist tendencies of the movement of 1977 rather than a return to communist orthodoxy or social democratic reformism.[45]

Without always directly referring to the multitude, many enthusiastic observers and participants in the world social forums that began with Porto Alegre generally agree that the contemporary world is marked by a plurality of diverse and overlapping struggles to create new institutions and forms of life. These forums have sprung up in conjunction with what in France is referred to as *altermondialisme*. This is the term used to describe the extremely diffuse alliance of trade unions, churches, NGOs (nongovernmental organisations such as Greenpeace, Friends of the Earth, Earth First, Oxfam, Doctors without Borders, Amnesty International, Human Rights Watch, etc.), established social movements (peace, gay rights, greens) and new social movements and networks such as SOS Rascisme (founded in France in 1984) and the internationally active ATTAC (Association pour la Taxation des Transactions Financières pour l'aide aux Citoyens, an association created in 1998 defending just taxation of financial transactions on an international scale, abolition of Third World debt, and an array of related issues), which are currently aligned in a broad struggle against neo-liberal globalisation.[46] The prefix 'alter' in *altermondialisme* is expressly used instead of 'anti' in order to indicate that the unions, NGOs, social movements and other associations in question are not against internationalism as such. On the contrary, and in consonance with a number of the theoretical positions examined earlier in this chapter, the de facto international character of the economy, culture, identities and other aspects of contemporary society is embraced in opposition to the obsolete and reactionary politics of what in international relations is called the 'state system'.

The state system presupposes the inevitability of antagonistically juxtaposed nations in constant anticipation of war with one another. By contrast, the new internationalism is exemplified by the Zapatista movement in Mexico and the contestations associated with Seattle in the United States, Porto Alegre in Brazil, the European social forums and other spontaneous instances of struggle where the terrain of conflict is fluid and in constant evolution. In various ways the supporters of these movements and protests suggest, in the manner of Hardt and Negri, that the state system paradigm passed with the transition from imperialism to empire, and that the empire's enemies are now flourishing *within* its global territory. Unsurprisingly, Hardt and Negri explain that they are opposed to ostensibly left-wing republican arguments for the reconstitution of the nation state as a political framework capable of instituting at least limited forms of democratic control over international capitalism. This attitude is shared by many of the participants in the global forums and counter summits. The idea is that states, borders and boundaries are in an irreversible process of dissolution. Moreover, this is a positive development in view of the fact that the state represents an unacceptable form of false (i.e. in reality authoritarian) political community. What unites many contemporary theorists and activists is the perception that if internationalism and globalisation are realities, there is nothing inevitable about the neo-liberal version of international trade and development that is vaunted by the G8 and WTO as the only viable system in a post-1989 world. That is, the *altermondialiste* position is that the weakening of the state should not mean that the WTO, IMF, World Bank and other prominent players in the project to de-regulate markets should be allowed to continue to impose their narrow vision of international peace under the aegis of private accumulation and fiscal austerity.[47]

It is worth noting in this context that countries such as Argentina have been brought to the brink of economic collapse by organisations such as the World Bank and WTO, and have responded in various sectors with syndicalist and anarchist movements calling for worker self-management of factories. Hence it is possible to detect moments of overlap between the forms of struggle adopted by the traditional revolutionary left and those taken up by the protagonists of what might be called the new internationalism. This raises some pertinent questions for the conclusion about the relationship between the left and contemporary society. Can the left reinvent itself and work together with the new forms of contestation without losing what has been distinct about revolutionary left politics from Marx to the critique of daily life, or has the time come to say that the time of the left has passed with the crisis of the nation state and the transition from imperialism to empire? Does the left need to reinvent or abandon humanism? Can the left be both Foucauldian and pluralist as well as Marxist and rigorously coherent?

Suggestions for Further Reading

Best, Steven and Kellner, Douglas. *Postmodern Theory: Critical Interrogations*, London, Macmillan, 1991.

Butler, Judith, Laclau, Ernesto and Zizek, Slavoj. *Contingency, Hegemony, Universality: Contemporary Dialogues on the Left*, London, Verso, 2000.

Fisher, William F. and Ponniah, Thomas. *Another World is Possible: Popular Alternatives to Globalization at the World Social Forum*, London, Zed, 2003.

Holloway, John. *Changing the World Without Seizing it*, London, Pluto, 2005.

Murphy, Timothy S. and Mustapha, Abdul-Karim (eds). *The Philosophy of Antonio Negri: Resistance in Practice*, London, Pluto, 2005.

Simons, Jon (ed.), *Contemporary Critical Thought: From Lacan to Said*, Edinburgh, EUP, 2004.

Thomson, Alex. *Deconstruction and Democracy: Derrida's Politics of Friendship*, London and New York, Continuum, 2005.

Tormey, Simon. *Anti-Capitalism: A Beginner's Guide*, Oxford, One-World Books, 2004.

Notes

1 A more extensive history of the left would certainly devote an entire chapter to Pasolini. Although a committed Marxist, he experienced the twilight of Gramscian humanism as a crisis of Western civilisation which in his estimation extended well beyond the left-right divide. His poem 'The Ashes of Gramsci' (1957) succeeds in conveying this profound sense of malaise without melodrama. The poem is contained in the collection *Le ceneri di Gramsci* [*The Ashes of Gramsci*], and is also available in English translation. Readers interested in his films should consult Vighi, *Traumatic Encounters in Italian Film*.

2 Haraway, *Simians, Cyborgs, and Women*; Deleuze Guattari, *Capitalisme et schizo-phrénie I: L'anti-oedipe [Capitalism and Schizophrenia I: The Anti-Oedipus]* and *Capitalisme et schizophrénie II: Mille Plateaux [Capitalism and Schizophrenia II: A Thousand Plateaux]*. Both of these works have been translated into English along with virtually everything else written by these highly influential authors, whose work is looked at in the second half of this chapter. The first chapter of *The Anti-Oedipus* is famous for conjuring up the image of the desiring machine as an alternative to the traditional humanist subject. The Italian sociologist Alberto Melucci analyses NSMs in the light of the post-humanist theoretical positions taken up by Foucault and Deleuze and Guattari. See his *Nomads of the Present*.

3 Freud's clearest statement of this position is formulated in *Das Unbehagen in der Kultur [Civilisation and its Discontents]*, pp. 52–54.

4 Heidegger, *Sein und Zeit [Being and Time]*, Introduction and Chapter 1.

5 Another powerful statement of the problem is formulated by Jacques Derrida in *L'écriture et la différence [Writing and Difference]*, Chapters 1, 4, 7, 8 and 10. For an analysis that draws out the political significance of this and other Derrida texts, see Thomson, *Deconstruction and Democracy*. Some readers may be tempted to regard these theories as ulterior developments in the quest to rethink the difference between divinity and humanity. As will be seen, the Dutch philosopher Spinoza's (1632–77) idea that the divine is collective and immanent rather than individual and transcendent has been taken up by Deleuze and by Hardt and Negri with their theory of the multitude.

6 In Chapter 2 on Western Marxism it is seen that theorists such as Althusser attempt to avoid this problem by adapting Lacan's notion of over-determination to the theoretical framework of structuralism in an attempt to show that capitalist society is a de-centred totality. The problems with this idea are also discussed in that chapter.

7 See Foucault, *Raymond Roussel*, Chapter 6, entitled 'The surface of things', and Gros, 'Michel Foucault, lecteur de Roussel et Brisset', pp. 40–42.

8 Foucault, op. cit., pp. 208–12; Foucault, 'Dire et voir chez Raymond Roussel' ('Saying and seeing in the work of Raymond Roussel'), in *Dits et écrits I, 1954–1975 [Discourses and Writings I]*, pp. 233–36, 239–43. Roussel wrote the play *Impressions of Africa* (1910) and a number of poems and novels. Foucault's reading of artists such as Roussel is greatly influenced by the surrealists and the work of the literary critic Maurice Blanchot (1907–2003), author of *L'éspace littéraire [The Space of Literature]*, and *Michel Foucault, tel que je l'imagine [Michel Foucault as I Imagine him]*. Both of these works by Blanchot are available in English.

9 Foucault, 'Nietzsche, Freud, Marx' in *Dits et écrits I, 1954–1975 [Discourses and Writings I]*, pp. 595–96, and 'Nietzsche, généalogie, histoire' in the same volume, pp. 1006–9. Also see his *Les mots et les choses [Words and Things]* (translated into English in 1970 as *The Order of Things*), Chapter 9.

10 For a lucid explanation of these issues in Foucault, see Dreyfus and Rabinow, *Michel Foucault: Beyond Structuralism and Hermeneutics*. The volume also contains an afterword by and an interview with Foucault.

11 Not enough work has been done on Gramsci and Foucault and the possibility of comparing and contrasting their ideas on power, emancipation and self-transformation. Like Foucault, Gramsci is a student of linguistics and literature

as well as an analyst of the links between language and social power. Gramsci shares Foucault's belief that power is diffuse, but nonetheless retains the idea that power is organised in relation to economic, political, and national specificities that are knowable and transformable by a collective subject. In the *Prison Notebooks* Gramsci discusses the question of hegemony in relation to the national-popular bases of literature. In his work on Roussel and bio-power Foucault suggests that if language and power were once national-popular, in the twentieth century they assume a more universal character. For Foucault this universality is not humanistic, however. It is an ontological and anonymous universality implying a much more uncertain political programme than the construction of a new hegemony under the leadership of a communist party designated as the modern successor to Machiavelli's prince. In the encounter between Gramsci and Foucault one glimpses the point where the most flexible form of dogmatism meets the most epistemologically rigorous form of relativism. The epistemological and political potential of that encounter has not been explored in sufficient detail.

12 Foucault, *Naissance de la biopolitique* [*The Birth of Bio-politics*], pp. 272–75.

13 Deleuze, *Foucault*, pp. 77–99. This book has been translated into English and offers what is probably the best concise account of Foucault's main ideas on epistemology, language, power and self-transformation.

14 Foucault, *Surveiller et punir* [*Discipline and Punish*] (translated into English in 1979), and *Naissance de la biopolitique* [*The Birth of Bio-politics*], pp. 67–69.

15 Foucault, *L'archéologie du savoir* [*The Archaeology of Knowledge*] (translated into English in 1971), pp. 44–54; Deleuze, *Foucault*, pp. 55–75.

16 Foucault, op. cit., Part I, Chapter 3; Deleuze, op. cit., pp. 55–60.

17 Foucault, *Naissance de la biopolitique* [*The Birth of Bio-politics*], pp. 55–56.

18 Foucault, *L'ordre du discours* [*The Order of Discourse*], pp. 20–23; Dreyfus and Rabinow, *Michel Foucault*, second edition, Part II, Chapters 7, 8 and 9.

19 Hardt and Negri, *Empire*, p. 30; Virno, *Grammatica della moltitudine* [*A Grammar of the Multitude*] (available in English translation), p. 16.

20 This argument is developed in Schecter, *Beyond Hegemony*, especially Chapter 2.

21 Foucault, 'La pensée du dehors' ['Thought from the outside'] (available in translation), and *L'archéologie du savoir* [*The Archaeology of Knowledge*], Part I, Chapters 2–3.

22 Foucault, *Surveiller et Punir* [*Discipline and Punish*], Parts 3–4; *La pensée du dehors* [*Thought from the Outside*], pp. 545–46.

23 If one considers the post–World War II period to date, it is quite possibly the case that Foucault is the most original and difficult-to-categorise thinker with a broadly left-wing profile. Yet there are many other important thinkers whose relations with the left are also difficult to define with adequate clarity. There is unfortunately not enough space to examine the ideas of Frantz Fanon, Cornelius Castoriadis, Slavoj Zizek, Homi Baba, G. C. Spivak, Jacques Derrida, Judith Butler, Julia Kristeva, Edward Said, Donna Haraway, Pierre Bourdieu, Hélène Cixous, Luce Irrigary, Frederic Jameson, and many others. This confirms the point made at the outset of this section on Foucault: that although a history of the left would be incomplete without a substantial discussion of Foucault, he is not part of an identifiable left-wing tradition or movement in the same way as Western Marxists, anarchists, council communists and other thinkers considered in previous chapters. Hardt and Negri are

arguably the pre-eminent thinkers of contemporary global anticapitalism, which is why they are discussed in some detail below. If one tried to examine the thought of all the thinkers just mentioned in this footnote, the argument in this book would dissipate into a very superficial series of summaries. Foucault is included for reasons that should be clear. What is less clear is the answer to the question posed above, namely: if there is no way to integrate Foucault's critique of power, reified thinking and humanism into a recognisably left-wing political programme, is it time to say that the left has ceased to be relevant to the experience of most people in advanced capitalist societies? Hardt and Negri say that there is definitely a way to do this. As will be seen in the next section, the work of Deleuze and Guattari constitutes the link joining the bio-political theories of Foucault with Hardt and Negri's theory of the multitude.

24 Deleuze, *Spinoza el le problème de l'expression* [*Spinoza and the Problem of Expression*], pp. 247–48 and *Différence et répétition* [*Difference and Repetition*], Chapter 5; Zourabichvici, 'Une philosophie de l'événement' ['A Philosophy of the Event'], pp. 6–8.

25 Adorno, *Zur Metakritik der Erkennnistheorie* [*Against Epistemology*], pp. 60–63, *Negative Dialektik* [*Negative Dialectics*], pp. 18–33, and *Ontologie und Dialektik* [*Ontology and Dialectics*], pp. 117–18, 426–27.

26 Deleuze, *Le bergsonisme* [*Bergsonism*] (translated into English in 1988), pp. 25–30.

27 Deleuze, *Cinéma I: l'image-mouvement* [*Cinema I: The Image-Movement*], Chapter 7, and *Cinéma II: l'image-temps* [*Cinema II: The Time-Image*], Chapter 1. Both volumes are available in English. In Chapter 1 of the second volume Deleuze explains his theory of the transition from the image-movement dimension of the cinematic structure of experience to the ontology of cinematic time. Readers of French can also consult Hême de Lacotte, *Deleuze, philosophie et cinema*.

28 Spinoza, *Ethica*, Parts 3–5; Deleuze, *Spinoza el le problème de l'expression* [*Spinoza and the Problem of Expression*], pp. 15, 125, 197, 247–48, 322.

29 Deleuze and Guattari, *Capitalisme et schizophrénie I: l'anti-Oedipe* [*Capitalism and Schizophrenia I: Anti-Oedipus*], Chapter 2.

30 Best and Kellner, *Postmodern Theory*, p. 89. This book offers lucid explanations of the ideas of Foucault, Deleuze and Guattari, Baudrillard, Lyotard, Fredric Jameson, feminists and other important social theorists. For a concise summary of Deleuze and Guattari's main ideas, see also Goodchild, 'Gilles Deleuze and Félix Guattari' in Simons (ed.), *Contemporary Critical Theorists: From Lacan to Said*, pp. 168–84. This is an excellent collection of essays containing chapters on Derrrida, Irrigary, Cixous, Kristeva, Foucault, Said and others.

31 Deleuze and Guattari, op. cit., Chapter 4.

32 Freud shows that all people are neurotic to some extent and that it is therefore erroneous to suppose a clear distinction between healthy people and neurotic people. The more pertinent issue for him concerns the possibility of ascertaining at what point neurosis becomes pathological and dysfunctional. Deleuze and Guattari make an analogous point regarding the cultural meanings attached to disability. If everyone is handicapped in some ways, there is a great deal at stake in the medical and psychiatric designations of what counts as disabled and dysfunctional and why. Op. cit., Chapter 4 and Appendix.

33 Deleuze and Guattari, op. cit., pp. 352–71.

34 Deleuze and Guattari, *Capitalisme et schizophrénie II: mille plateaux* [*Capitalism and Schizophrenia II: A Thousand Plateaux*], pp. 9–10. The term *agencement* is variously translatable as an arrangement, a putting together, or a laying out of several elements.

35 Deleuze and Guattari, *Kafka*, Chapters 2–4, 6 and 8–9.

36 Hardt and Negri, *Empire*, Introduction and Conclusion.

37 Ibid., pp. 53–56.

38 Ibid., pp. 178–79.

39 Ibid., pp. 236–37. It remains unclear if Foucault envisages a hybrid between disciplinary and pastoral society, or if he thinks we are on the way to a fully pastoral society. Instead of taking this question up in any detail, Hardt and Negri focus on the potential implications of the emergence of the postmodern and post-Fordist multitude.

40 Ibid., pp. 285–87.

41 Ibid., pp. 178–79.

42 Ibid., pp. 373–76. See also Hardt and Negri's Foreword to Fisher and Ponniah, *Another World is Possible*, pp. xvi–xix. This volume includes a contribution by the ATTAC activist Bernard Cassen.

43 For a much more sober assessment of the political potential of the multitude, see Jappe and Kurz, *Les habits de l'empire*.

44 Virno, *Grammatica della moltitudine* [*A Grammar of the Multitude*], pp. 14, 32.

45 Ibid., pp. 103–4, 118–20. A similar argument is made by Oskar Negt and Alexander Kluge in *Öffentlichkeit und Erfahrung* [*The Public Sphere and Experience*].

46 For the specific case of ATTAC, see Walters, 'Á l'ATTAC'. In addition to its dynamic activist profile, ATTAC is a versatile movement with a number of important theorists including Susan George, Bernard Cassen, Christophe Aguiton and Ignatio Ramonet. Readers of French should consult Cassen, *Tout a commencé à Porto Alegre* [*Everything Began in Porto Alegre*]. It is fairly safe to assume that the idea of a thousand social forums is a direct allusion to *A Thousand Plateaux*, and that Cassen regards the proliferation of social forums as the multitude's realisation of new forms of direct democracy. The positions of Cassen and ATTAC are usually parallel to those taken by the French monthly journal *Le Monde Diplomatique*, which is simultaneously translated into English and other languages.

47 Hardt and Negri, *Empire*, pp. 53–56. For the relation between the theoretical terrain staked out in *Empire* and contemporary forms of global anticapitalism, see also the collection of essays contained in Murphy and Mustapha, *The Philosophy of Antonio Negri*.

CONCLUSION

The first number of the journal *Internationale Situationiste* in June 1958 begins with an anonymous article entitled 'The Bitter Victory of Surrealism'. Almost forty years later, in 1996, Gianfranco Marelli wrote an important historical account of the SI entitled *The Bitter Victory of Situationism*. There can be little doubt that what is meant in both cases is a negative victory referring to the urgent, but to date impossible, task of translating the critique of political economy *and* the critique of daily life from Marx and Rimbaud to Breton and Debord into a coherent political programme of the left. The importance of rearticulating this political programme may well be obvious to many militants active in contemporary struggles. There is much evidence to suggest that the political forces and powerful interests organised in social democratic parties are in the process of devising different strategies to accommodate the regimes governed in their names to the production and consumption rhythms of globalised neo-liberal capitalism. The surrealists and situationists score a brilliant victory by showing that, despite a tremendous amount of theoretical and practical endeavour to the contrary, the dialectical basis of the modernist revolution is not really the philosophical dialectic between materialism and idealism or even the socioeconomic dialectic between the economy and the superstructure. Breton and Lefebvre suggest that it is in fact the dialectic between the critique of political economy and the critique of daily life. The relevance of this project assumes renewed importance today, when social democracy everywhere seems ready to emulate liberal democracy by capitulating to the needs of capital, and state socialism is probably less attractive than ever for most people. If the critique of political economy without the critique of daily life is likely to culminate in authoritarian state socialism and stale socialist realist art with very little appeal in the twenty-first century, the critique of daily life without the critique of political economy tends to run into the dead ends of ineffectual aesthetic protest, dandyism and academic abstraction. Unless one is convinced by Hardt and Negri's theory of the immanent revolutionary desire of the multitude, the surrealist-situationist victory may seem all the more bitter in light of the manifest absence of a collective subject capable of reconciling the two critiques in theory and practice.[1]

But there is also another possible tentative conclusion to the history of the left offered in this book. That is, there may be a way out of the impasses reached when juxtaposing the negative dialectics of some strands of critical theory with postmodernist immanence on the one hand, or indecisive social democratic reformism with 'revolutionary' dogmatism on the other, to name just a couple of the unsatisfactory alternatives suggested by the different crises that have confronted the left since the end of World War II. Given that Lefebvre and Debord are theorists of everyday life working within a broadly Marxist framework, it is imprecise to regard the dialectic of the two critiques as a simple case of thesis and antithesis. But it would also be imprecise to regard it as an issue internal to and resolvable within Marxism, and indeed, it was seen in Chapter 2 and at various other points that Marxism experienced a series of crises well before the authoritarian turn of the Russian Revolution. The more pertinent point is that social democracy's unwillingness or incapacity to envisage an economy that is not subordinate to the requirements of international capital does not alter the reality that the needs of capital are not synonymous with the modalities of what Foucault, developing a number of Nietzsche's ideas, designates as bio-power. The discussion in Chapters 5 and 6 suggests that Foucault's analysis of bio-power can be regarded as the most brilliant and politically promising development in the critique of everyday life and the society of the spectacle.

In Chapter 5 it was shown that the critique of everyday life has literary and avant-garde origins in the writings of Rimbaud and the anti-art performances of the Dada movement. It is a critique that took a more recognisably political turn with surrealism and even more so with situationism. In Chapter 6 it was seen that Foucault's wide-ranging contribution begins with the reflections on language, power and visibility in his *Raymond Roussel* of 1963, and branches out in several directions thereafter. Despite the undeniable theoretical suggestiveness of works such as *A Thousand Plateaus*, *Empire* and others, it is the analysis of bio-power begun by Foucault and the related possibility of a qualitative transformation in the daily lives of individuals that must be developed further and rethought. This rethinking must be done in conjunction with a renewed analysis of Marx on the epistemological and juridical implications of the transformation of external nature in the labour process (Chapter 1), Gramsci on hegemony (Chapter 2), Neumann and Kichheimer on structural transformations and the conditions of nonpopulist conceptions of legitimacy (Chapter 3), as well as with a fresh look at G. D. H. Cole's proposals for a radically different economy beyond the plan/market straitjacket (Chapter 4).

Hence the conclusion of this book is that if there is a future for left politics in the sense used here, it depends on the ability of its thinkers and activists to rearticulate the relation between the critique of political economy and capital with the critique of daily life and bio-power. This requires a nonauthoritarian co-ordination of the transformation of external nature in the labour process with the transformation of internal, human nature in artistic creativity. This may sound utopian. But the traditional idea of art as a sphere of creativity reserved for a select few and removed from everyday concerns has been undermined for reasons cited by the surrealists and situationsists.[2] The epistemological and aesthetic implications of the transformation of human nature are poetically celebrated by Rimbaud and Nietzsche, and touched on to some extent in a more systematic fashion by Adorno. This transformation is bound up with the potential for individual self-overcoming which is taken considerably further by Foucault with methodological innovation and finesse. The project of self-overcoming needs further elaboration in order to evolve towards a coherent critique of daily life capable of sustaining and completing the critique of political economy begun by Marx.[3]

It may seem odd in a book on the left to attach great importance to an instance of originally aesthetic expression and refusal that has such obviously avant-garde and arguably elitist connotations. Yet a key aspect of the existing hegemony is the continual intersection and dispersion of the apparently contradictory forces of capitalist exploitation, which tend to stratify and marginalise, and of bio-power, which tend to integrate and assimilate. Chapters 3, 5 and 6 indicate that one of the salient features of coerced integration in practice is the technocratic management of revolt, which is consolidated by the prerogative of political parties to channel the articulation of protest into left and right populist discourses and institutions. These discourses and institutions act as channels that in very different ways reaffirm the identity of the people (as class on the left or as the nation on the right) as well as the unity of the state (as sovereignty and territorial integrity). Within this constellation of forces the surrealist, situationist and bio-political critique of daily life is easily dismissed as either irrelevant or a luxury of the privileged. This dismissal serves only to reinforce the populist distortion of dissent, and ignores the point about the passing of the traditional work of art. It is important for the left to resist this tendency and to bear in mind that Hardt and Negri and Virno are absolutely correct to stress the general character of intelligence and the social dimension of productive creativity in the contemporary world.

The ideas of some of the surrealists, situationists and Foucault continue to be of central importance for the critique of everyday life. But today it also necessarily includes a range of issues taken up by feminism, postcolonialism and a number of NSMs, as well as some of the ideas defended by ATTAC and the participants in the World and European Social Forums. One of the great challenges is to articulate these concerns in conjunction with a thorough critique of capitalism that fully recognises the long-term futility of liberal democratic, social democratic and state socialist modes of organising the labour process. This will take some time and struggle, but it is certainly not impossible. Henri Lefebvre eloquently states the matter thus:

> We are still learning to think via metaphysical, abstract—alienated—forms of thought. The danger of dogmatic, speculative, and abstract attitudes lies ever in wait for us. How long will it take to create a *dialectical consciousness,* as long as our consciousness still feels it necessary to rise above its own self—in the metaphysical way—in order to think dialectically? It is impossible to fix a date; it may need generations before the dialectic can penetrate life by means of a regenerated culture.
>
> And as for love—which for nearly all of us oscillates between coarse biological need and the fine abstractions of passion's rhetoric—what is there to say?[4]

Notes

1 'Amère victoire du surréalisme'; Marelli, *L'amère victoire du situationisme* [*The Bitter Victory of Situationism*].
2 The traditional 'work of art' has for the most part been replaced by installations and other hybrid forms of artistic production that actually confirm some of the theses in Debord's *Society of the Spectacle*. See in particular thesis 191.
3 A very good introduction to some of these issues is provided by John Roberts in *Philosophising the Everyday*. Roberts offers an engaging study which includes analyses of a number of the thinkers considered in the present book, such as Lukács, Gramsci, Benjamin, Lefebvre and Vaneigem. His book includes an examination of important theorists of daily life not covered here, such as Roland Barthes (1915–80). Some readers may object that it is precisely a rearticulation of the relation between the critique of political economy and capital with the critique of daily life and bio-power that the authors of *A Thousand Plateaux* and *Empire* strive to formulate. This could be the topic of a very useful debate in the immediate future. But for reasons that should be clear from the exposition in Chapters 5 and 6, in this book it is suggested that in its existing versions the idea of the multitude is still undertheorised, somewhat vague, and more indebted to the populist and humanist traditions it seeks to break with than its authors seem willing to admit. The theory celebrates the inherent revolutionary capacity of the multitude, though without ever really posing the important issue of self-overcoming. In terms of the cri-

tique of daily life, Deleuze and Guattari's idea of *becoming* a minority seems a more fruitful idea. This could also provide the topic of a very valuable future debate.

4 Lefebvre, *Critique de la vie quotidienne I: Introduction* [*Critique of Everyday Life I: Introduction*], p. 184 (his emphases).

BIBLIOGRAPHY

Acton, Edward. *Rethinking the Russian Revolution*, London, Edward Arnold, 1990.

Adorno, T. W. *Ästhetische Theorie [Aesthetic Theory]*, Frankfurt, Suhrkamp, 1970.

Adorno, T. W. *Aesthetic Theory*, trans. and Introduction by Robert Hullot-Kentor, Continuum, London, 1997.

Adorno, T. W. *Drei Studien zu Hegel [Hegel: Three Studies]*, Frankfurt, Suhrkamp, 1963.

Adorno, T. W. *The Jargon of Authenticity*, London, Methuen, 1978.

Adorno, T. W. *Kant's Critique of Pure Reason* (trans. Rodney Livingston), Stanford, Stanford University Press, 2001.

Adorno, T. W. *Zur Metakritik der Erkenntnistheorie: Studien über Husserl und die phänomenologischen Antinomien [Against Epistemology]*, Frankfurt, Suhrkamp, 1970.

Adorno, T. W. *Negative Dialektik [Negative Dialectics]*, Frankfurt, Suhrkamp, 1966.

Adorno, T. W. *Noten zur Literatur [Notes on Literature]*, Frankfurt, Suhrkamp, 1974.

Adorno, T. W. *Ontologie und Dialektik [Ontology and Dialectics]* (published lectures from 1960–61), Frankfurt, Suhrkamp, 2002.

Adorno, T. W. *Stichworte: Kritische Modelle 2*, Frankfurt, Suhrkamp, 1969.

Adorno, T. W. *Vorlesung über Negative Dialektik, [Lectures on Negative Dialectics]*, Frankfurt, Suhrkamp, 2003.

Ali, Tariq. *Street Fighting Years*, New York, Citadel, 1980.

Allison, Henry E. *Kant's Transcendental Idealism: An Interpretation and Defence*, New Haven, Yale University Press, 1983.

Althusser, Louis. *Ecrits philosophiques et politiques [Philosophical and political writings]*, Vol. II, Paris, Stock/Mec, 1995.

Althusser, Louis. *Lenin and Philosophy*, New York, Monthly Review Press, 1971.

Althusser, Louis (with Etienne Balibar, Roger Establet, Pierre Macherey and Jacques Rancière). *Lire le Capital [Reading Capital]*, Paris, PUF, 1965.

Althussser, Louis. *Pour Marx [For Marx]*, Paris, François Maspero, 1965.

'Amère victoire du surréalisme', in *SI*, 1 (1958), 3–4.

Andersen, Thornton. *Masters of Russian Marxism*, New York, Appelton, 1963.

Anderson, Perry. *Considerations on Western Marxism*, London, Verso, 1976.

Anderson, Perry. *In the Tracks of Historical Materialism*, Chicago, University of Chicago Press, 1984.

Anikin, Andrei. *Russian Thinkers: Essays on Socio-Economic Thought in the Eighteenth and Nineteenth Centuries*, Moscow, Progress Publishers, 1988.

Ansouline, Pierre. *Cartier-Bresson*, Paris, Gallimard, 1999.

Apter, David and Joll, James (eds.). *Anarchism Today*, London, Macmillan, 1970.

Aragon, Louis. *Le paysan de Paris* [*The Paris Peasant*] (1926), Paris, Gallimard, 1953.

Arato, Andrew and Gebhardt, Eike (eds.). *The Essential Frankfurt School Reader*, London and New York, Continuum, 1982.

Arendt, Hannah. *The Human Condition*, Chicago, University of Chicago Press, 1958.

Arendt, Hannah. *On Revolution*, New York, Penguin, 1963.

Asor-Rosa, Alberto. *Scrittori e popolo* [*Writers and the People*], Rome, Riuniti, 1965.

Bakunin, Mikhail. *God and the State*, New York, Dover, 1970.

Bakunin, Mikhail. *Marxism, Freedom and the State*, London, Freedom Press, 1950.

Baldwin, Roger N. (ed.). *Kropotkin's Revolutionary Pamphlets*, New York, Dover, 1970.

Baudelaire, Charles. *L'art romantique* [*Romantic Art*] (1861) Paris, Flammarion, 1968.

Behan, Tom. *Dario Fo: Revolutionary Theatre*, London, Pluto, 2000.

Bellamy, Richard (ed.). *Gramsci: Pre-Prison Writings*, Cambridge, CUP, 1994.

Bellamy, Richard. *Liberalism and Modern Society: An Historical Argument*, Cambridge, Polity, 1992.

Bellamy, Richard. *Modern Italian Social Theory: Ideology and Politics from Pareto to the Present*, Stanford, Stanford University Press, 1987.

Bellamy, Richard and Schecter, Darrow. *Gramsci and the Italian State*, Manchester, MUP, 1993.

Benjamin, Walter. *Illuminations*, New York, Schocken, 1969.

Benjamin, Walter. *Das Passagen-Werk* [*The Paris Arcades Project*], 2 vols, Frankfurt, Suhrkamp, 1983.

Benjamin, Walter. *Reflections*, New York, Schocken, 1975.

Best, Steven and Kellner, Douglas. *Postmodern Theory: Critical Interrogations*, London, Macmillan, 1991.

Blanchot, Maurice. *L'éspace littéraire* [*The Space of Literature*], Paris, Gallimard, 1955.

Blanchot, Maurice. *Michel Foucault, tel que je l'imagine* [*Michel Foucault as I Imagine him*], Montpellier, Fata Morgana, 1986.

Bobbio, Norberto. *Ideological Profile of the Twentieth Century*, Princeton, PUP, 1995.

Bobbio, Norberto. *Destra e sinistra: ragioni e significati di una distinzione politica* [*Left and Right*], Rome, Donzelli, 1994.

Bookchin, Murray. *The Spanish Anarchists: The Heroic Years*, New York, Free Life Editions, 1977.

Borkenau, Franz. *The Spanish Cockpit*, London, Faber, 1937.

Bottomore, Tom (ed.). *A Dictionary of Marxist Thought*, second edition, Oxford, Basil Blackwell, 1991.

Bottomore, Tom and Goode, Patrick (eds.). *Austro-Marxism*, Oxford, Clarendon Press, 1978.

Brenan, Gerald. *The Spanish Labyrinth: An Account of the Social and Political Background of the Spanish Civil War*, Cambridge, CUP, 1943.

Breton, André. *Amour Fou* [*Mad Love*, 1937]. Paris: Gallimard, 1991.

Breton, André. *Manifestes du surréalisme* [*Manifesto of Surrealism*] (1924), Paris, Gallimard, 1963.

Breton, André. *Nadja* (1928), Paris, Gallimard, 1964.

Breton, André. *Les pas perdus* [*The Lost Steps*] (1924), Paris, Gallimard, 1969.

Breton, André. *La position politique du surréalisme* [*The Political Position of Surrealism*], Paris, Pauvert, 1971.

Breton, André. *Les vases communicants* [*The Communicating Vases*] (1932), Paris, Gallimard, 1955.

Breton, André and Soupault, Philippe. *Les champs magnétiques* [*The Magnetic Fields*] (1919), Paris, Gallimard, 1968.

Bronner, Stephen Eric and Kellner, Douglas (eds.) *Critical Theory and Society: A Reader*, London, Routledge, 1989.

Brown, Tom. *Tom Brown's Syndicalism*, London, Phoenix Press, 1990.

Callinicos, Alex. *Althusser's Marxism*, London, Pluto, 1976.

Carpenter, L.P. *G.D.H. Cole: An Intellectual Biography*, Cambridge, CUP, 1973.

Carr, E.H. *Bakunin*, New York, Simon and Schuster, 1961.

Cassen, Bernard. *Tout a commencé à Porto Alegre: mille forums sociaux!* [*Everything Began in Porto Alegre: A Thousand Social Forums!*], Paris, Fayard, 2003

Caygill, Howard. *A Kant Dictionary*, Oxford, Blackwell, 1995.

Caygill, Howard. *Walter Benjamin: The Colour of Experience*, London: Routledge 1988.

Chun, Lin. *The British New Left*, Edinburgh, Edinburgh University Press, 1993.

Clark, Martin. *Antonio Gramsci and the Revolution that Failed*, New Haven, Yale University Press, 1983.

Cohen, Stephen. *Bukharin and the Bolshevik Revolution*, Princeton, PUP, 1987.

Cole, G. D. H. *Guild Socialism Re-stated*, London, Leonard Parsons, 1920.

Cole, G. D. H. *Social Theory*, London, Methuen, 1920.

Cole, G. D. H. *The World of Labour*, London, George Bell & Sons, 1913.

Colletti, Lucio (ed.). *Marx: Early Writings*, London, Penguin, 1975.

Crowder, George. *Classical Anarchism: The Political Thought of Godwin, Proudhon, Bakunin, and Kropotkin*, Oxford, Clarendon Press, 1991.

Debord, Guy. *La société du spectacle* [*The Society of the Spectacle*] (1967, first published by Buchet-Chastel), Paris, Gallimard, 1992.

Deleuze, Gilles. *Le bergsonisme* [*Bergsonism*], Paris, PUF, 1966.

Deleuze, Gilles. *Cinéma I: l'image-mouvement* [*Cinema I: The Image-Movement*], Paris, Minuit, 1983.

Deleuze, Gilles. *Cinéma II: l'image-temps* [*Cinema II: The Time-Image*], Paris, Minuit, 1985.

Deleuze, Gilles. *Différence et répétition* [*Difference and Repetition*], Paris, PUF, 1968.

Deleuze, Gilles. *Foucault*, Paris, Minuit, 1986.

Deleuze, Gilles. *Spinoza et le problème de l'expression* [*Spinoza and the Problem of Expression*], Paris, Minuit, 1968.

Deleuze, Gilles and Guattari, Félix. *Capitalisme et schizophrénie I: l'anti-Oedipe* [*Capitalism and Schizophrenia I: Anti-Oedipus*], Paris, Minuit, 1973.

Deleuze, Gilles and Guattari, Félix. *Capitalisme et schizophrénie II: mille plateaux* [*Capitalism and Schizophrenia II: A Thousand Plateaux*], Paris, Minuit, 1980.

Deleuze, Gilles and Guattari, Félix. *Kafka: pour une littérature mineure*, Paris, Minuit, 1975.

Deleuze, Gilles and Félix Guattari. *Qu'est-ce que la Philosophy? (What is Philosophy?)*, Paris, Minuit, 1991.

Derrida, Jacques. *L'écriture et la différence [Writing and Difference]*, Paris, Seuil, 1967.

Deutscher, Isaac. *The Prophet Armed: Trotsky, 1879–1921*, Oxford, OUP, 1954.

Deutscher, Isaac. *The Prophet Outcast: Trotsky, 1929–1940*, Oxford, OUP, 1963.

Deutscher, Isaac. *The Prophet Unarmed: Trotsky, 1922–1928*, Oxford, OUP, 1959.

D'Hotel, André. *Rimbaud et la révolte moderne*, Paris, Gallimard, 1952.

Djilas, Milovan. *The New Class: An Analysis of the Communist System*, New York, Harcourt, 1983.

Dreyfus, Hubert and Rabinow, Paul. *Michel Foucault: Beyond Structuralism and Hermeneutics*, second edition, Chicago, University of Chicago Press, 1983.

Eyck, Frank. *The Revolutions of 1848–49*, Edinburgh, Oliver & Boyd, 1972.

Feldner, Heiko and Vighi, Fabio. *Beyond Foucault: On Zizek and Consequences*, London, Palgrave, 2006.

Fetscher, Iring. *Marx und Engels: Studienausgabe*, vols I and IV, Frankfurt, Fischer, 1990.

Feuerbach, Ludwig. *Ludwig Feuerbach: Philosophische Kritiken und Gegensätze, 1839–1846*, Leipzig, Reclam, 1966.

Feuerbach, Ludwig. *Das Wesen des Christentums [The Essence of Christianity]* (1841), Stuttgart, Reclam, 1969.

Finlayson, Gordon. *Habermas: A Very Short Introduction*, Oxford, OUP, 2004.

Fisher, William F. and Ponniah, Thomas (eds.). *Another World is Possible: Popular Alternatives to Globalization at the World Social Forum*, second edition, London, Zed, 2004.

Foucault, Michel. *L'archéologie du savoir [The Archaeology of Knowledge]*, Paris, Gallimard, 1969.

Foucault, Michel. *Dits et écrits I, 1954–75 [Discourses and Writings I]*, Paris, Gallimard, 2001.

Foucault, Michel. *Dits et écrits II, 1976–88 [Discourses and Writings II]*, Paris, Gallimard, 2001.

Foucault, Michel. *Les mots et les choses [Words and Things]*, Paris, Gallimard, 1966.

Foucault, Michel. *Naissance de la biopolitique [The Birth of Bio-politics]*, Cours au Collège de France 1978–79, Paris, Gallimard, 2004.

Foucault, Michel. *L'ordre du discours [The Order of Discourse]*, Paris, Gallimard, 1971.

Foucault, Michel. 'La pensée du dehors' ['Thought from the outside'], in *Critique*, 229 (1966).

Foucault, Michel. *Raymond Roussel*, Paris, Gallimard, 1963.

Foucault, Michel. *Surveiller et punir [Discipline and Punish]*, Paris, Gallimard, 1977.

Freud, Sigmund. *Die Traumdeutung [The Interpretation of Dreams]* (1900), Frankfurt, Fischer, 1999.

Freud, Sigmund. *Das Unbehagen in der Kultur [Civilisation and its Discontents]* (1930), Frankfurt, Fischer, 2000.

Frisby, David. *Fragments of Modernity: Theories of Modernity in the Work of Simmel, Krakauer, and Benjamin*, Cambridge, MIT Press, 1986.

Frith, Simon and Horne, Howard. *Art into Pop*, London, Methuen, 1987.

Fromm, Erich. *The Art of Being*, London, Constable, 1978.

Fromm, Erich. *Beyond the Chains of Illusion: My Encounter with Marx and Freud*, New York, Simon & Schuster, 1962.

Fromm, Erich. *Die Gesellschaft als Gegenstand der Psychoanalyse* [*Society as an Object of Psychoanalysis*], Frankfurt, Suhrkamp, 1993.

Fromm, Erich. *The Greatness and Limitations of Freud's Thought,* New York, Simon & Schuster, 1979.

Fromm, Erich. *To Have or to Be?* New York, Harper & Row, 1976.

Fromm, Erich. *Marx's Concept of Man,* New York, Continuum, 1961.

Gascar, Pierre. *Rimbaud et la Commune* [*Rimbaud and the Commune*], Paris, Gallimard, 1971.

Geoghegan, Vincent. *Reason and Eros: The Social Theory of Herbert Marcuse,* London, Pluto, 1981.

Gerber, John. *Anton Pannekoek and the Socialism of Workers' Self-Emancipation, 1873–1960,* London, Kluwer Academic, 1989.

Gill, Stephen (ed.). *Gramsci's Historical Materialism and International Relations,* Cambridge, CUP, 1993.

Goldmann, Lucien. *Lukács and Heidegger,* London, Verso, 1977.

Gombin, Richard. 'The Ideology and Practice of Contestation seen through Recent Events in France Today', in Apter and Joll, *Anarchism Today.*

Gombin, Richard. *The Origins of Modern Leftism,* London, Penguin, 1975.

Goodchild, Philip. 'Gilles Deleuze and Félix Guattari', in Simons (ed.), *Contemporary Social Theorists.*

Goode, Patrick. *Karl Korsch: A Study in Western Marxism,* London, Verso, 1979.

Gramsci, Antonio. *Americanismo e fordismo* [*Americanism and Fordism*], Rome, Riuniti, 1977.

Gramsci, Antonio. *Gli intellettuali e l'organizzazione della cultura* [*Intellectuals and the Organisation of Culture*], Rome, Riuniti, 1978.

Gramsci, Antonio. *Il materialismo storico* [*Historical Materialism*], Rome, Riuniti, 1977.

Gramsci, Antonio. *Note sul Machiavelli e sullo stato moderno* [*Notes on Machiavelli and the Modern State*], Rome, Riuniti, 1975.

Gramsci, Antonio. *Il Risorgimento* [*The Risorgimento*], Rome, Riuniti, 1975.

Gramsci, Antonio. *Scritti politici, 1921–26* [*Political Writings, 1921–26*], Turin, Einaudi, 1975.

Gramsci, Antonio. *Selections from the Political Writings, 1921–26,* London, Lawrence and Wishart, 1977.

Grave, Jean. *L'anarchisme: son but, ses moyens,* Paris, Stock, 1924.

Gros, Fréderic. 'Michel Foucault, lecteur de Roussel et Brisset', in *Magazine Littéraire,* 410 (2002).

Habermas, Jürgen. *Between the Facts and the Norms* (1992), Cambridge, Polity, 1998.

Habermas, Jürgen. *Knowledge and Human Interests,* Boston, Beacon Press, 1971.

Habermas, Jürgen. *Legitimation Crisis,* Boston, Beacon Press, 1978.

Habermas, Jürgen. *The Structural Transformation of the Public Sphere* (1962), Cambridge, Polity, 1989.

Habermas, Jürgen. *The Theory of Communicative Action* (1981), 2 vols, Cambridge, Polity, 1988.

Haraway, Donna. *Simians, Cyborgs, and Women: The Reinvention of Nature,* London, Free Association Books, 1991.

Harding, Neil. *Lenin's Political Thought,* 2 Volumes, Oxford, OUP, 1977.

Hardt, Michael and Negri, Antonio. *Empire: The New Order of Globalization,* Cambridge, Harvard University Press, 2000.

Hardt, Michael and Virno, Paolo. *Political Thought in Italy: A Potential Politics*, Minneapolis, University of Minnesota Press, 1996.

Hegel, G. W. F. *Grundlinien der Philosophie des Rechts* [*Philosophy of Right*] (1821), Frankfurt, Suhrkamp, 1970.

Hegel, G. W. F. *Lectures on the Philosophy of World History*, Cambridge, CUP, 1975.

Hegel, G. W. F. *The Phenomenology of Spirit*, Oxford, OUP, 1977.

Heidegger, Martin. *Sein und Zeit* [*Being and Time*] (1927), Tübingen, Max Niemeyer, 1993.

Hême de Lacotte, Suzanne. *Deleuze, philosophie et cinéma: le passage de l'image-mouvement à l'image-temps*, Paris, l'Harmatton, 2001.

Henry, Michel. *Marx, A Philosophy of Human Reality*, Bloomington, University of Indiana Press, 1983.

Hobson, S. G. *National Guilds: An Inquiry into the Wage System and the Way Out*, London, G. Bell & Sons, 1914.

Hobson, S. G. *National Guilds and the State*, London, G. Bell & Sons, 1920.

Hollis, Catherine. 'Walter Benjamin: beyond instrumental politics', DPhil thesis, University of Sussex, 2006.

Honneth, Axel. *The Struggle for Recognition*, Cambridge, Polity, 1990.

Horkheimer, Max. *The Critique of Instrumental Reason*, New York, Seabury, 1974.

Horkheimer, Max. *Critical Theory: Selected Essays*, New York, Seabury, 1972.

Horkheimer, Max. *Gesammelte Schriften*, Vol. 6, Frankfurt, Fischer, 1991.

Horkheimer, Max. *Selected Essays*, New York, Seabury, 1972.

Horkheimer, Max. *Traditionelle und kritische Theorie: Fünf Aufsätze* [*Traditional and Critical Theory: Five Essays, 1935*], Frankfurt, Fischer, 1970.

Horkheimer, Max and T. W. Adorno, *Dialektik der Aufklärung: Philosophische Fragmente* [*The Dialectic of Enlightenment*] (1947), Frankfurt, Fischer, 1995.

Horowitz, Irving. *Radicalism and the Revolt against Reason: The Social Theories of Georges Sorel*, London, Routledge & Kegan Paul, 1961.

Hughes, H. Stuart. *Consciousness and Society: The Re-orientation of European Social Thought, 1870–1930*, New York, Vintage, 1977.

Husserl, Edmund. *The Crisis of the European Sciences and Transcendental Phenomenology* (1938), London, Routledge, 1990.

Jacobson, Eric. *Metaphysics of the Profane: The Political Theology of Walter Benjamin and Gershom Scholem*, New York, Columbia University Press, 2003.

Jameson, Frederic. *Marxism and Form: Twentieth-Century Theories of Literature*, New Jersey, Princeton University Press, 1971.

Jappe, Anselm and Kurz, Robert, *Les habits de l'empire: remarques sur Negri, Hardt, et Rufin*, Paris, Lignes, 2003.

Jarvis, Simon. *Adorno: A Critical Introduction*, Cambridge, Polity, 1998.

Jay, Martin. *The Dialectical Imagination: A History of the Frankfurt School and the Institute for Social Research*, Boston, Little and Brown, 1973.

Jay, Martin. *Marxism and Totality*, Cambridge, Polity, 1984.

Jennings, Jeremy. *Syndicalism in France: A Study of Ideas*, London, Macmillan, 1990.

Joll, James. *The Anarchists*, London, Methuen, 1979.

Kant, Immanuel. *Kritik der reinen Vernunft* [*Critique of Pure Reason*] (1781), Frankfurt, Suhrkamp, 1968.

Kant, Immanuel. *Kritik der Urteilskraft* [*The Critique of Judgement*] (1790), Stuttgart, Reclam, 1963.

Kant, Imanuel. *Schriften zur Anthropologie, Geschichtsphilosophie, Politik und Päda-gogik I*, Frankfurt, Suhrkamp, 1977.

Kellner, Douglas (ed.). *Karl Korsch: Revolutionary Theory*, Austin, University of Texas Press, 1977.

Kelly, Aileen. *Mikhail Bakunin: A Study in the Psychology and Politics of Utopianism*, New Haven, Yale University Press, 1987.

Khayati, Mustapha. *De la misère en milieu étudiant considérée sous ses aspects économique, politique, psychologique, sexuel et notamment intellectuel, et de quelques moyens pour y remédier* [*On the Poverty of Student Life*], Arles, Sulliver, 1995.

Kinna, Ruth. *Anarchism: A Beginners's Guide*, Oxford, Oneworld Books, 2005.

Kirchheimer, Otto. 'Bemerkungen zu Carl Schmitts *Legalität und Legitimität*' ['Remarks on Carl Schmitt's *Legality and Legitimacy*'], in Wolfgang Luthardt (ed.), *Von der Weimarer Republik zum Faschismus*.

Kirchheimer, Otto. 'Changes in the structure of political compromise' (1941), in Arato and Gebhardt, *The Essential Frankfurt School Reader*.

Knei-Paz, Baruch. *The Social and Political Thought of Leon Trotsky*, Berkeley, University of California Press, 1978.

Konrad, George and Szelenyi, Ivan. *The Intellectuals on the Road to Class Power*, Brighton, Harvester, 1976.

Kool, Fritz. *Die Linke gegen die Parteiherrschaft* [*The Left against the Domination of the Party*], Olten, Walter Verlag, 1970.

Korsch, Karl. *Arbeitsrecht für Betriebsräte* [*Industrial Law for Workers' Councils*] (1922), Frankfurt and Vienna, Europäische Verlagsanstalt, 1968.

Korsch, Karl. *Karl Marx* (1938), Vienna and Frankfurt, Europäische Verlagsanstalt, 1968.

Korsch, Karl. *Marxismus und Philosophie* [*Marxism and Philosophy*], Vienna and Frankfurt, Europäische Verlagsanstalt, 1966.

Korsch, Karl. *Die materialistische Geschichtsauffassung* [*The Materialist Conception of History*] (1929), Vienna and Frankfurt, Europäische Verlagsanstalt, 1977.

Korsch, Karl. *Was ist Sozialisierung?* [*What is Socialisation?*], Hannover, Freies Deutschland, 1919.

Kropotkin, Peter. 'Anarchist Communism' in Woodcock (ed.), *The Anarchist Reader*, and Baldwin, *Kropotkin's Revolutionary Pamphlets*.

Kropotkin, Peter. *The Conquest of Bread*, London, Elephant Editions, 1985.

Kropotkin, Peter. *Fields, Factories and Workshops*, London, Hutchinson, 1899.

Kropotkin, Peter. 'Modern Science and Anarchism' (1913) in Woodcock, *The Anarchist Reader*.

Kropotkin, Peter. *Mutual Aid*, Hermondsworth, Penguin, 1939.

Kuo, Wil. 'Adorno and Habermas as public figures', DPhil thesis, University of Sussex, 2007.

Labriola, Arturo. *Sindacalismo e riformismo* [*Syndicalism and Reformism*], Florence, G. Nerbini, 1905.

Labriola, Arturo. *Storia di dieci anni, 1899–1909* [*The History of Ten Years: 1899–1909*], Milan, Il Viandante, 1910.

Lacan, Jacques. *Les quatre concepts fondamentaux de la psychanalyse* [*The Four Fundamental Concepts of Psychoanalysis*], Paris, Seuil, 1973.

Laclau, Ernesto and Mouffe, Chantal. *Hegemony and Socialist Strategy*, London, Verso, 1985.

Landauer, Gustav. *Aufruf zum Sozialismus* [*Call to Socialism*] (1911), Cologne, Marcan-Block, 1923.

Landshut, Siegfried (ed.). *Marx: Frühe Schriften*, Stuttgart, Alfred Kröner, 1953.

Lefebvre, Henri. *Critique de la vie quotidienne I: Introduction* [*Critique of Everyday Life I: Introduction*] (1947), Paris, Arche, 1958.

Lefebvre, Henri. *Critique de la vie quotidienne II: fondements d'une sociologie de la quotidienneté* [*Critique of Everyday Life II: Foundations of a Sociology of Daily Life*], Paris, Arche, 1961.

Lefebvre, Henri. *Critique de la vie quotidienne III: Critique de la modernité* [*Critique of Everyday Life III: Critique of Modernity*], Paris, Arche, 1981.

Lefebvre, Henri. *Critique of Everyday Life,* London, Verso, 1991.

Lefebvre, Henri. *L'irruption de Nanterre au sommet* [*The Irruption of Nanterre at the Summit*], Paris, Anthropos, 1968.

Lefort, Claude. 'L'insurrection hongroise', in *Socialisme ou Barbarie?,* 20 (1957).

Lefort, Claude. 'Le nouveau désordre', in Morin et. al., *Mai 68*.

Lenin, Vladimir J. *Left-Wing Communism, an Infantile Disorder,* Moscow, Progress Publishers, 1977.

Lenin, Vladimir J. *State and Revolution,* in *Collected Works,* Volume 25, Moscow, Progress Publishers, 1975.

Leval, Gaston. *Collectives in the Spanish Revolution,* London, Freedom Press, 1975.

Lotringer, Sylvere and Marazzi, Christian. *Italy, Autonomia: Post-Political Politics,* New York, Semiotext(e), 1980.

Luhn, Eugene. *Marxism and Modernism: An Historical Study of Lukács, Brecht, Benjamin and Adorno,* Berkeley, University of California Press, 1982.

Lukács, Georg. *Chvostismus und Dialektik* [*Tailism and the Dialectic*], London, Verso, 2000.

Lukács, Georg. *Geschichte und Klassenbewusstsein. Studien über marxistischen Dialektik* [*History and Class Consciousness*] (1923), Amsterdam, De Munter, 1967.

Lukács, Georg. *Lenin* (1924), London, Verso, 1985.

Lukacs, Georg. *Die Theorie des Romans* (*The Theory of the Novel,* written in 1916, first appears as book in 1920), Munich, DTV, 1994.

Lukács, Georg. *Soul and Form* (1911), London, Penguin, 1973.

Lumley, Robert. *States of Emergency: Cultures of Revolt in Italy from 1968 to 1978,* London, Verso, 1990.

Luthardt, Wolfgang (ed.). *Von der Weimarer Republik zum Faschismus: Die Auflösung der demokratischen Rechtsordnung* [*From the Weimar Republic to Fascism: The Dissolution of the Democratic Legal Order*], Frankfurt, Suhrkamp, 1976.

Luxemburg, Rosa. *The Mass Strike and other Writings,* New York, Pathfinder, 1970.

Macdonald, Ramsay. *Syndicalism,* London, Constable & Co., 1912.

Machiavelli, Niccolò. *Il principe* [*The Prince*] (1513), Milan, Garzanti, 1967.

Magraw, Roger. *France 1815–1915: The Bourgeois Century,* London, Fontana, 1983.

Maitron, Jean. *Histoire du movement anarchiste en France, 1880–1914* [*History of the Anarchist Movement in France, 1880–1914*], Paris, Société Universitaire d'Edition et de Libraire, 1955.

Marcus, Greil. *Lipstick Traces: A Secret History of the Twentieth Century,* Cambridge, Harvard University Press, 1989.

Marcuse, Herbert. *Eros and Civilisation,* London, Penguin, 1969.

Marcuse, Herbert. Foreword to Pross, *Franz Neumann, Demokratischer und autoritärer Staat*.

Marcuse, Herbert. *Konterrevolution und Revolte* [*Counter-Revolution and Revolt*], Frankfurt, Suhrkamp, 1972

Marcuse, Herbert. *Nachgelassene Schriften, Band 2: Kunst und Befreiung*, Berlin, Zu Klampen, 2000.

Marcuse, Herbert. *Nachgelassene Schriften, Band 3: Philosophie und Psychoanalyse*, Berlin, Zu Klampen, 2002.

Marcuse, Herbert. *Negations: Essays in Critical Theory*, London, Penguin, 1968.

Marcuse, Herbert. *One-Dimensional Man*, London, Routledge, 1991.

Marcuse, Herbert. *Reason and Revolution: Hegel and the Rise of Social Theory*, London, Routledge & Kegan Paul, 1954.

Marcuse, Herbert. *Soviet Marxism: A Critical Analysis*, London, Routledge & Kegan Paul, 1958.

Marelli, Gianfranco. *L'amère victoire du situationisme: Pour une histoire de l'internationale situationiste, 1957–1971* [*The Bitter Victory of Situationism*], Arles, Sulliver, 1998.

Marshall, Peter. *Demanding the Impossible: A History of Anarchism*, London, Collins, 1992.

Marx, Karl and Engels, Frederick. *The German Ideology*, edited by Chris Arthur, London, Lawrence and Wishart, 1970.

Marx, Karl. *Preface and Introduction to a Contribution to the Critique of Political Economy*, Peking, Foreign Languages Press, 1976.

Marx, Karl and Engels, Frederick. *Selected Works in 1 Volume*, London, Lawrence and Wishart, 1980.

Mattick, Paul. *Anti-Bolshevik Communism*, London, Merlin, 1978.

McLellan, David. *Karl Marx and the Young Hegelians*, London, Houghton Mifflin, 1979.

McLellan, David. *Marx: Modern Masters*, London, Fontana, 1975.

McLellan, David. *Marxism After Marx*, Boston, Houghton Mifflin, 1979.

McLellan, David. *The Thought of Karl Marx: An Introduction*, London, Macmillan, 1971.

Melucci, Alberto. *Nomads of the Present: Social Movements and Individual Needs in Contemporary Society*, London, Hutchinson, 1989.

Mentinis, Mihalis. *Zapatistas: The Chiapas Revolt and what it means for Radical Politics*, London, Pluto, 2006.

Merleau-Ponty, Maurice. *Les adventures de la dialectique* [*Adventures of the Dialectic*], Paris, Gallimard, 1955.

Miller, David. *Anarchism*, London, J.M. Dent & Son, 1984.

Morin, Edgar, Lefort, Claude and Coudray, Jean-Marc. *Mai 68: le brèche*, Paris, Fayard, 1968.

Mosconi, Patrick (ed.). *Internationale Situationiste*, Paris, Fayard, 1997.

Mouffe, Chantal (ed.). *Gramsci and Marxist Theory*, London, Lawrence and Wishart, 1979.

Murphy, Thomas S. and Mustapha, Abdul-Karim (eds.). *The Philosophy of Antonio Negri: Resistance in Practice*, London, Pluto, 2005.

Nadeau, Maurice. *The History of Surrealism*, Cambridge, Harvard University Press, 1989.

Negri, Antonio. *Marx Beyond Marx: Lessons on the Grundrisse*, London, Pluto, 1983.

Negri, Antonio. *Il potere costituente: saggi sulle alternative del moderno*, Rome, Manifestolibri, 2002.

Negt, Oskar and Lugge, Alexander. *Öffentlichkeit und Erfahrung: Zur Organisations-analyse von bürgerlicher and proletarischer Öffentlichkeit* [*The Public Sphere and Experience*], Frankfurt, Suhrkamp, 1973.

Neumann, Franz. *Behemoth: The Structure and Practice of National Socialism, 1933–44*, New York, Harper & Row, 1966.

Neumann, Franz (ed. Helge Pross). *Demokratischer und autoritärer Staat: Studien zur politischen Theorie* [*The Democratic and Authoritarian State: Studies in Political Theory*], Munich, Fischer, 1986.

Nicholls, Peter. *Modernisms: A Literary Guide*, Berkeley, University of California Press, 1995.

Nietzsche, Friedrich. *Die fröhliche Wissenschaft* [*The Gay Science*] (1882), Munich, Goldmann, 1982.

Nietzsche, Friedrich. *Die Geburt der Tragödie aus dem Geiste der Musik* [*The Birth of Tragedy*] (1872), Munich: Goldmann, 1990.

Pasolini, Pier Paolo. *Le ceneri di Gramsci* [*The Ashes of Gramsci*], Milan, Grazanti, 1976.

Pasolini, Pier Paolo. *Scritti corsari* [*Pirate Writings*], Milan, Garzanti, 1974.

Pateman, Carole. *Participation and Democratic Theory*, Cambridge, CUP, 1970.

Pelloutier, Fernand. *Histoire des Bourses du Travail* [*History of the Bourses du Travail*], Paris, Schleicheur Frères, 1902.

Penty, A. J. *Old Worlds for New: A Study of the Post-Industrial State*, London, George Allen & Unwin, 1917.

Piccone, Paul. *Italian Marxism*, Berkeley, University of California Press, 1983.

Pike, David. *Lukács and Brecht*, Chapel Hill and London, University of North Carolina Press, 1985.

Pippin, Robert. *Kant's Theory of Form: An Essay on the Critique of Pure Reason*, New Haven, Yale University Press, 1982.

Plant, Sadie. *The Most Radical Gesture: The Situationist International in a Postmodern Age*, London, Routledge, 1992.

Pollock, Friedrich. 'State capitalism: its possibilities and limitations' (1941), in Arato and Gebhardt, *The Essential Frankfurt School Reader*.

Portis, Larry. *Georges Sorel*, London, Pluto, 1980.

Poster, Mark. *Existentialist Marxism in Postwar France: From Sartre to Althusser*, Princeton, Princeton University Press, 1975.

Poster, Mark. *Sartre's Marxism*, London, Pluto, 1979.

Poulantzos, Nicos. *Political Power and Social Classes*, London, NLB, 1978.

Pross, Helge (ed.). *Franz Neumann, Demokratischer und autoritärer Staat: Studien zur politischen Theorie* [*Franz Neumann, The Democratic and Authoritarian State: Studies in Political Theory*], Munich, Fischer, 1986.

Proudhon, P. J. *De la capacité politique des classes ouvrières* [*On the Political Capacity of the Working Classes*] (1865), Paris, Librairie Internationale, 1873.

Reiss, Hans (ed.). *Kant: Political Writings*, Cambridge, CUP, 1970.

Richards, Vernon. *Lessons of the Spanish Revolution*, London, Freedom Press, 1983.

Ritter, Alan. *The Political Thought of Pierre-Joseph Proudhon*, New Jersey, Princeton University Press, 1969.

Roberts, John. *Philosophising the Everyday: Revolutionary Praxis and the Fate of Cultural Theory*, London, Pluto, 2006.

Ross, Kristin. *The Emergence of Social Space: Rimbaud and the Paris Commune*, Minneapolis, University of Minnesota Press, 1988.

Sadler, Simon. *The Situationist City,* Cambridge, MIT Press, 1998.

Sanguinetti, Gianfranco and Debord, Guy. *La véritable scission dans l'internationale: circulaire publique de l'internationale situationiste* [*The Real Split in the SI*], Paris, Fayard, 1972.

Sartre, Jean-Paul. *Critique de la raison dialectique, tome I: théorie des ensembles pratiques* [*Critique of Dialectical Reason*], Paris, Gallimard, 1960.

Sartre, Jean-Paul. *L'être et le néant: essai d'ontologie phénoménologique* [*Being and Nothingness*], Paris, Gallimard, 1943.

Sartre, Jean-Paul. *L'existentialisme est un humanisme* [*Existentialism is a Humanism*], Paris, Nagel, 1946.

Schecter, Darrow. *Beyond Hegemony: Towards a New Philosophy of Political Legitimacy,* Manchester, MUP, 2005.

Schecter, Darrow. *Gramsci and the Theory of Industrial Democracy,* Aldershot, Avebury, 1991.

Schecter, Darrow. *Radical Theories: Paths Beyond Marxism and Social Democracy,* Manchester, MUP, 1994.

Schecter, Darrow. *Sovereign States or Political Communities? Civil Society and Contemporary Politics,* Manchester, MUP, 2000.

Scheuerman, William E. *Between the Norm and the Exception: The Frankfurt School and the Rule of Law,* Cambridge, MIT Press, 1994.

Scheuerman, William E.(ed.). *The Rule of Law under Siege: Selected Essays by Franz Neumann and Otto Kirchheimer,* Berkeley, University of California Press, 1996.

Schmidt, Alfred. *The Concept of Nature in Marx,* Cambridge, Polity, 1985.

Shilliam, Robbie. 'Hegemony and the unfashionable problem of primitive accumulation', in *Millenium,* 33 (2004), 59–88.

Simmel, Georg. *Die Philosophie des Geldes* [*The Philosophy of Money*] (1900), London, Routledge, 1998.

Simmel, Georg. *Soziologie: Untersuchungen über die Form der Vergesellschaftung* [*Sociology*] (1908), Frankfurt, Suhrkamp, 1992.

Simons, Jon (ed.), *Contemporary Critical Theorists: From Lacan to Said,* Edinburgh, EUP, 2004.

Smith, David. *Left and Right in Twentieth-Century Europe,* London, Longman, 1970.

Sohn-Rethel, Alfred. *Geistige und körperliche Arbeit,* Frankfurt, Suhrkamp, 1973.

Sohn-Rethel, Alfred. *Soziologische Theorie der Erkenntnis* [*The Sociological Theory of Knowledge*], Frankfurt, Suhrkamp, 1985.

Sorel, Georges. 'L'avenir socialiste des syndicats' ['The socialist future of the unions'], in *L'Humanité Nouvelle,* 3 (1899).

Sorel, Georges. *La décomposition du marxisme* [*The Decomposition of Marxism*], Paris, Marcel Rivière, 1908.

Sorel, Georges. 'Étude sur Vico' ['Study of Vico'], in *Le Devenir Social* 11–12 (1986), 1033–34.

Sorel, Georges. *Les illusions du progrès* [*The Illusions of Progress*], Paris, Marcel Rivière, 1908.

Sorel, Georges. *Réflexions sur la violence* [*Reflections on Violence*], Paris, Marcel Rivière, 1908.

Spinoza, Baruch. *Ethica* (1675), London, Penguin, 1958.

Thomas, Hugh. *The Spanish Civil War,* London, Penguin, 1977.

Thomas, Paul. *Karl Marx and the Anarchists,* London, Routledge, 1980.

Thompson, Edward P. *The Poverty of Theory and Other Essays*, London, Merlin, 1978.

Thomson, Alex. *Adorno: A Guide for the Perplexed*, London, Continuum, 2006.

Thomson, Alex. *Deconstruction and Democracy: Derrida's Politics of Friendship*, London, Contimuum, 2005.

Thornhill, Chris. *Political Theory in Modern Germany: An Introduction*, Cambridge, Polity, 1999.

Timms, Edward and Kelley, David (eds.). *Unreal City: Urban Experience in Modern European Literature and Art*, Manchester, MUP, 1985.

Tronti, Mario. 'The Strategy of Refusal' in Lotringer and Marazzi, *Italy, Autonomia*.

Tucker, Robert (ed.). *The Marx-Engels Reader*, New York, Norton, 1978.

Vaneigem, Raoul. *Traité de savoir-vivre à l'usage des jeunes générations*, Paris, Gallimard, 1967; translated by John Fullerton and Paul Sieveking as *The Revolution of Everyday Life*, London, Rising Free Collective, 1979.

Vienet, René. *Enragés et situationistes dans le movement des occupations* [*Enragés and Situationists in the Movement of the Occupations*], Paris, Gallimard, 1968.

Vighi, Fabio. *Traumatic Encounters in Italian Film: Locating the Cinematic Unconscious*, Bristol, Intellect, 2006.

Virno, Paolo. *Una grammatica della moltitudine* [*A Grammar of the Multitude*], Rome, Derriveapprodi, 2003.

Virno, Paolo and Hardt, Michael (eds). *Radical Thought in Italy: A Potential Politics*, Minneapolis, University of Minnesota Press, 1996.

Walker, Ian. *City Gorged with Dreams: Surrealism and Documentary Photography in Interwar Paris*, Manchester, MUP, 2002.

Walters, Sarah. 'Á l'ATTAC: Globalisation and the Ideological Renewal of the French Left', in *Modern and Contemporary France*, 14 (2006).

Ward, Colin. *Anarchism: A Very Short Introduction*, Oxford, OUP, 2004.

Ward, Colin. *Anarchy in Action*, London, Allen & Unwin, 1973.

Ward, Colin. Introduction, in Kropotkin, *Fields, Factories and Workshops*.

Weber, Max. *The Protestant Ethic and the Spirit of Capitalism* (1904), London, Methuen, 1971.

Weischedel, Wilhelm (ed.). *Immanuel Kant: Schriften zur Anthropolgie, Geschichtsphilosophie, Politik und Pädagogik I*, Frankfurt, Suhrkamp, 1977.

Wiggershaus, Rolf. *The Frankfurt School*, Cambridge, MIT Press, 1999.

Williams, Gwyn. *Proletarian Order: Italy 1919–1920*, London, Pluto, 1977.

Woodcock, George (ed.). *The Anarchist Reader*, London, Fontana, 1977.

Wright, Steve. *Storming Heaven: Class Composition and Struggle in Italian Autonomous Marxism*, London, Pluto, 2002.

Wyatt, Chris. 'G. D. H. Cole: Emancipatory politics and organisational democracy', DPhil thesis, University of Sussex, 2004.

Wyatt, Chris. 'A recipe for a cookshop of the future: G. D. H. Cole and the Conundrum of Sovereignty', in *Capital and Class*, 90 (2007).

Zegel, Sylvan. *Les idées de mai*, Paris, Gallimard, 1968.

Zourabichvili, François. 'Une philosophie de l'évenément' ['A Philosophy of the Event'], in Zourabichvili et al., *La philosophie de Deleuze*.

Zourabichvili, François, Sauvagnargues, Anne and Marrati, Paola. *La Philosophie de Deleuze*, Paris, PUF, 2004.

INDEX

political strategy, 32
Preface and Introduction to a Contribution to a Critique of Political Economy, 31–32
proletariat, 17–18, 21, 49, 53, 55, 78
reification, 12, 14, 15, 53, 74, 85, 87
religion, 11, 12, 14, 158, 181
sociological deficit, 155
state, 9, 14, 21, 22–23, 37, 94
superstructure, 7, 23, 27, 29n19, 31–34, 43–44, 46, 51, 57, 148
totality, 3, 5, 112, 183–84, 202, 213n6
universal suffrage, 18, 25
working class, 35, 43, 53, 59, 76, 81, 85
Matteotti, Giacomo, 37
Millerand, Alexandre, 108
Miskole Council, 119–20
Mitterand, François, 113
Moro, Aldo, 166, 177n44
Morris, William, 120–21
Mouffe, Chantal, 38, 65n7, 228
Movimento Sociale Italiano (MSI), 166

Nagy, Imre, 119–20
Nanterre, University of, 162, 164
National Confederation of Labour (CNT), 133, 134
'National guilds', 121, 139n26, 139n28, 227
National Union of French Students (UNEF), 161–62
Negri, Antonio, 146, 156, 168, 169, 171n4, 179–81, 191
Neumann, Franz, 81, 91, 94, 96
  'The change in the function of law in modern society', 94, 95, 105n35
Nietzsche, Friedrich, 2, 9, 143, 186, 187
  Birth of Tragedy, 80, 231

Ordine Nuovo (journal), 40, 41

Pannekoek, Anton, 116, 118, 121
Paris Commune, 23–27, 40, 131, 140n40, 142, 146, 173n18, 179
Partito Comunista Italiano (PCI), 34, 137n14, 165, 166–68, 176n42, 181
Partito Socialista Italiano (PSI), 35, 37, 42, 108, 113–14, 117, 118, 165
Pasolini, Pier Paolo, 46, 66n22, 180, 202, 212n1, 231
Pelloutier, Fernand, 109–110, 137n6, 231
Penty, A. J., 122, 125, 139n28–29, 231
Petöfi, Sandor, 119
Plekhanov, Georgi, 34

Poe, Edgar Allan, 148, 171n5
Pollock, Friedrich, 90, 91, 105n30, 231
Pompidou, Prime Minister Georges, 166
post-Fordism, 154, 169, 207
Potere Operaio. *See* Workers' Power (Potere Operaio)
Poulantzas, Nicos, 62, 70n55
Proudhon, P.J., 129–33, 140n41, 141n44, 231
PSF. *See* French Socialist Party (PSF)

Quaderni Rossi (*Red Notebooks*) (journal), 168, 177n46

Red Brigades (BR), 166
Revolutions of 1848, 18–20
Rimbaud, Arthur, 146–47, 149, 151, 152, 158, 171n6, 173n18
Risorgimento, 39, 40
Roussel, R., 183, 184, 192, 197, 206, 213n8, 214n11
Rühle, Otto, 119
Ruskin, John, 120
Russian Revolution, 22, 25–26, 30n25, 37, 40, 176n34, 203, 218

Salvemini, Gaetano, 44
Sartre, Jean-Paul, 51–60, 111
  Being and Nothingness, 54, 57, 68n40, 232
  Critique of Dialectical Reason, 54–57, 59, 69n40–41, 69n45, 232
'scandal of Strasbourg', 161
Schmitt, Carl, 93, 127, 140n38, 207
  Legality and Legitimacy, 93, 105n33, 139n25, 228
Schumpeter, Joseph, 127, 140n38
Second International Workingman's Association, 33, 35, 38, 49
SI. *See* Situationist International (SI)
Simmel, Georg, 49, 52, 85, 86, 156
  The Philosophy of Money, 124, 139n32, 174n26, 232
Situationist International (SI), 152–53, 159–60, 170
social democracy, 108
  biopower, 218
  crisis of, 207
  European, 116
  French, 113
  German, 115, 119
  Italian, 43
  liberal democracy, 217